SECTOR

AV7 TRS

TRANSFORMERS

7

IDW

www.IDWPublishing.com

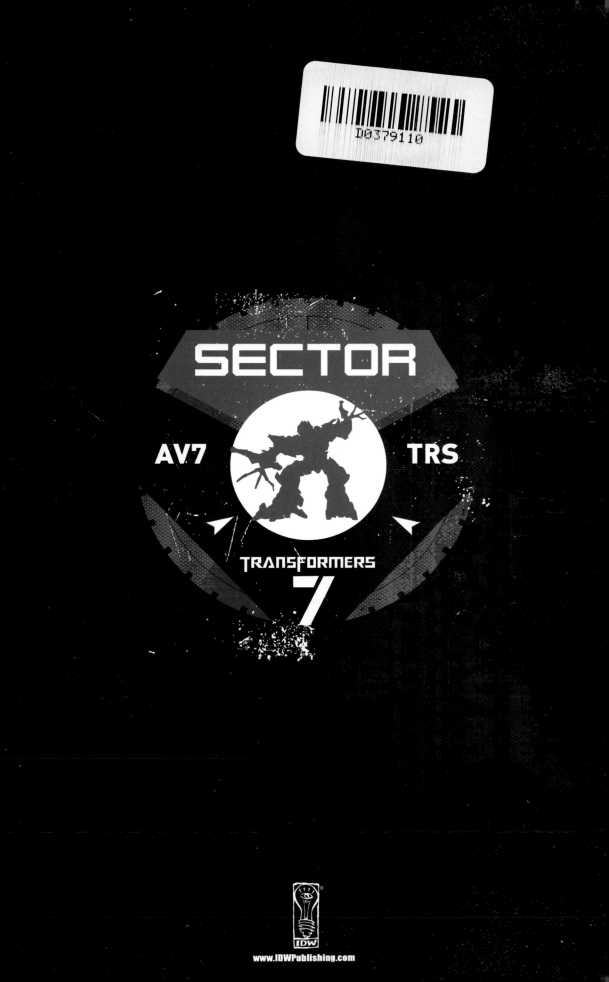

TRANS FORMERS

Licensed by: Hasbro

Special thanks to Hasbro's Aaron Archer, Elizabeth Griffin, Sheri Lucci, Richard Zambarano, Jared Jones, Michael Provost, Michael Richie, and Michael Verrecchia for their invaluable assistance.

ISBN: 978-1-60010-066-6
10 09 08 07   1 2 3 4 5

IDW Publishing is:
Ted Adams, Co-President
Robbie Robbins, Co-President
Chris Ryall, Publisher/Editor-in-Chief
Kris Oprisko, Vice President
Alan Payne, Vice President of Sales
Neil Uyetake, Art Director
Dan Taylor, Editor
Justin Eisinger, Editorial Assistant
Chris Mowry, Graphic Artist
Matthew Ruzicka, CPA, Controller
Alonzo Simon, Shipping Manager
Alex Garner, Creative Director
Yumiko Miyano, Business Development
Rick Privman, Business Development

To discuss this issue of *Transformers*, or join the IDW Insiders, or to check out exclusive Web offers, check out our site:

WWW.IDWPUBLISHING.COM

DREAMWORKS PICTURES

Paramount
A VIACOM COMPANY

story by **Chris Ryall**

written by **Simon Furman
and Chris Ryall**

art by **Don Figueroa**

colors by **Josh Burcham**

color assist by **Mark Bristow**

letters by **Robbie Robbins**

edits by **Dan Taylor**

design by **Robbie Robbins
and Neil Uyetake**

TRANSFORMERS: MOVIE PREQUEL TPB. JUNE 2007. FIRST PRINTING. IDW Publishing, a division of Idea and Design Works, LLC. Editorial offices: 4411 Morena Blvd., Suite 106, San Diego, CA 92117. HASBRO and its logo. TRANSFORMERS, and all related characters are trademarks of Hasbro and are used with permission. © 2007 Hasbro. All Rights Reserved. © 2007 DreamWorks LLC and Paramount Pictures Corporation. ® and/or TM & © 2007 Hasbro, Pawtucket, RI 02862 USA. All Rights Reserved. TM & ® denote U.S. Trademarks. Hasbro Canada, Longueuil, QC, Canada J4G 1G2. Pave Low™, Sikorsky® and the Pave Low helicopter design is used under license from Sikorsky Aircraft Corporation. Camaro and all related Emblems and vehicle body designs are General Motors Trademarks used under license to Hasbro, Inc. Pontiac Solstice and all related Emblems and vehicle body designs are General Motors Trademarks used under license to Hasbro, Inc. Hummer H2 and all related Emblems and vehicle body designs are General Motors Trademarks used under license to Hasbro, Inc.. Topkick and all related Emblems and vehicle body designs are General Motors Trademarks used under license to Hasbro, Inc. Saleen® and S281 are registered trademarks of Saleen Inc. used under license. LOCKHEED MARTIN, F-22 Raptor, associated emblems and logos, and body designs of vehicles are either registered trademarks or trademarks of Lockheed Martin Corporation in the USA and/or other countries, used under license by DreamWorks, LLC. Buffalo™ MPCV™ is used under license from Force Protection Industries. The IDW logo is registered in the U.S. Patent and Trademark Office. Any similarities to persons living or dead are purely coincidental. With the exception of artwork used for review purposes, none of the contents of this publication may be reprinted without the permission of Idea and Design Works, LLC. Printed in Korea.

IDW Publishing does not read or accept unsolicited submissions of ideas, stories, or artwork.

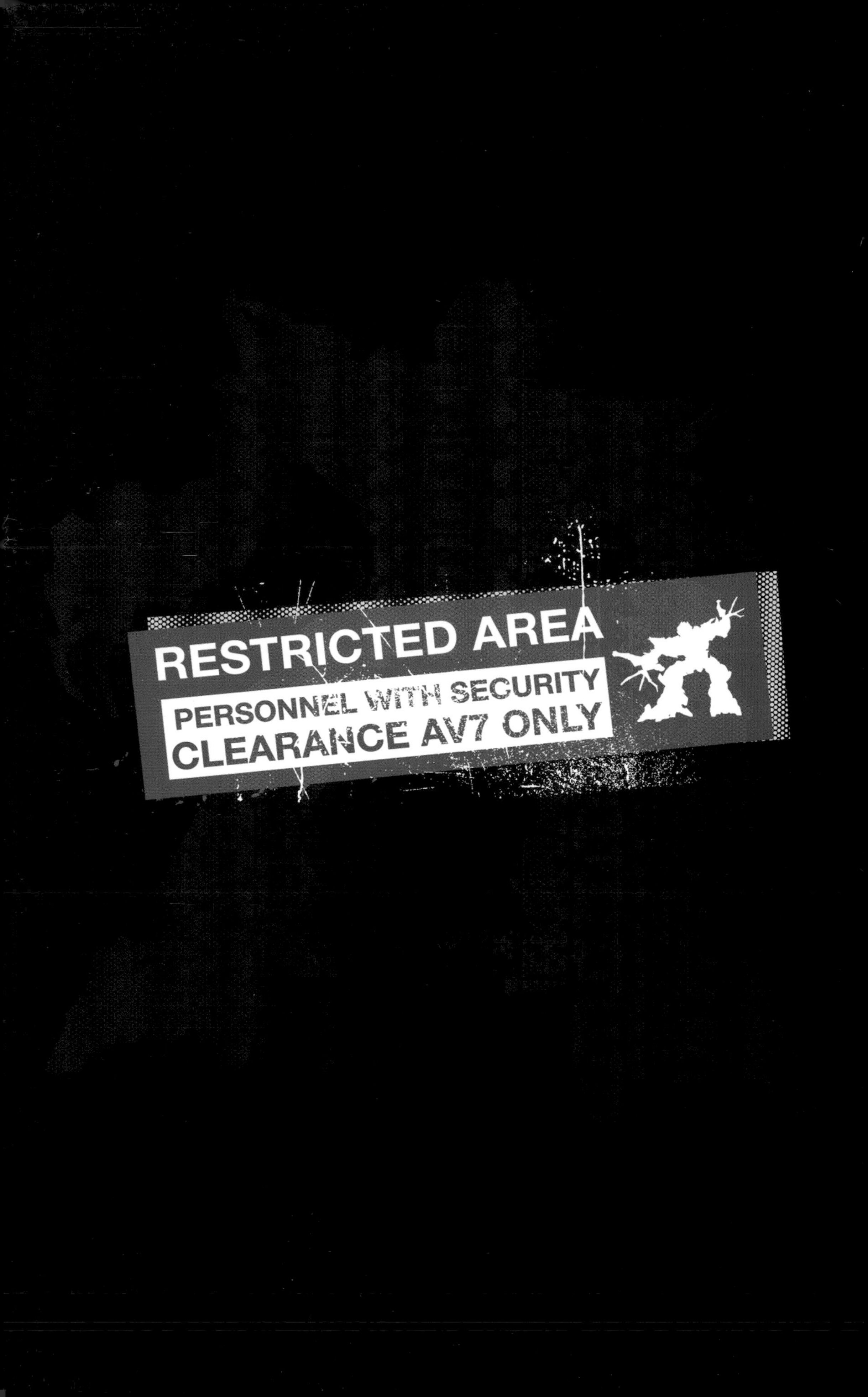
RESTRICTED AREA
PERSONNEL WITH SECURITY
CLEARANCE AV7 ONLY

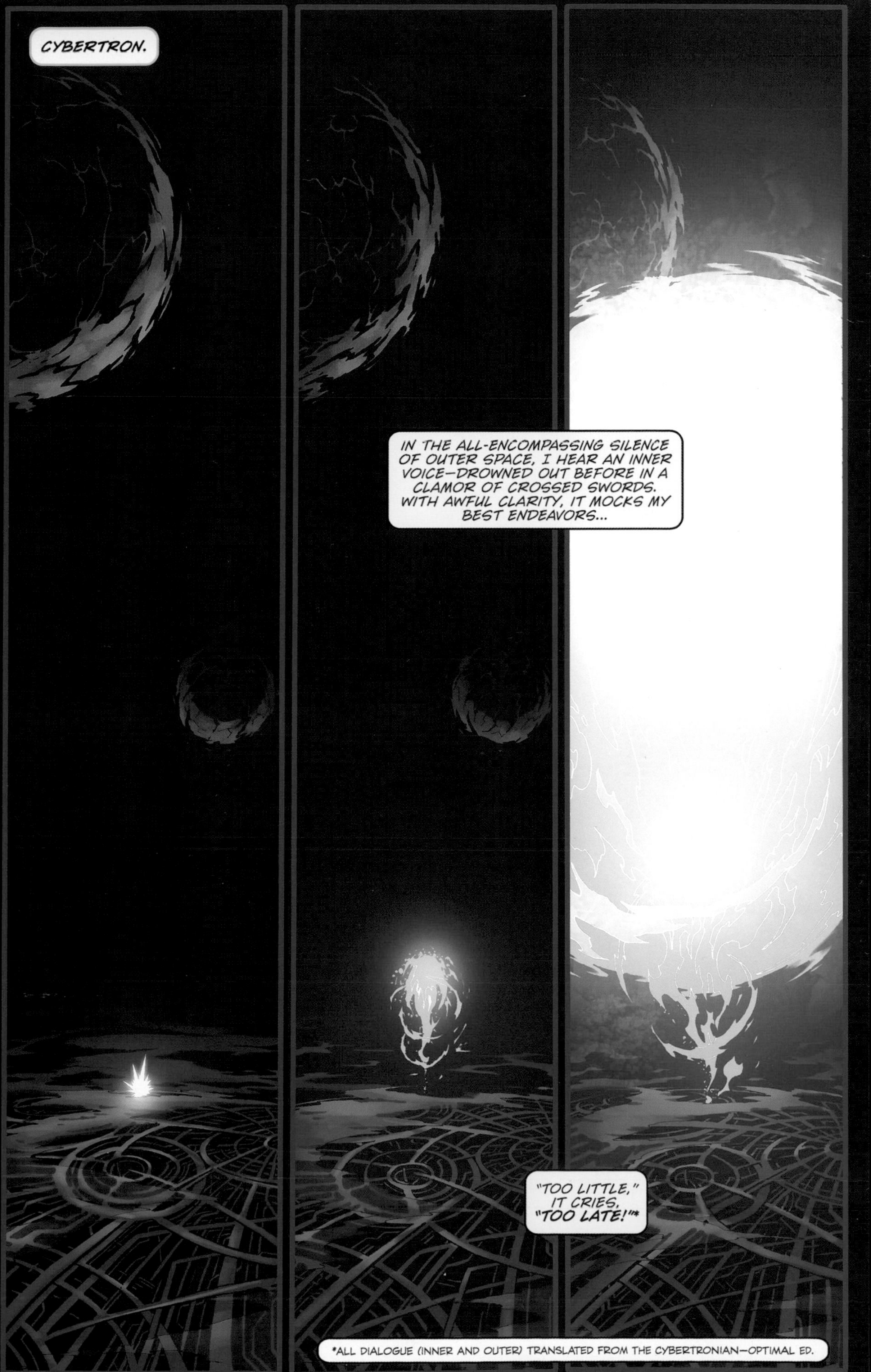
CYBERTRON.
IN THE ALL-ENCOMPASSING SILENCE OF OUTER SPACE, I HEAR AN INNER VOICE—DROWNED OUT BEFORE IN A CLAMOR OF CROSSED SWORDS. WITH AWFUL CLARITY, IT MOCKS MY BEST ENDEAVORS...
"TOO LITTLE," IT CRIES, "TOO LATE!"*
*ALL DIALOGUE (INNER AND OUTER) TRANSLATED FROM THE CYBERTRONIAN—OPTIMAL ED.

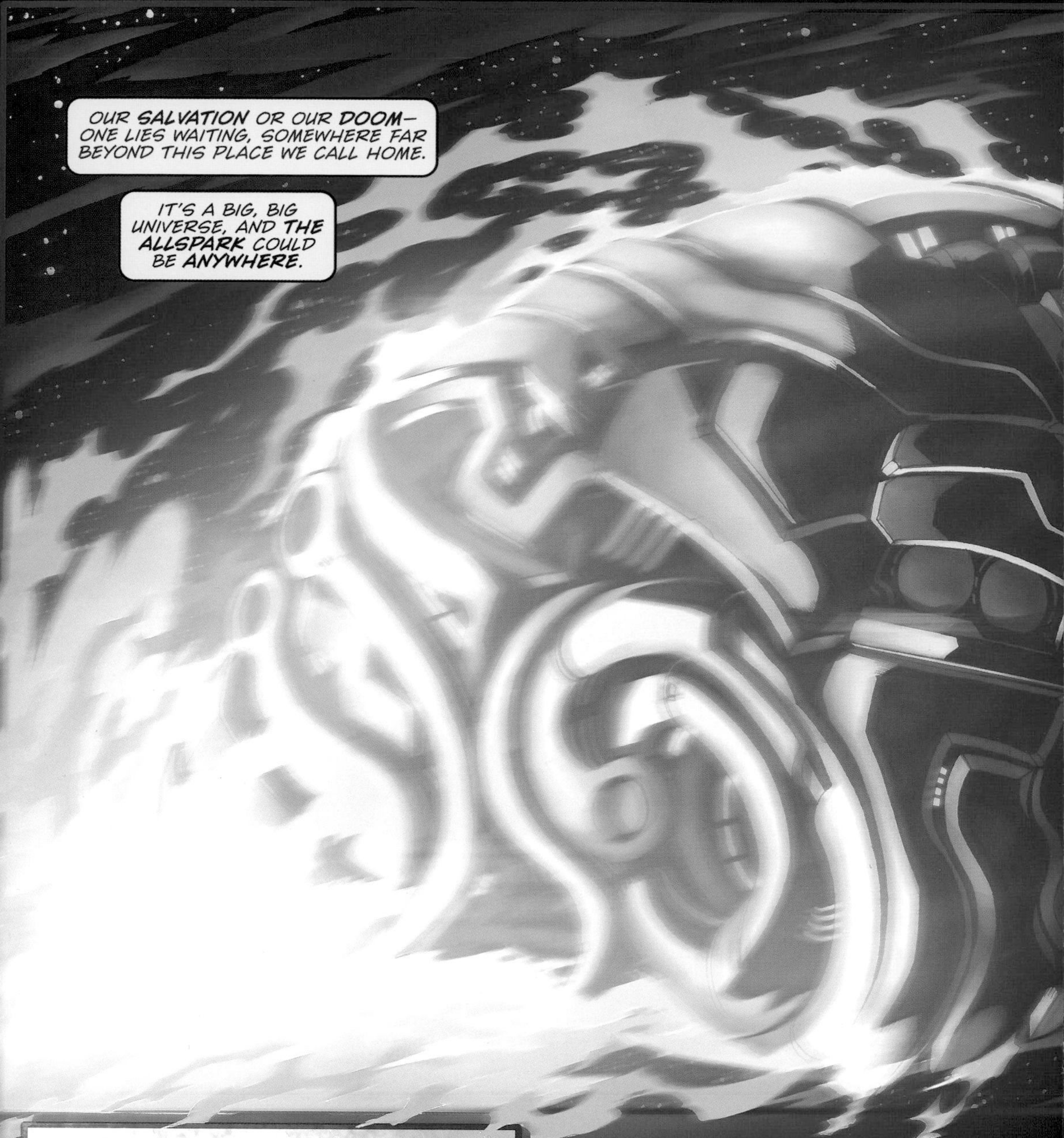
OUR **SALVATION** OR OUR **DOOM**— ONE LIES WAITING, SOMEWHERE FAR BEYOND THIS PLACE WE CALL HOME.
IT'S A BIG, BIG UNIVERSE, AND **THE ALLSPARK** COULD BE **ANYWHERE**.

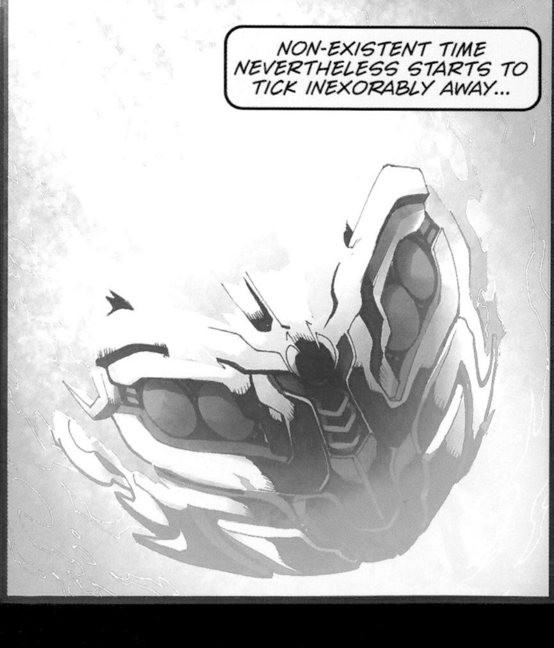
NON-EXISTENT TIME NEVERTHELESS STARTS TO TICK INEXORABLY AWAY...

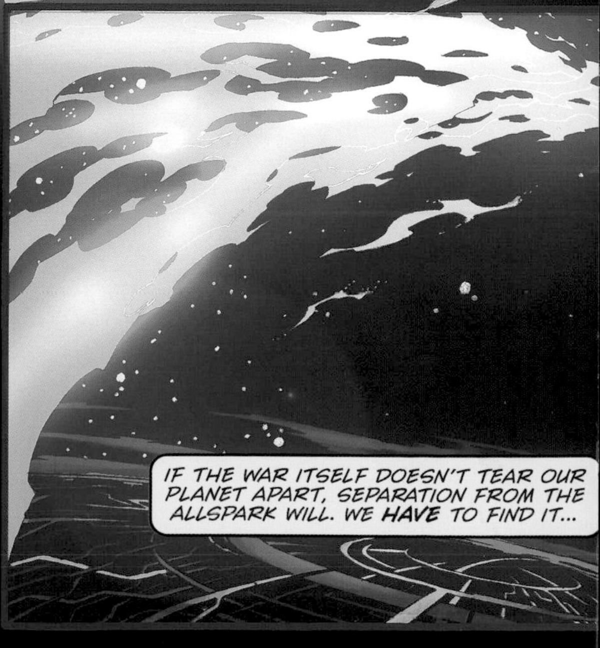
IF THE WAR ITSELF DOESN'T TEAR OUR PLANET APART, SEPARATION FROM THE ALLSPARK WILL. WE **HAVE** TO FIND IT...

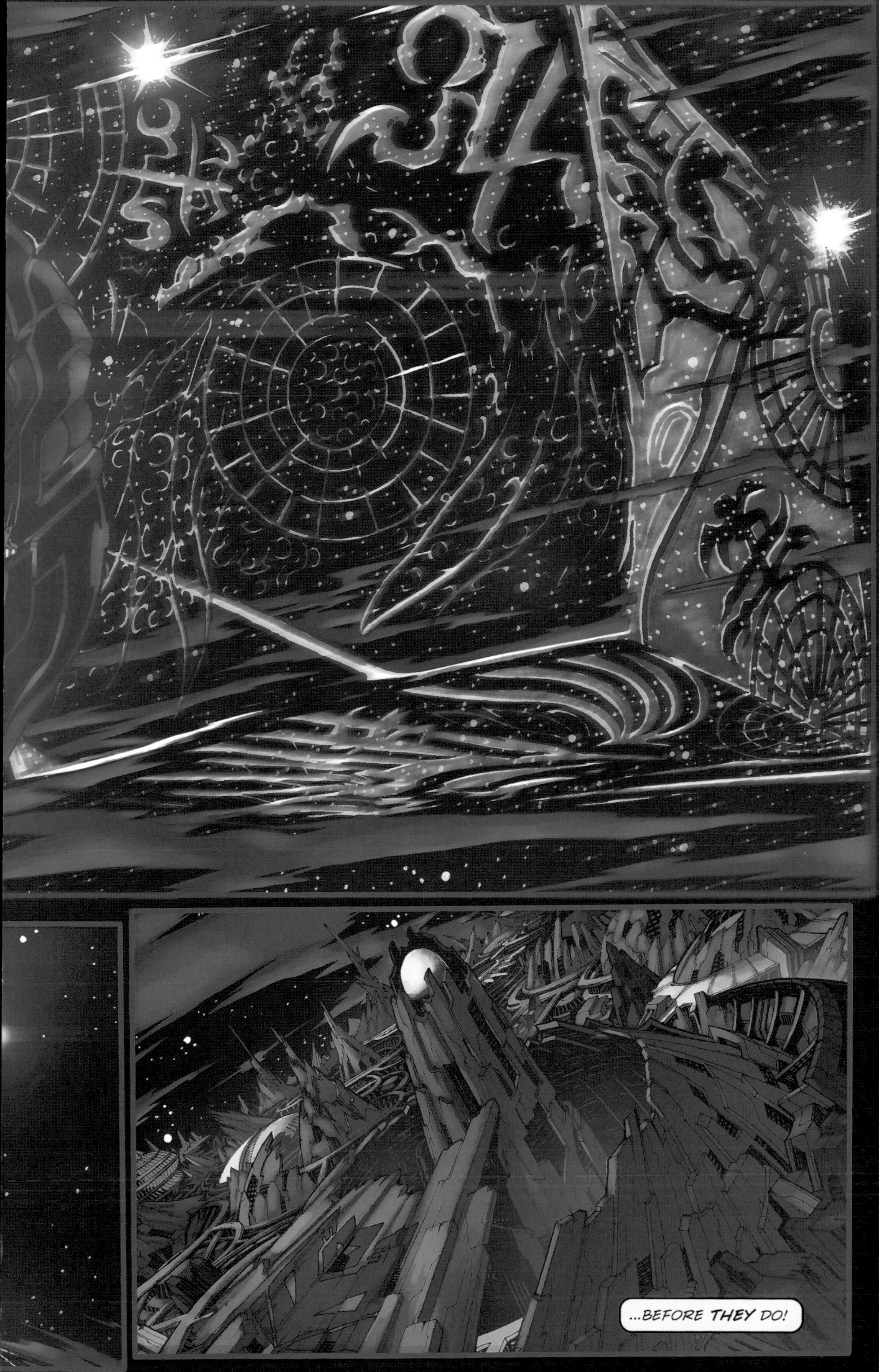
...BEFORE THEY DO!

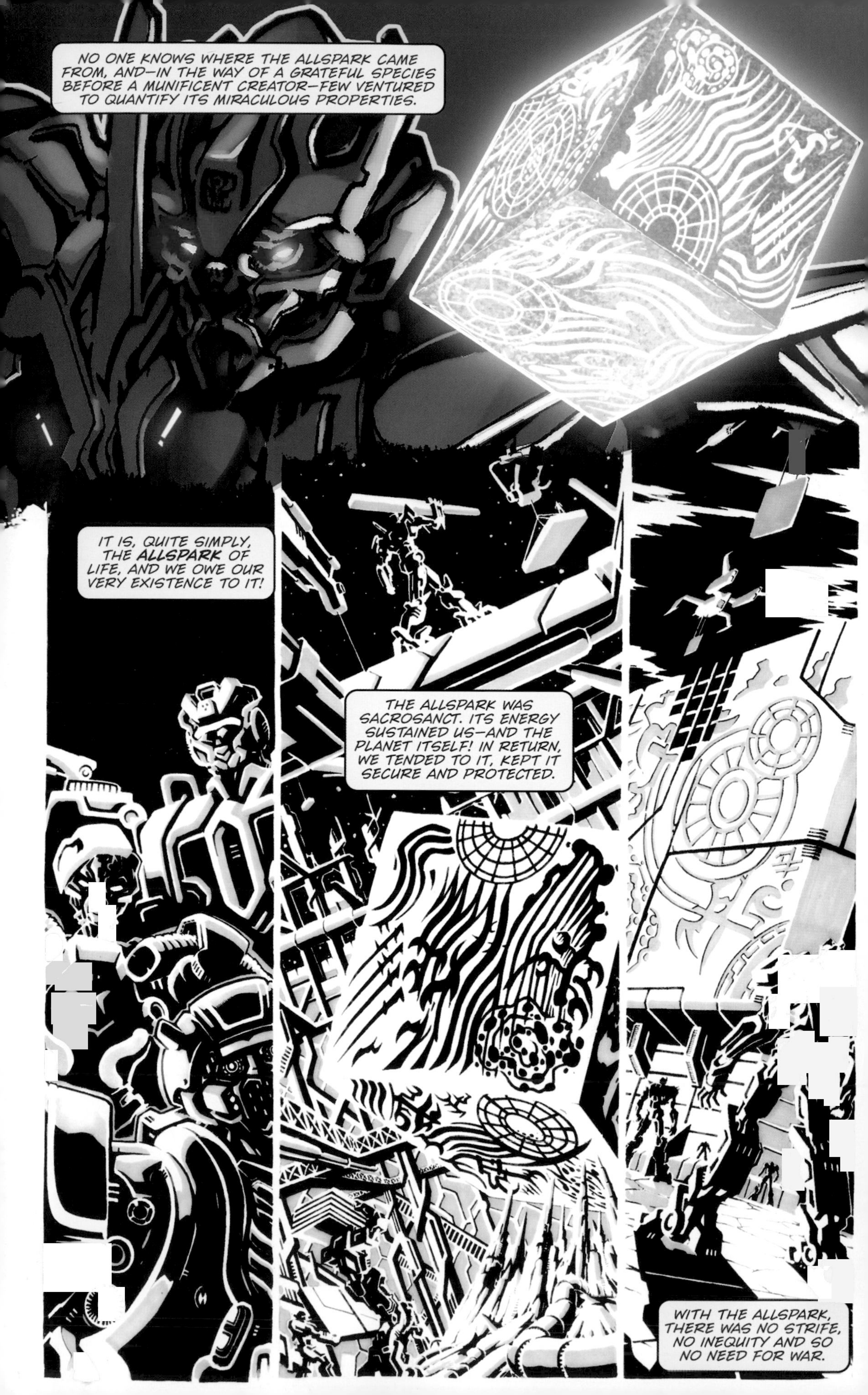
NO ONE KNOWS WHERE THE ALLSPARK CAME FROM, AND—IN THE WAY OF A GRATEFUL SPECIES BEFORE A MUNIFICENT CREATOR—FEW VENTURED TO QUANTIFY ITS MIRACULOUS PROPERTIES.
IT IS, QUITE SIMPLY, THE **ALLSPARK** OF LIFE, AND WE OWE OUR VERY EXISTENCE TO IT!
THE ALLSPARK WAS SACROSANCT. ITS ENERGY SUSTAINED US—AND THE PLANET ITSELF! IN RETURN, WE TENDED TO IT, KEPT IT SECURE AND PROTECTED.
WITH THE ALLSPARK, THERE WAS NO STRIFE, NO INEQUITY AND SO NO NEED FOR WAR.

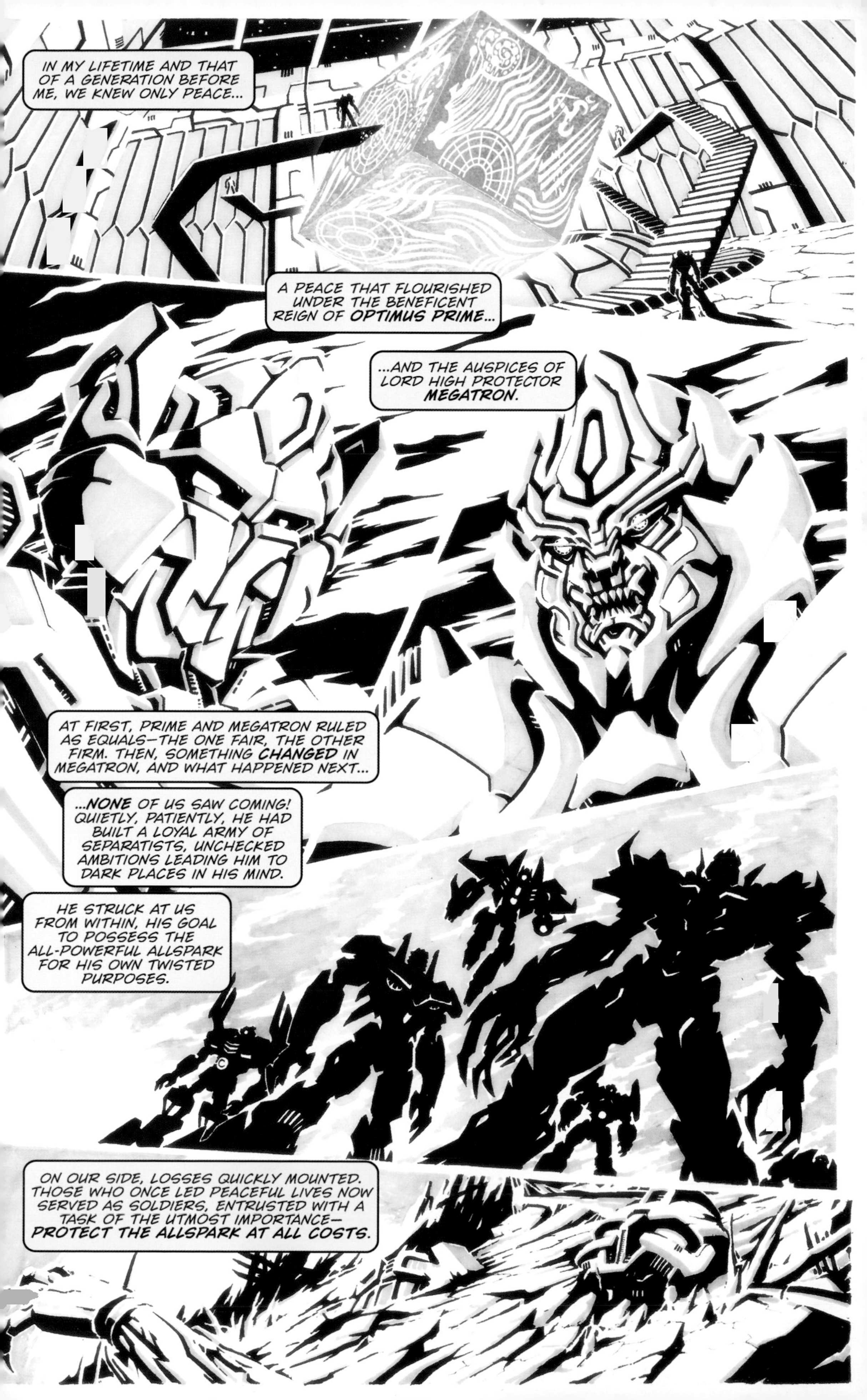
IN MY LIFETIME AND THAT OF A GENERATION BEFORE ME, WE KNEW ONLY PEACE...
A PEACE THAT FLOURISHED UNDER THE BENEFICENT REIGN OF OPTIMUS PRIME...
...AND THE AUSPICES OF LORD HIGH PROTECTOR MEGATRON.
AT FIRST, PRIME AND MEGATRON RULED AS EQUALS—THE ONE FAIR, THE OTHER FIRM. THEN, SOMETHING CHANGED IN MEGATRON, AND WHAT HAPPENED NEXT...
...NONE OF US SAW COMING! QUIETLY, PATIENTLY, HE HAD BUILT A LOYAL ARMY OF SEPARATISTS, UNCHECKED AMBITIONS LEADING HIM TO DARK PLACES IN HIS MIND.
HE STRUCK AT US FROM WITHIN, HIS GOAL TO POSSESS THE ALL-POWERFUL ALLSPARK FOR HIS OWN TWISTED PURPOSES.
ON OUR SIDE, LOSSES QUICKLY MOUNTED. THOSE WHO ONCE LED PEACEFUL LIVES NOW SERVED AS SOLDIERS, ENTRUSTED WITH A TASK OF THE UTMOST IMPORTANCE—PROTECT THE ALLSPARK AT ALL COSTS.

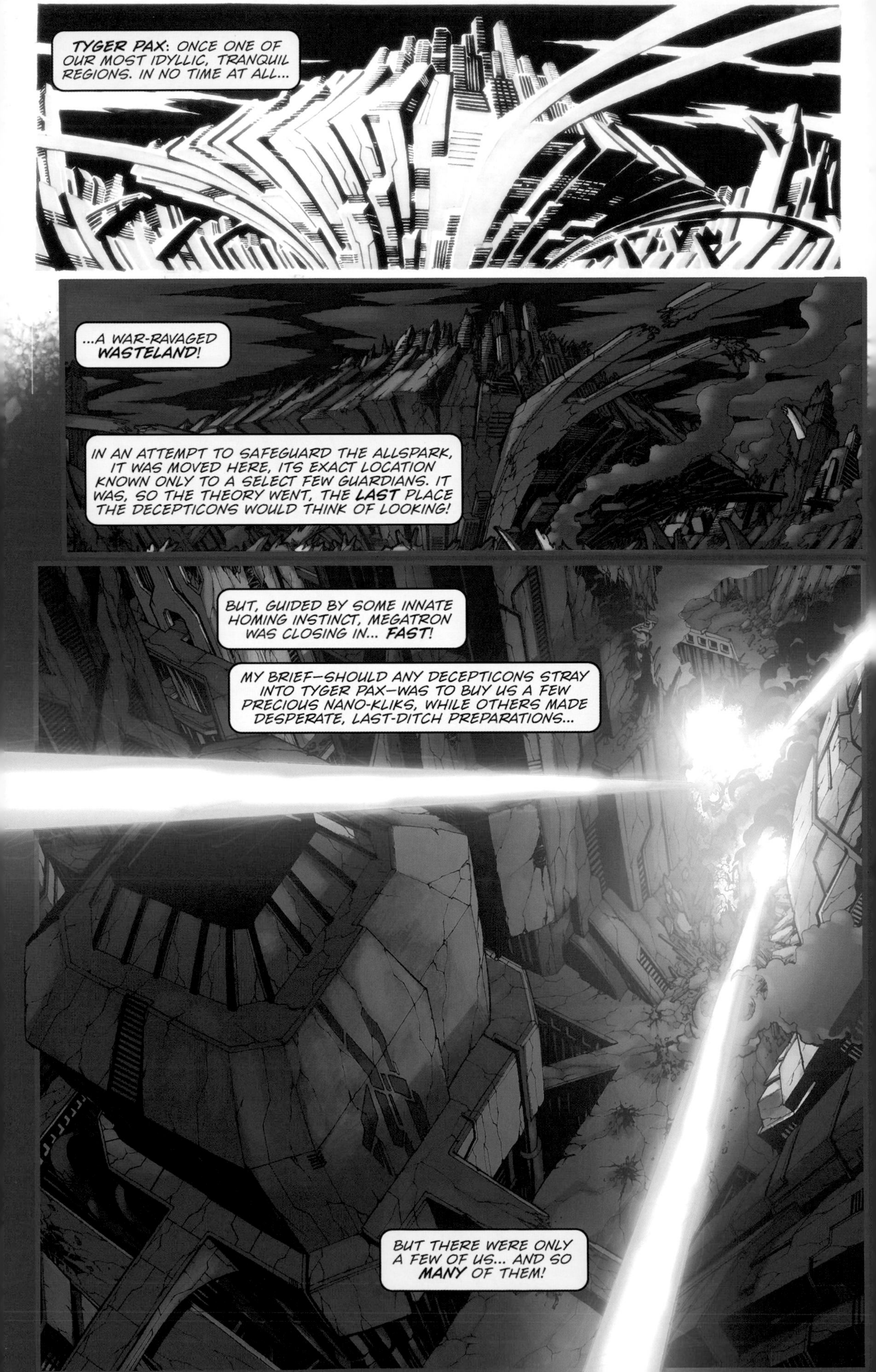
TYGER PAX: ONCE ONE OF OUR MOST IDYLLIC, TRANQUIL REGIONS. IN NO TIME AT ALL...
...A WAR-RAVAGED WASTELAND!
IN AN ATTEMPT TO SAFEGUARD THE ALLSPARK, IT WAS MOVED HERE, ITS EXACT LOCATION KNOWN ONLY TO A SELECT FEW GUARDIANS. IT WAS, SO THE THEORY WENT, THE LAST PLACE THE DECEPTICONS WOULD THINK OF LOOKING!
BUT, GUIDED BY SOME INNATE HOMING INSTINCT, MEGATRON WAS CLOSING IN... FAST!
MY BRIEF—SHOULD ANY DECEPTICONS STRAY INTO TYGER PAX—WAS TO BUY US A FEW PRECIOUS NANO-KLIKS, WHILE OTHERS MADE DESPERATE, LAST-DITCH PREPARATIONS...
BUT THERE WERE ONLY A FEW OF US... AND SO MANY OF THEM!

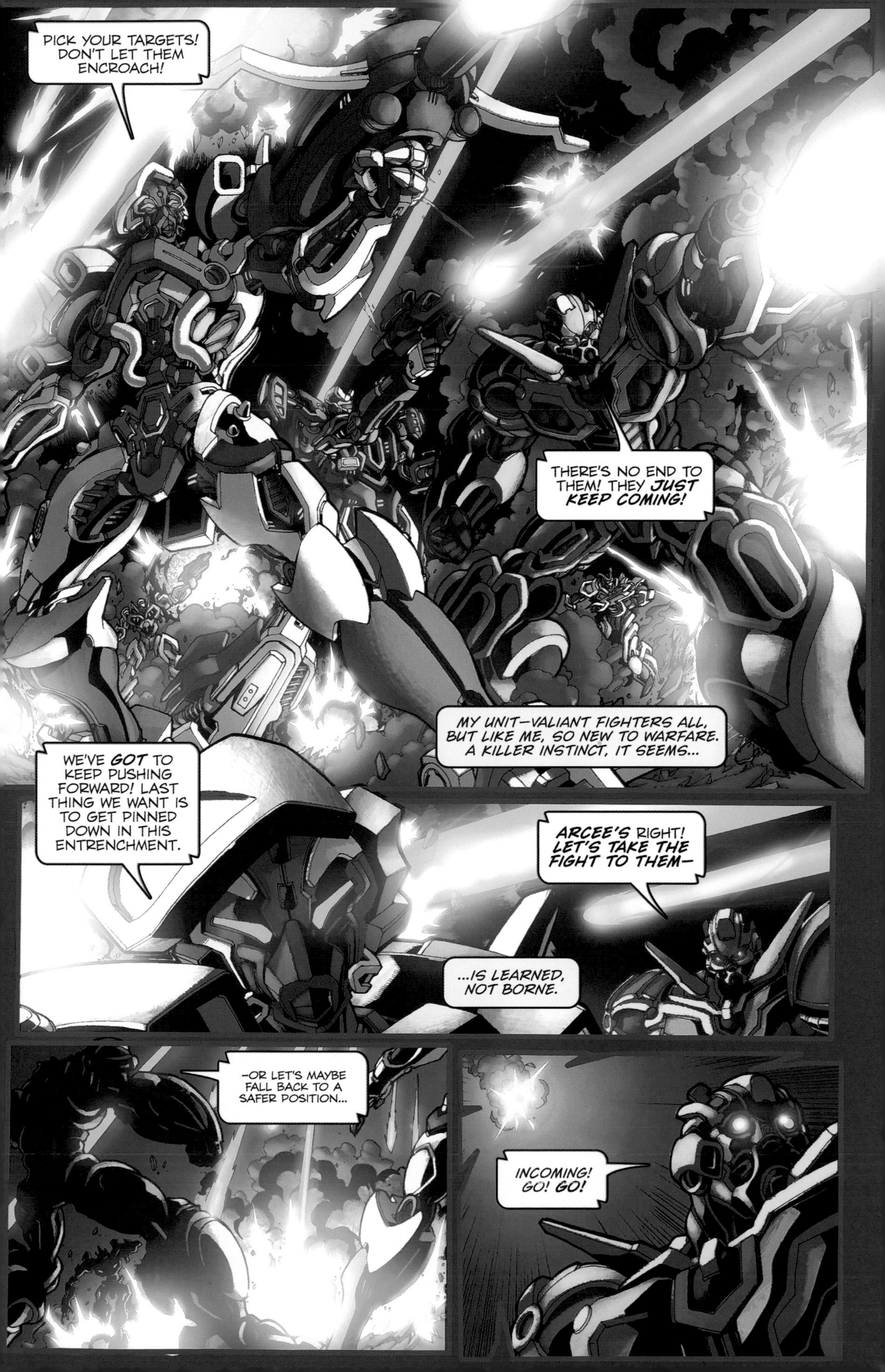

PICK YOUR TARGETS! DON'T LET THEM ENCROACH!
THERE'S NO END TO THEM! THEY JUST KEEP COMING!
MY UNIT—VALIANT FIGHTERS ALL, BUT LIKE ME, SO NEW TO WARFARE. A KILLER INSTINCT, IT SEEMS...
WE'VE GOT TO KEEP PUSHING FORWARD! LAST THING WE WANT IS TO GET PINNED DOWN IN THIS ENTRENCHMENT.
ARCEE'S RIGHT! LET'S TAKE THE FIGHT TO THEM—
...IS LEARNED, NOT BORNE.
—OR LET'S MAYBE FALL BACK TO A SAFER POSITION...
INCOMING! GO! GO!

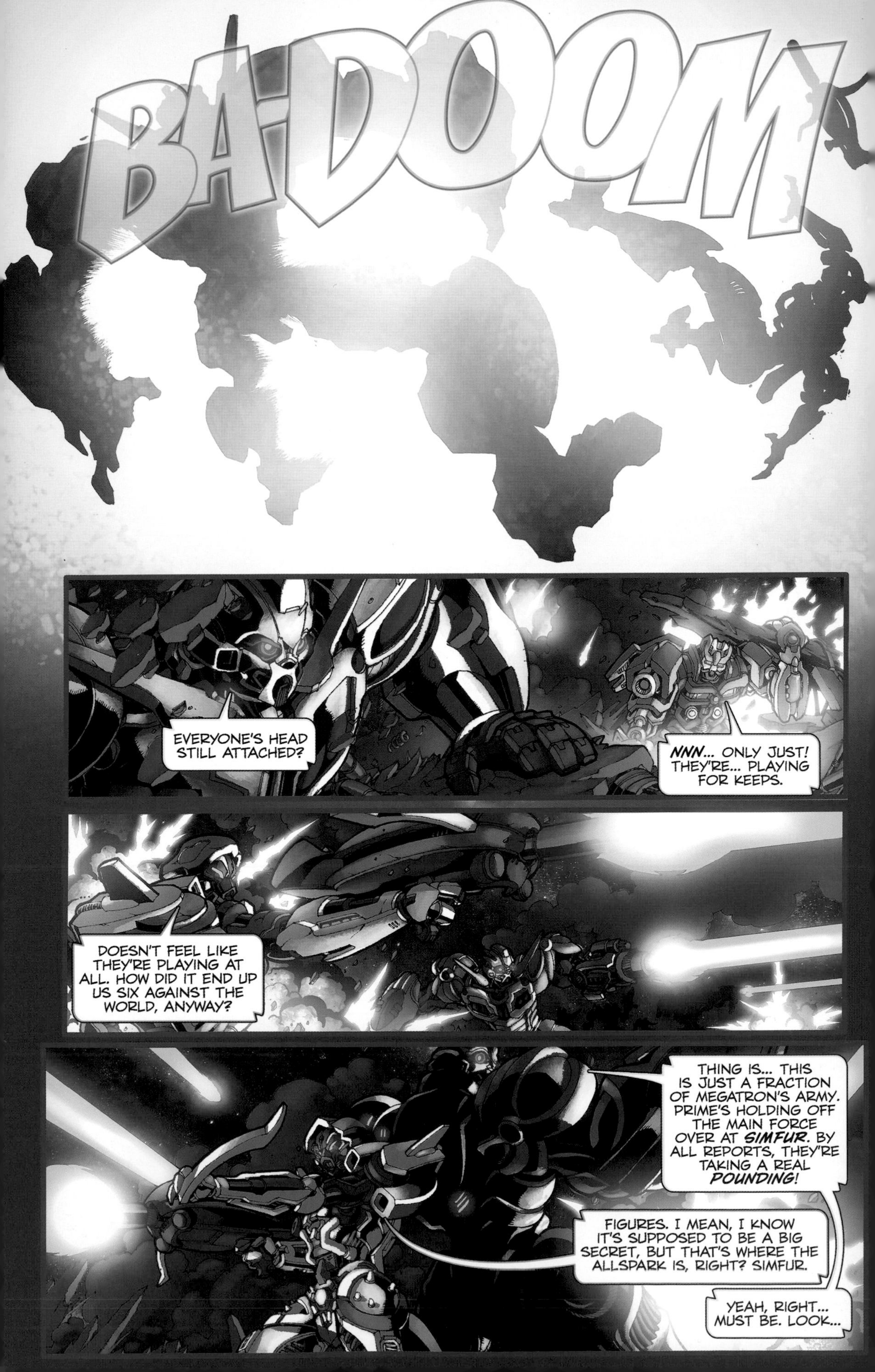
BA-DOOM
EVERYONE'S HEAD STILL ATTACHED?
NNN... ONLY JUST! THEY'RE... PLAYING FOR KEEPS.
DOESN'T FEEL LIKE THEY'RE PLAYING AT ALL. HOW DID IT END UP US SIX AGAINST THE WORLD, ANYWAY?
THING IS... THIS IS JUST A FRACTION OF MEGATRON'S ARMY. PRIME'S HOLDING OFF THE MAIN FORCE OVER AT SIMFUR. BY ALL REPORTS, THEY'RE TAKING A REAL POUNDING!
FIGURES. I MEAN, I KNOW IT'S SUPPOSED TO BE A BIG SECRET, BUT THAT'S WHERE THE ALLSPARK IS, RIGHT? SIMFUR.
YEAH, RIGHT... MUST BE. LOOK...

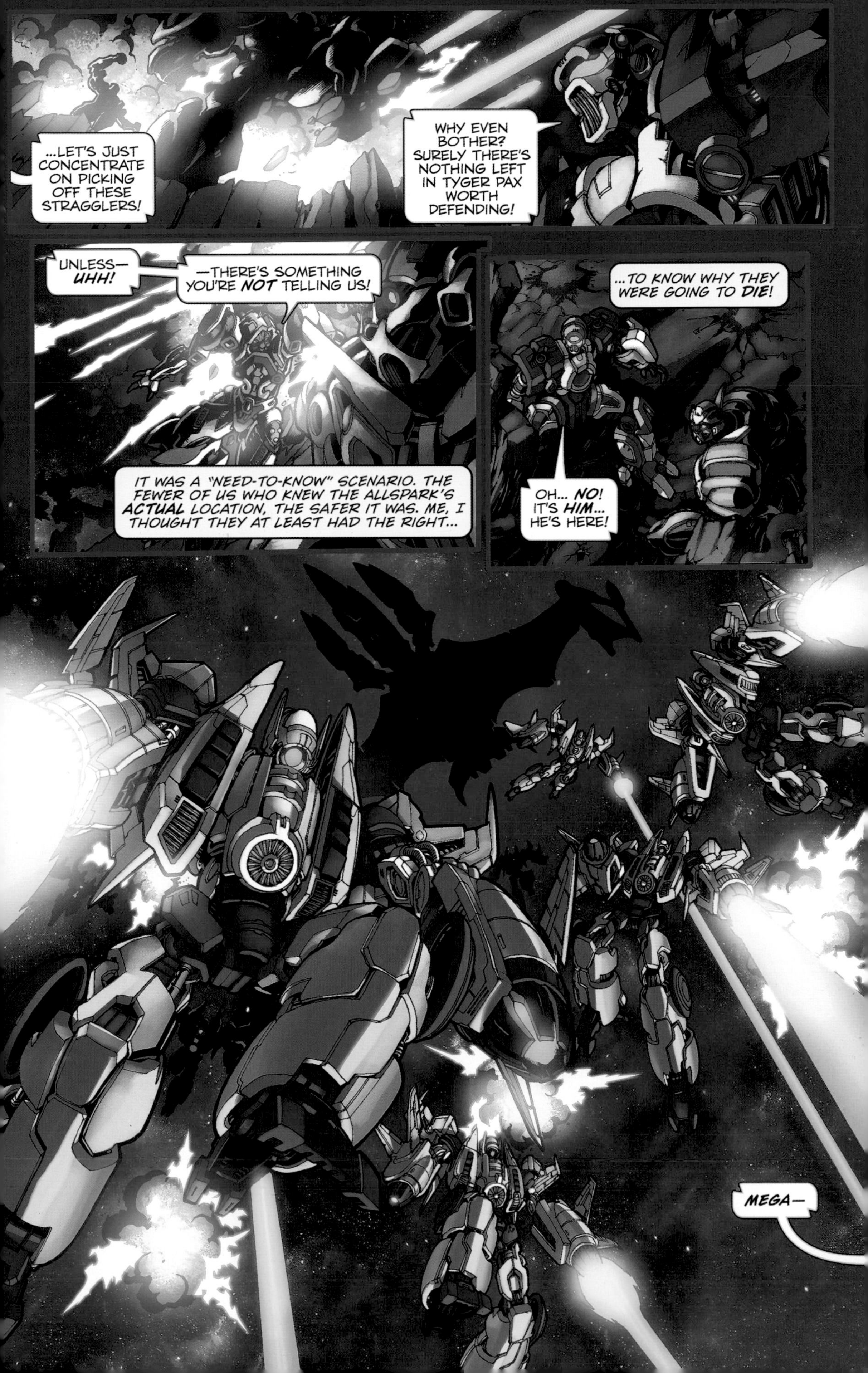
...LET'S JUST CONCENTRATE ON PICKING OFF THESE STRAGGLERS!
WHY EVEN BOTHER? SURELY THERE'S NOTHING LEFT IN TYGER PAX WORTH DEFENDING!
UNLESS— UHH!
—THERE'S SOMETHING YOU'RE NOT TELLING US!
IT WAS A "NEED-TO-KNOW" SCENARIO. THE FEWER OF US WHO KNEW THE ALLSPARK'S ACTUAL LOCATION, THE SAFER IT WAS. ME, I THOUGHT THEY AT LEAST HAD THE RIGHT...
...TO KNOW WHY THEY WERE GOING TO DIE!
OH... NO! IT'S HIM... HE'S HERE!
MEGA—

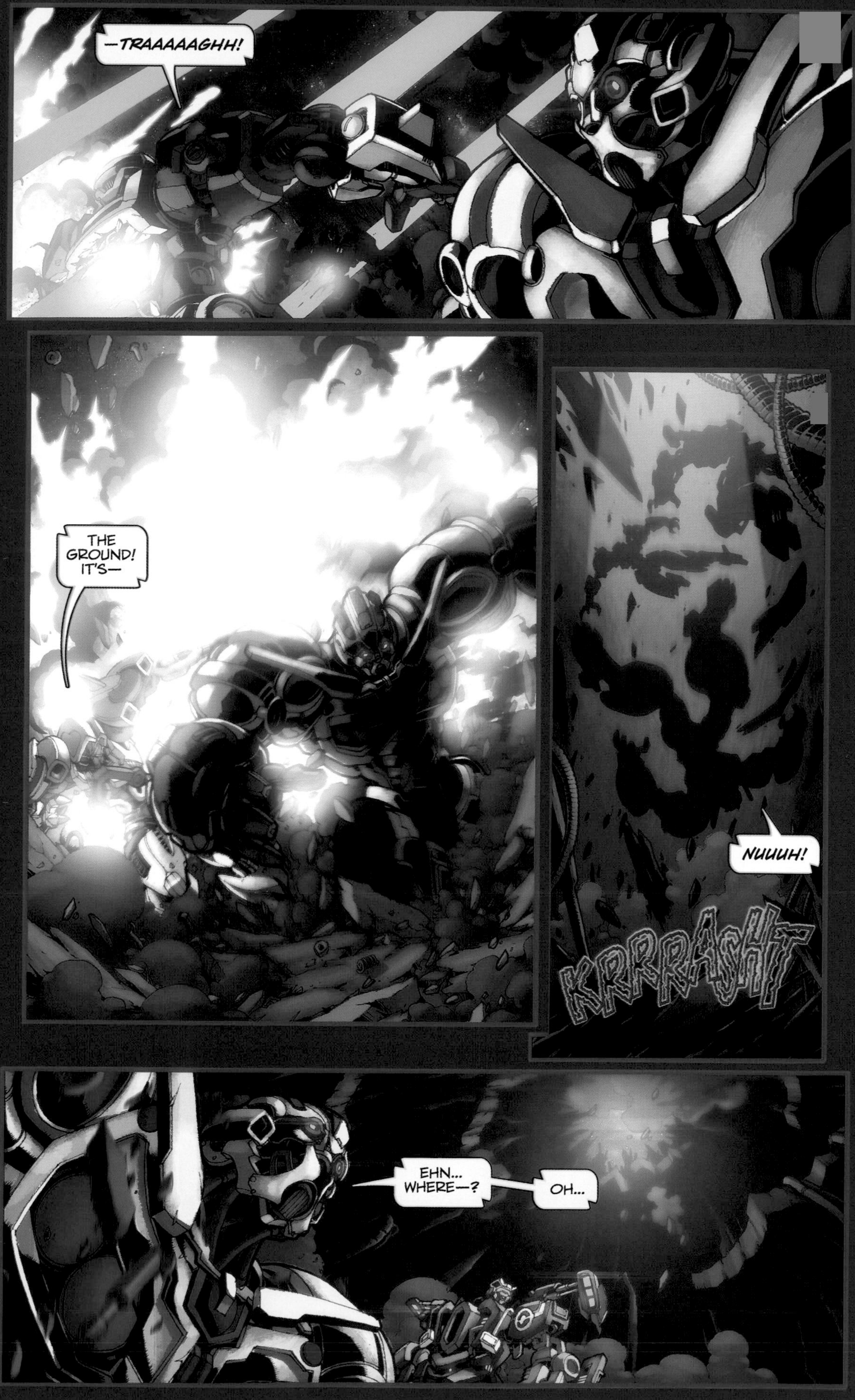
—TRAAAAAGHH!
THE GROUND! IT'S—
NUUUH!
KRRRASHT
EHN... WHERE—?
OH...

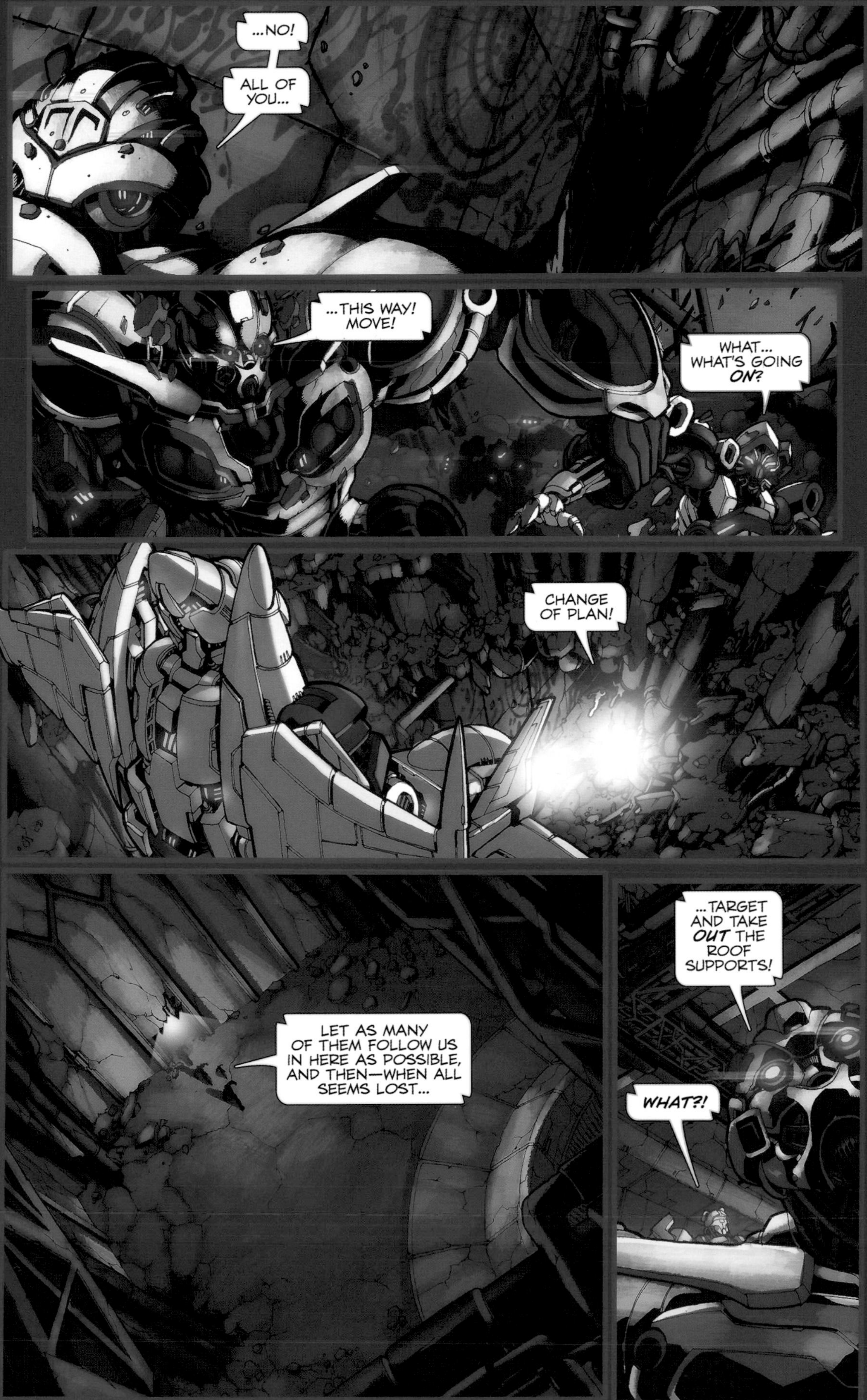
...NO!
ALL OF YOU...
...THIS WAY! MOVE!
WHAT... WHAT'S GOING ON?
CHANGE OF PLAN!
LET AS MANY OF THEM FOLLOW US IN HERE AS POSSIBLE, AND THEN—WHEN ALL SEEMS LOST...
...TARGET AND TAKE OUT THE ROOF SUPPORTS!
WHAT?!

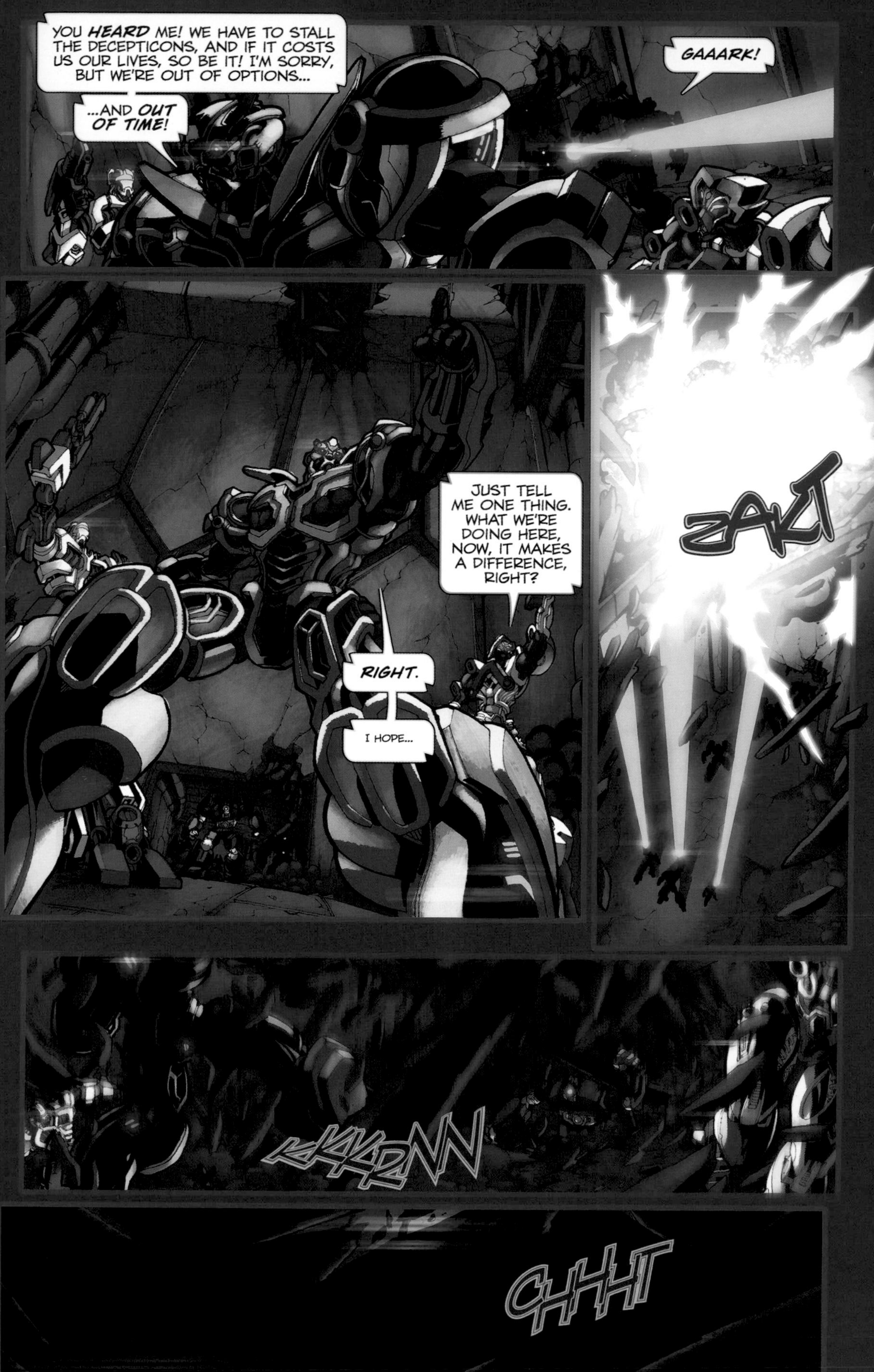
YOU HEARD ME! WE HAVE TO STALL THE DECEPTICONS, AND IF IT COSTS US OUR LIVES, SO BE IT! I'M SORRY, BUT WE'RE OUT OF OPTIONS...
...AND OUT OF TIME!
GAAARK!
JUST TELL ME ONE THING. WHAT WE'RE DOING HERE, NOW, IT MAKES A DIFFERENCE, RIGHT?
RIGHT.
I HOPE...
ZAKT
KKKKRNN
CHHHT

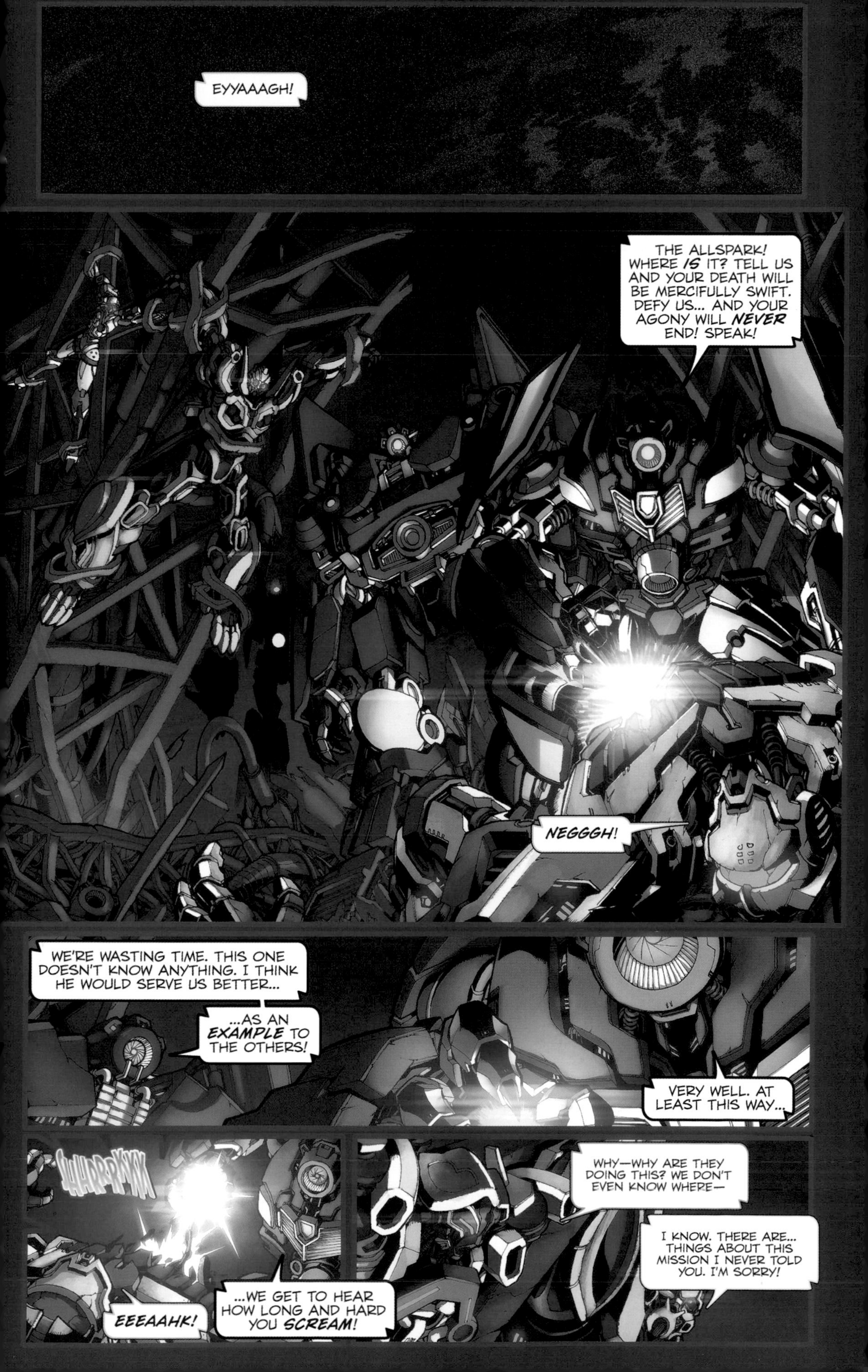
EYYAAAGH!
THE ALLSPARK! WHERE IS IT? TELL US AND YOUR DEATH WILL BE MERCIFULLY SWIFT. DEFY US... AND YOUR AGONY WILL NEVER END! SPEAK!
NEGGGH!
WE'RE WASTING TIME. THIS ONE DOESN'T KNOW ANYTHING. I THINK HE WOULD SERVE US BETTER...
...AS AN EXAMPLE TO THE OTHERS!
VERY WELL. AT LEAST THIS WAY...
...WE GET TO HEAR HOW LONG AND HARD YOU SCREAM!
EEEAAHK!
WHY—WHY ARE THEY DOING THIS? WE DON'T EVEN KNOW WHERE—
I KNOW. THERE ARE... THINGS ABOUT THIS MISSION I NEVER TOLD YOU. I'M SORRY!

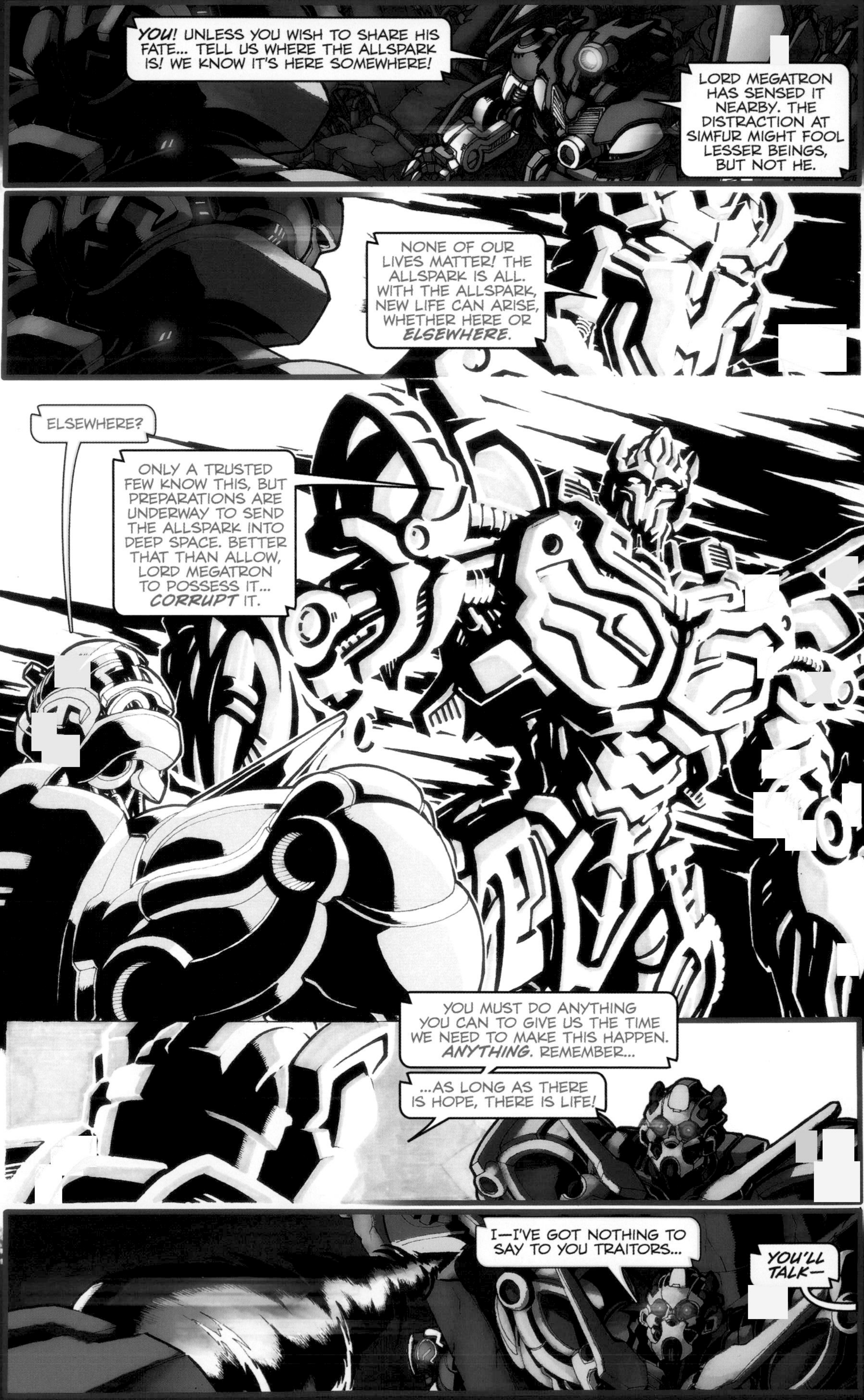
YOU! UNLESS YOU WISH TO SHARE HIS FATE... TELL US WHERE THE ALLSPARK IS! WE KNOW IT'S HERE SOMEWHERE!
LORD MEGATRON HAS SENSED IT NEARBY. THE DISTRACTION AT SIMFUR MIGHT FOOL LESSER BEINGS, BUT NOT HE.
NONE OF OUR LIVES MATTER! THE ALLSPARK IS ALL. WITH THE ALLSPARK, NEW LIFE CAN ARISE, WHETHER HERE OR ELSEWHERE.
ELSEWHERE?
ONLY A TRUSTED FEW KNOW THIS, BUT PREPARATIONS ARE UNDERWAY TO SEND THE ALLSPARK INTO DEEP SPACE. BETTER THAT THAN ALLOW, LORD MEGATRON TO POSSESS IT... CORRUPT IT.
YOU MUST DO ANYTHING YOU CAN TO GIVE US THE TIME WE NEED TO MAKE THIS HAPPEN. ANYTHING. REMEMBER...
...AS LONG AS THERE IS HOPE, THERE IS LIFE!
I—I'VE GOT NOTHING TO SAY TO YOU TRAITORS...
YOU'LL TALK—

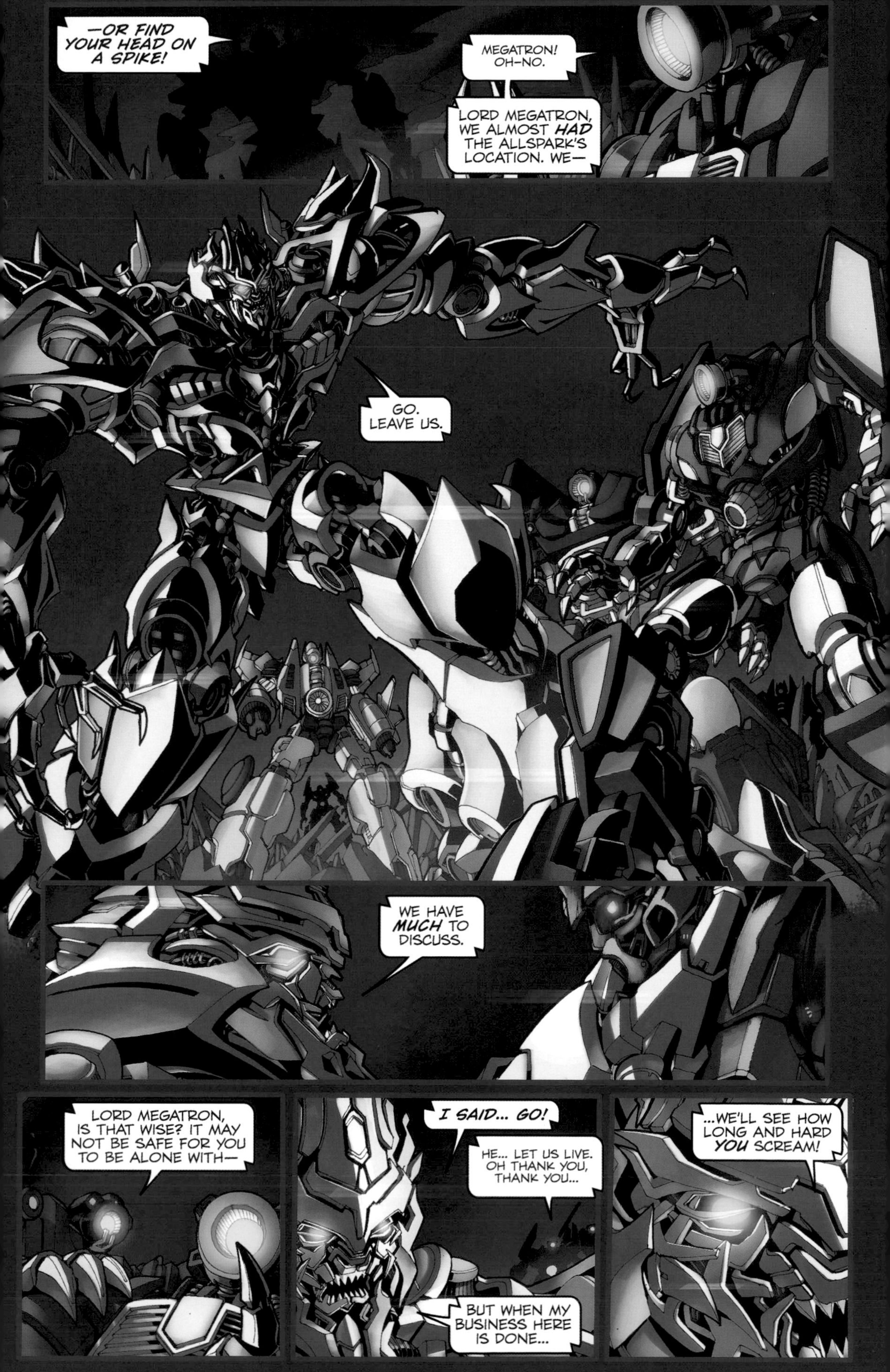
—OR FIND YOUR HEAD ON A SPIKE!
MEGATRON! OH—NO.
LORD MEGATRON, WE ALMOST HAD THE ALLSPARK'S LOCATION. WE—
GO. LEAVE US.
WE HAVE MUCH TO DISCUSS.
LORD MEGATRON, IS THAT WISE? IT MAY NOT BE SAFE FOR YOU TO BE ALONE WITH—
I SAID... GO!
HE... LET US LIVE. OH THANK YOU, THANK YOU...
BUT WHEN MY BUSINESS HERE IS DONE...
...WE'LL SEE HOW LONG AND HARD YOU SCREAM!

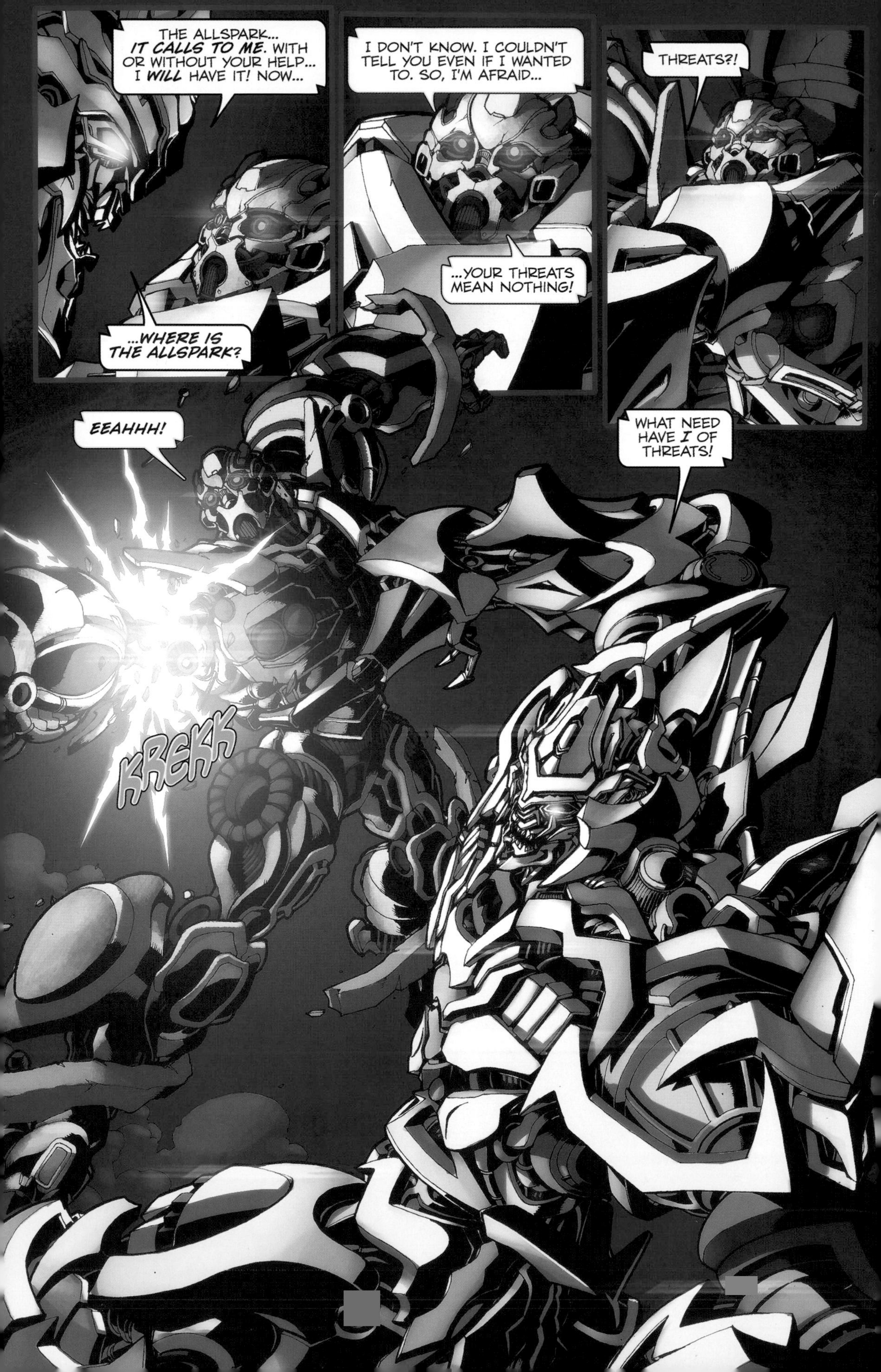
THE ALLSPARK... IT CALLS TO ME. WITH OR WITHOUT YOUR HELP... I WILL HAVE IT! NOW...
...WHERE IS THE ALLSPARK?
I DON'T KNOW. I COULDN'T TELL YOU EVEN IF I WANTED TO. SO, I'M AFRAID...
...YOUR THREATS MEAN NOTHING!
THREATS?!
WHAT NEED HAVE I OF THREATS!
EEAHHH!
KREKK

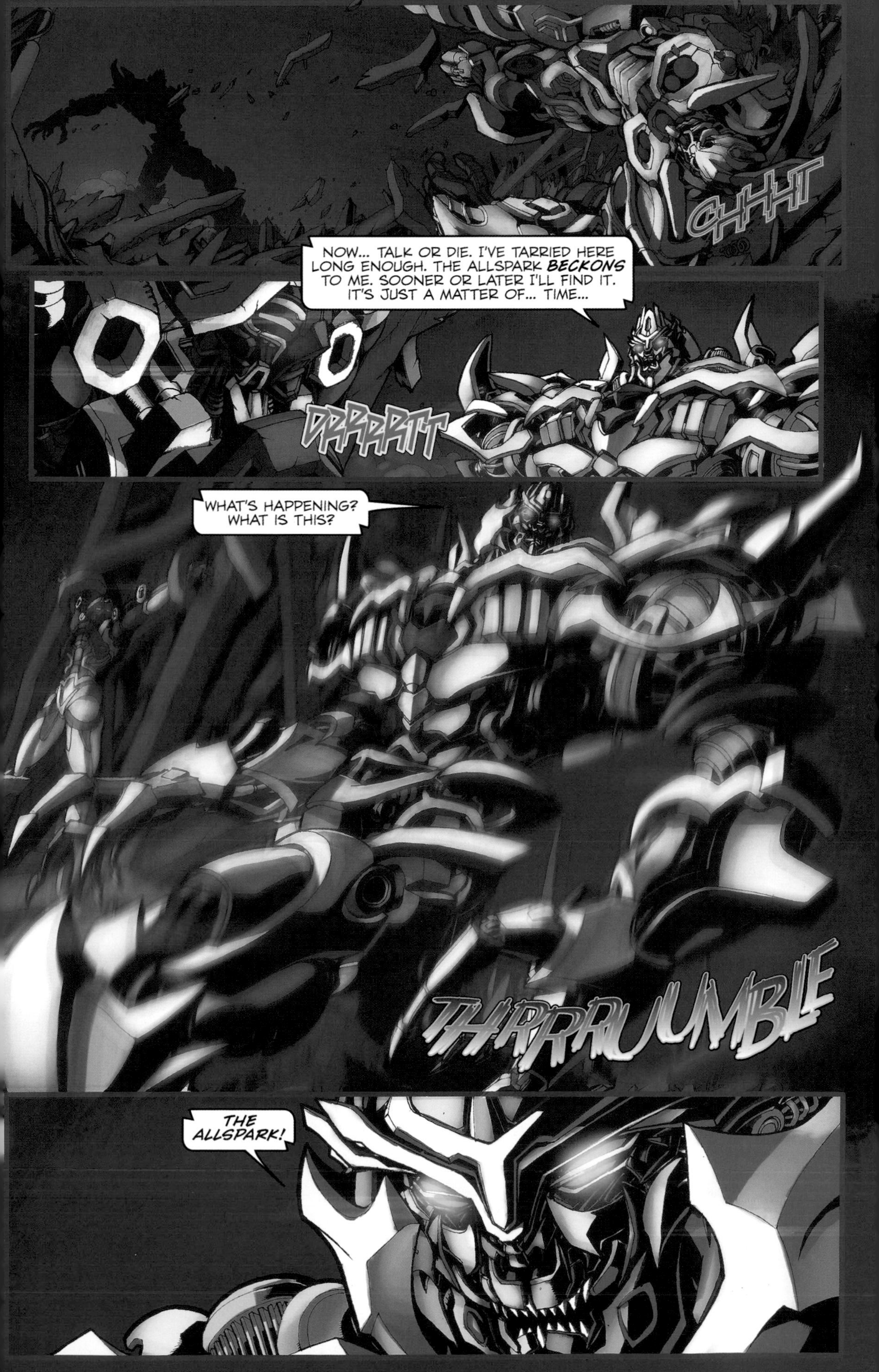
CHHHT
NOW... TALK OR DIE. I'VE TARRIED HERE LONG ENOUGH. THE ALLSPARK BECKONS TO ME. SOONER OR LATER I'LL FIND IT. IT'S JUST A MATTER OF... TIME...
DRRRRTT
WHAT'S HAPPENING? WHAT IS THIS?
THRRRUUMBLE
THE ALLSPARK!

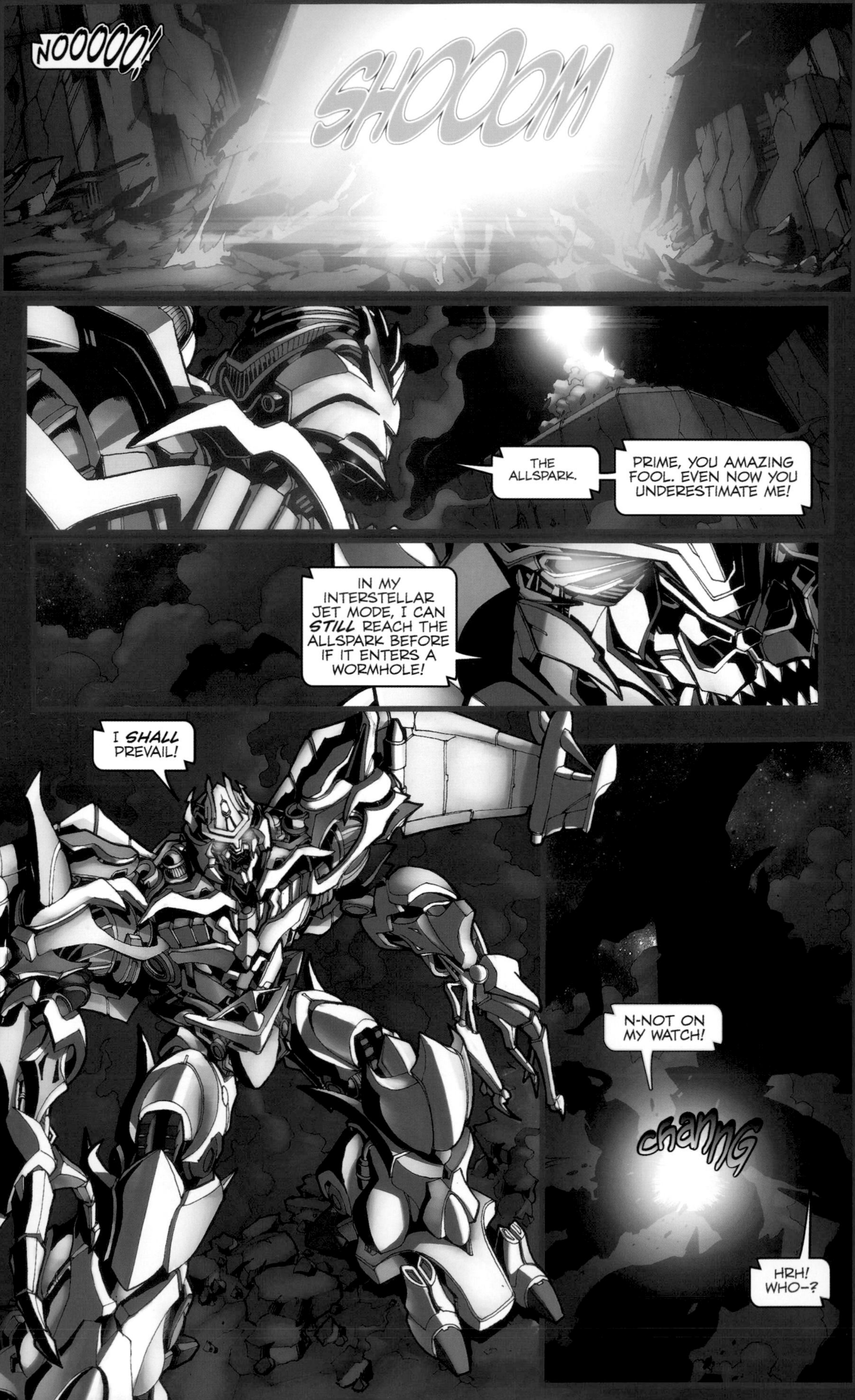
NOOOOO!
SHOOOM
THE ALLSPARK.
PRIME, YOU AMAZING FOOL. EVEN NOW YOU UNDERESTIMATE ME!
IN MY INTERSTELLAR JET MODE, I CAN STILL REACH THE ALLSPARK BEFORE IF IT ENTERS A WORMHOLE!
I SHALL PREVAIL!
N-NOT ON MY WATCH!
CHANNG
HRH! WHO-?

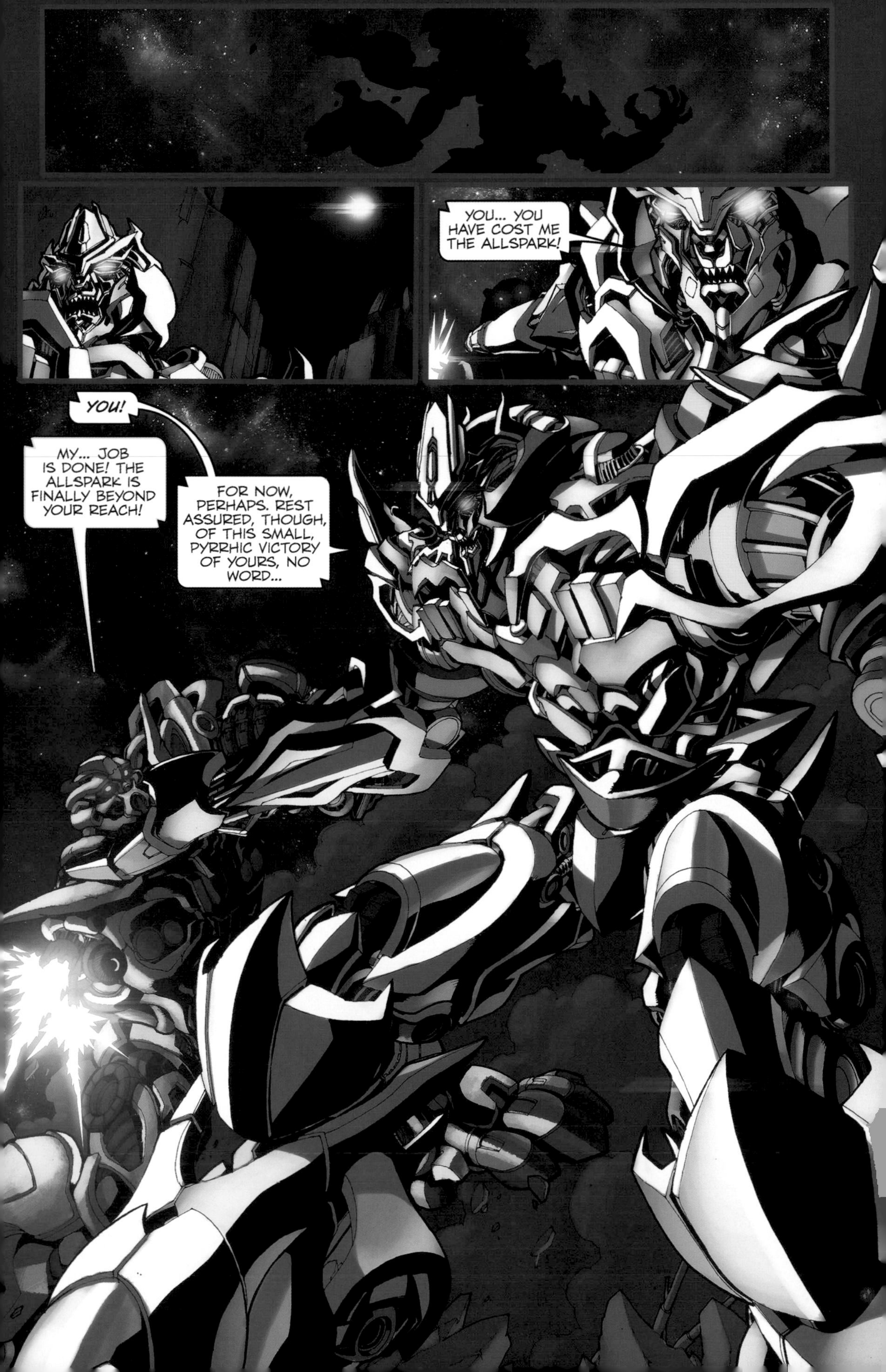
YOU... YOU HAVE COST ME THE ALLSPARK!
YOU!
MY... JOB IS DONE! THE ALLSPARK IS FINALLY BEYOND YOUR REACH!
FOR NOW, PERHAPS. REST ASSURED, THOUGH, OF THIS SMALL, PYRRHIC VICTORY OF YOURS, NO WORD...

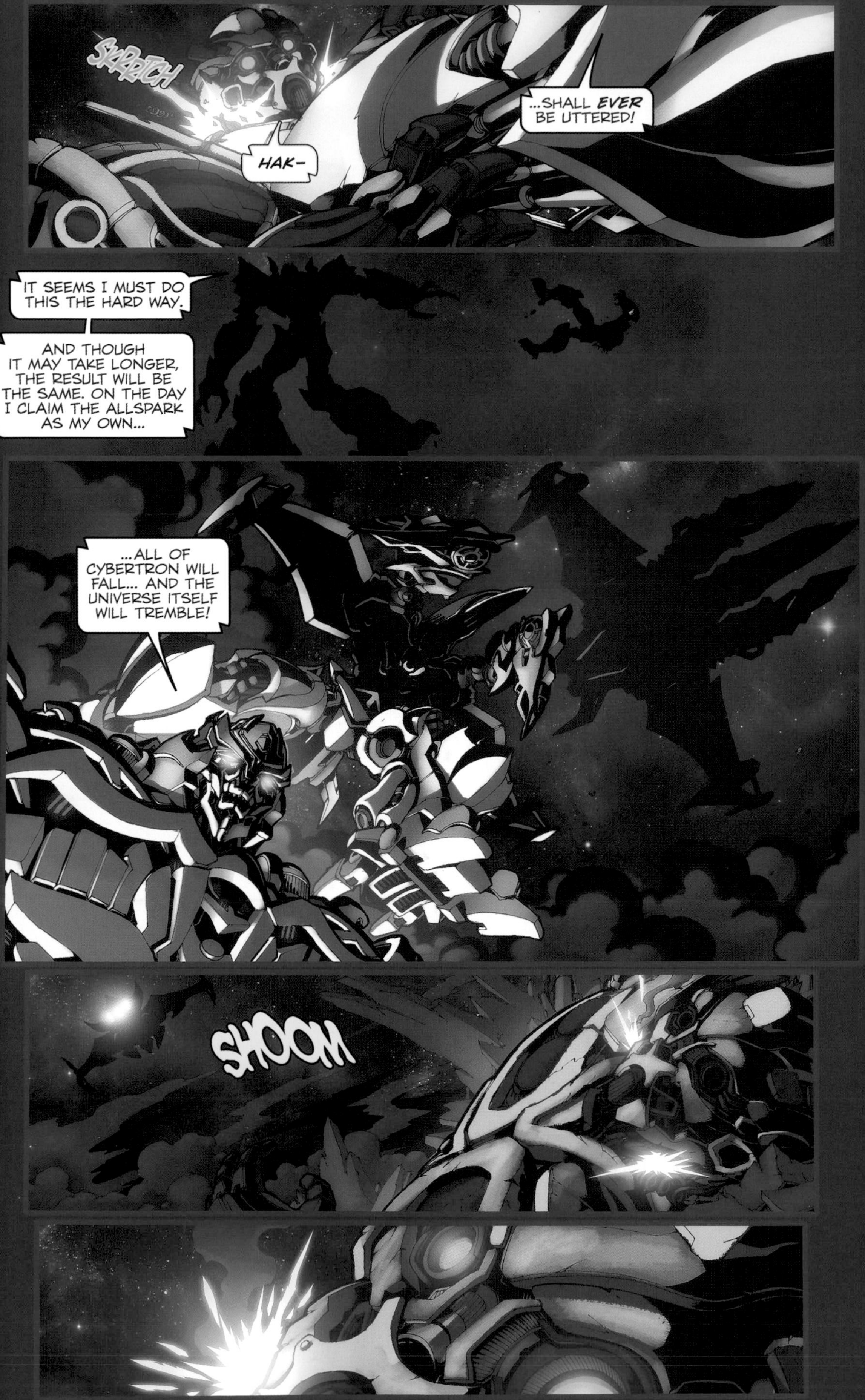
SKRRTCH
...SHALL EVER BE UTTERED!
HAK-
IT SEEMS I MUST DO THIS THE HARD WAY.
AND THOUGH IT MAY TAKE LONGER, THE RESULT WILL BE THE SAME. ON THE DAY I CLAIM THE ALLSPARK AS MY OWN...
...ALL OF CYBERTRON WILL FALL... AND THE UNIVERSE ITSELF WILL TREMBLE!
SHOOM

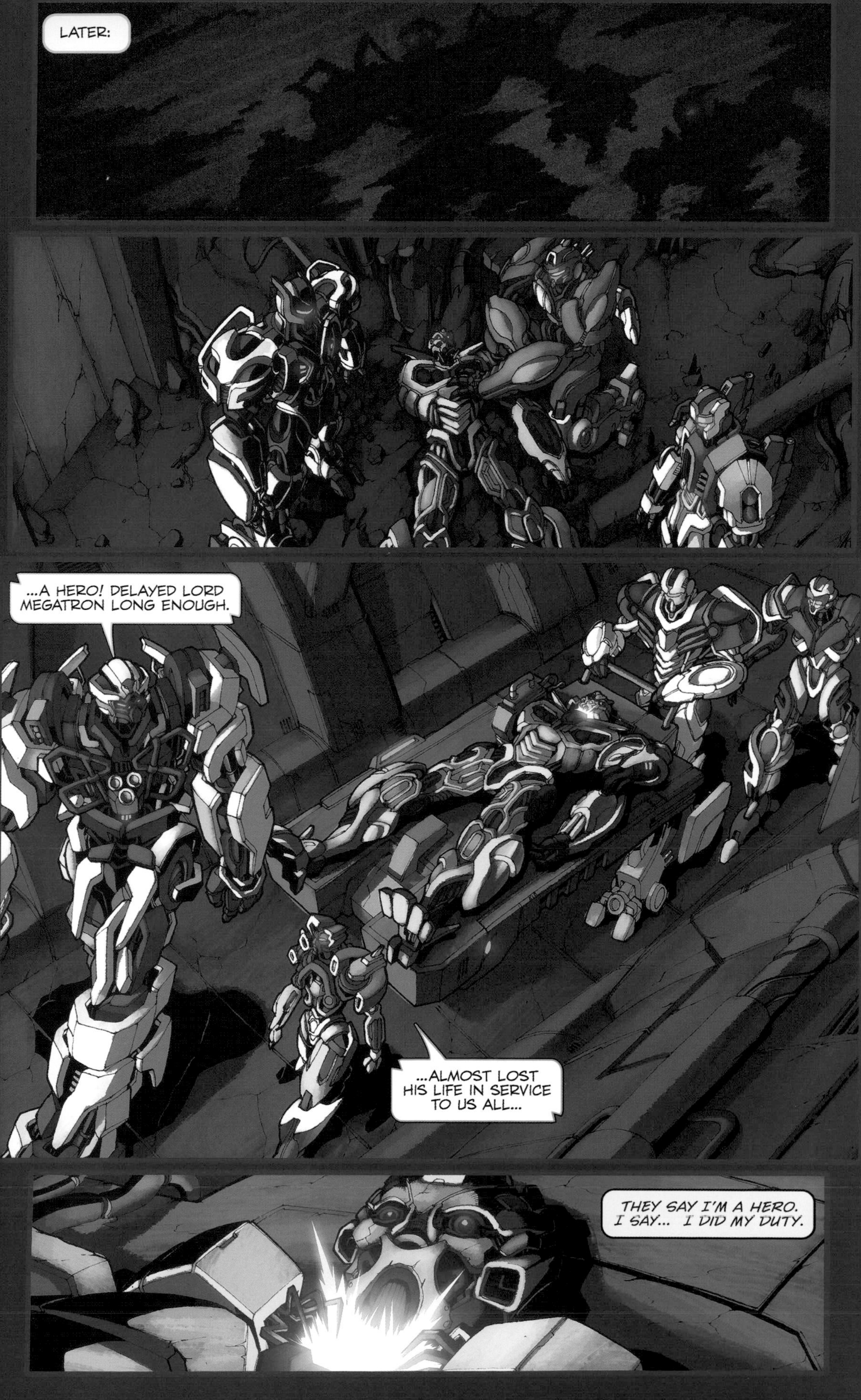
LATER:
...A HERO! DELAYED LORD MEGATRON LONG ENOUGH.
...ALMOST LOST HIS LIFE IN SERVICE TO US ALL...
THEY SAY I'M A HERO. I SAY... I DID MY DUTY.

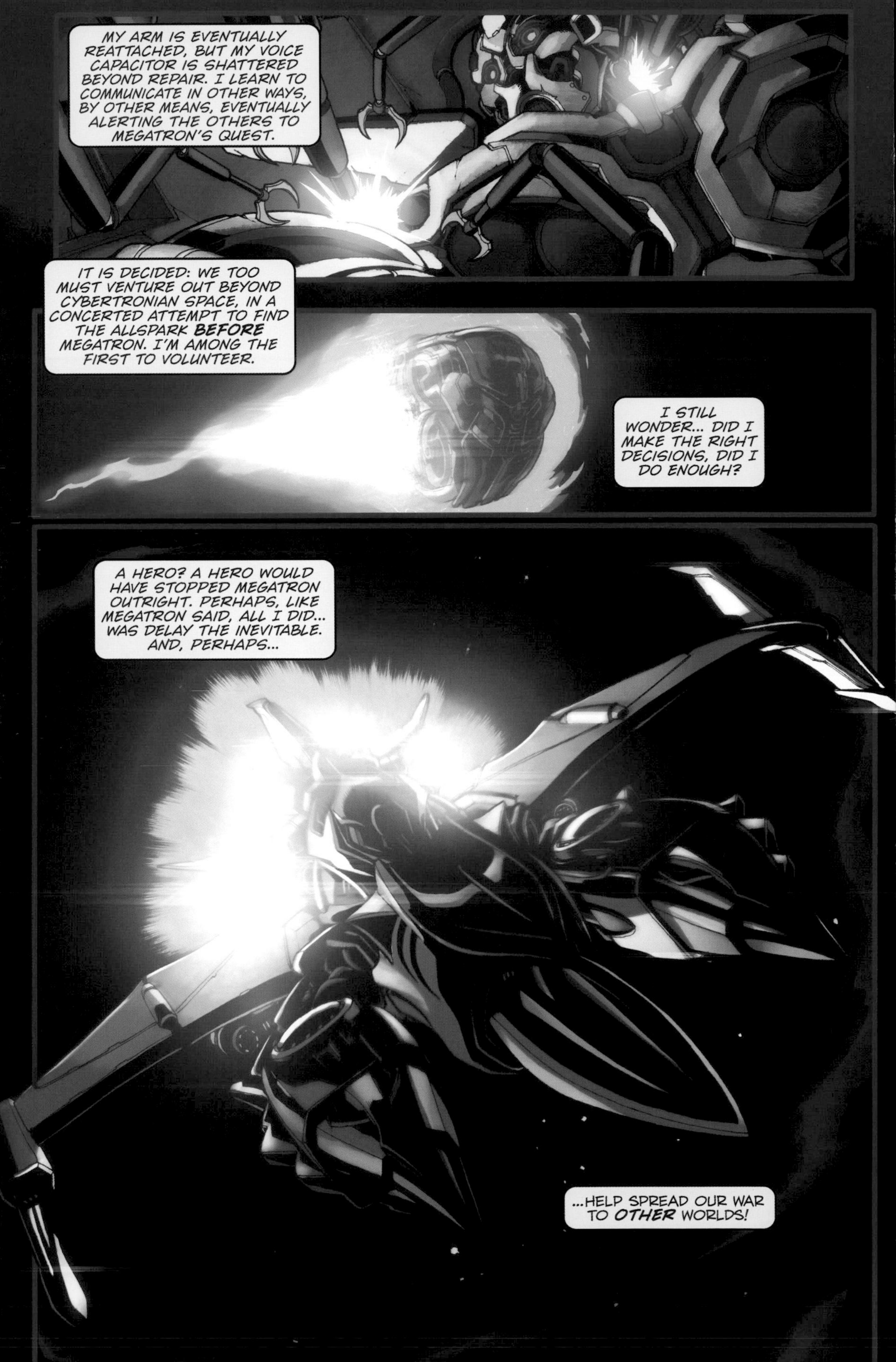
MY ARM IS EVENTUALLY REATTACHED, BUT MY VOICE CAPACITOR IS SHATTERED BEYOND REPAIR. I LEARN TO COMMUNICATE IN OTHER WAYS, BY OTHER MEANS, EVENTUALLY ALERTING THE OTHERS TO MEGATRON'S QUEST.
IT IS DECIDED: WE TOO MUST VENTURE OUT BEYOND CYBERTRONIAN SPACE, IN A CONCERTED ATTEMPT TO FIND THE ALLSPARK BEFORE MEGATRON. I'M AMONG THE FIRST TO VOLUNTEER.
I STILL WONDER... DID I MAKE THE RIGHT DECISIONS, DID I DO ENOUGH?
A HERO? A HERO WOULD HAVE STOPPED MEGATRON OUTRIGHT. PERHAPS, LIKE MEGATRON SAID, ALL I DID... WAS DELAY THE INEVITABLE. AND, PERHAPS...
...HELP SPREAD OUR WAR TO OTHER WORLDS!

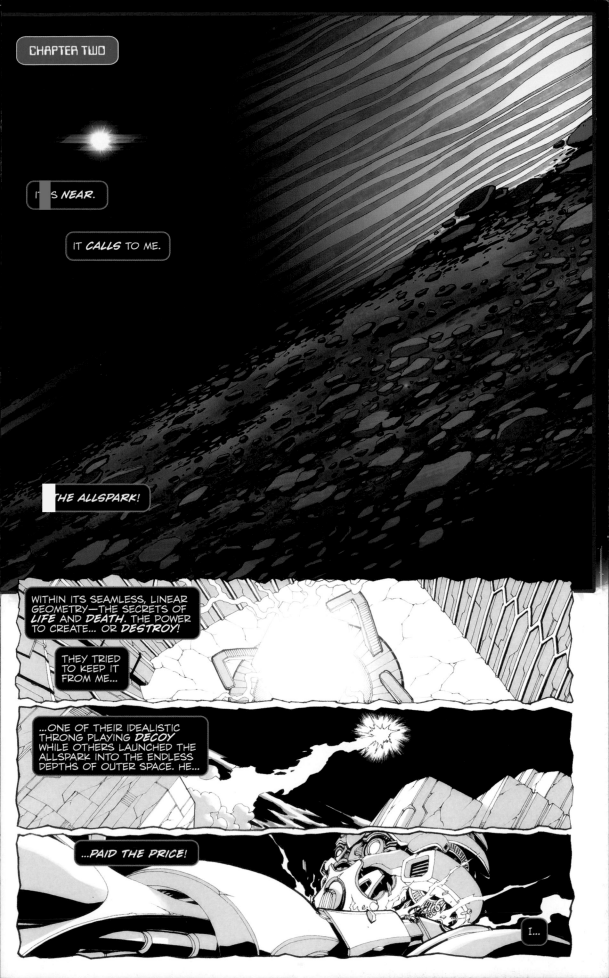

CHAPTER TWO

IT'S *NEAR.*

IT *CALLS* TO ME.

THE *ALLSPARK!*

WITHIN ITS SEAMLESS, LINEAR GEOMETRY—THE SECRETS OF *LIFE* AND *DEATH.* THE POWER TO CREATE... OR *DESTROY!*

THEY TRIED TO KEEP IT FROM ME...

...ONE OF THEIR IDEALISTIC THRONG PLAYING *DECOY* WHILE OTHERS LAUNCHED THE ALLSPARK INTO THE ENDLESS DEPTHS OF OUTER SPACE. HE...

...*PAID THE PRICE!*

I...

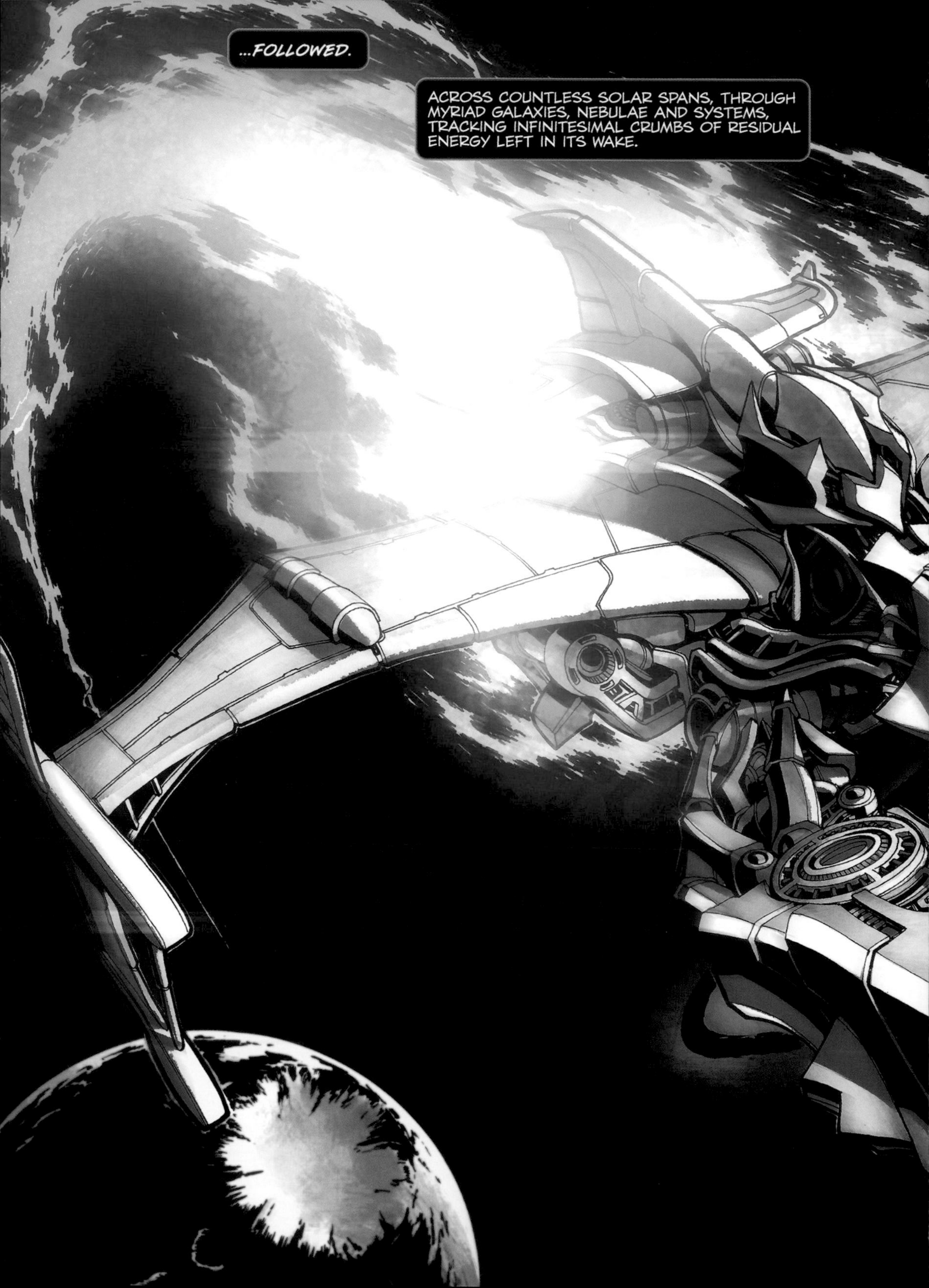
...FOLLOWED.
ACROSS COUNTLESS SOLAR SPANS, THROUGH MYRIAD GALAXIES, NEBULAE AND SYSTEMS, TRACKING INFINITESIMAL CRUMBS OF RESIDUAL ENERGY LEFT IN ITS WAKE.

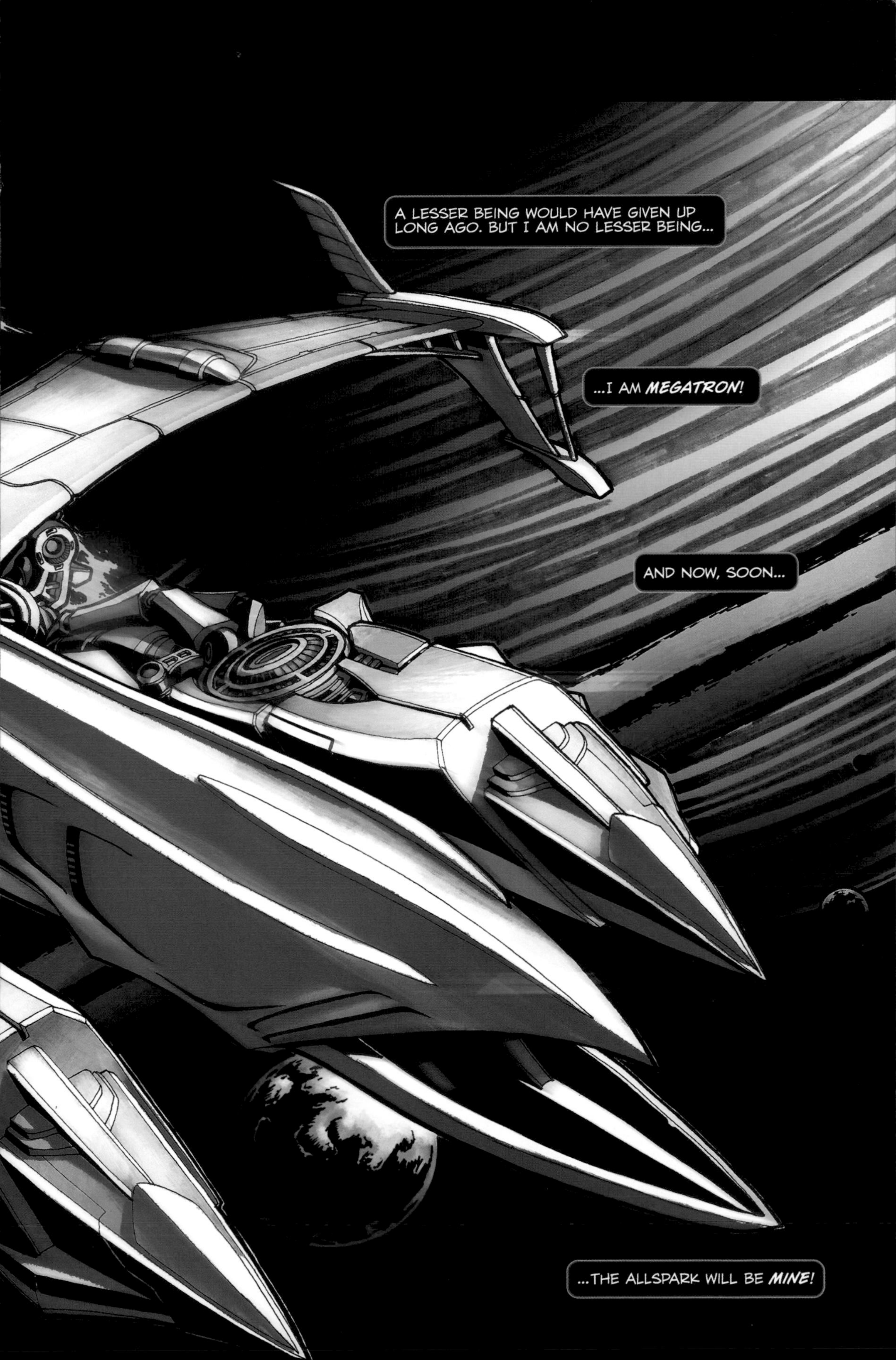
A LESSER BEING WOULD HAVE GIVEN UP LONG AGO. BUT I AM NO LESSER BEING...
...I AM MEGATRON!
AND NOW, SOON...
...THE ALLSPARK WILL BE MINE!

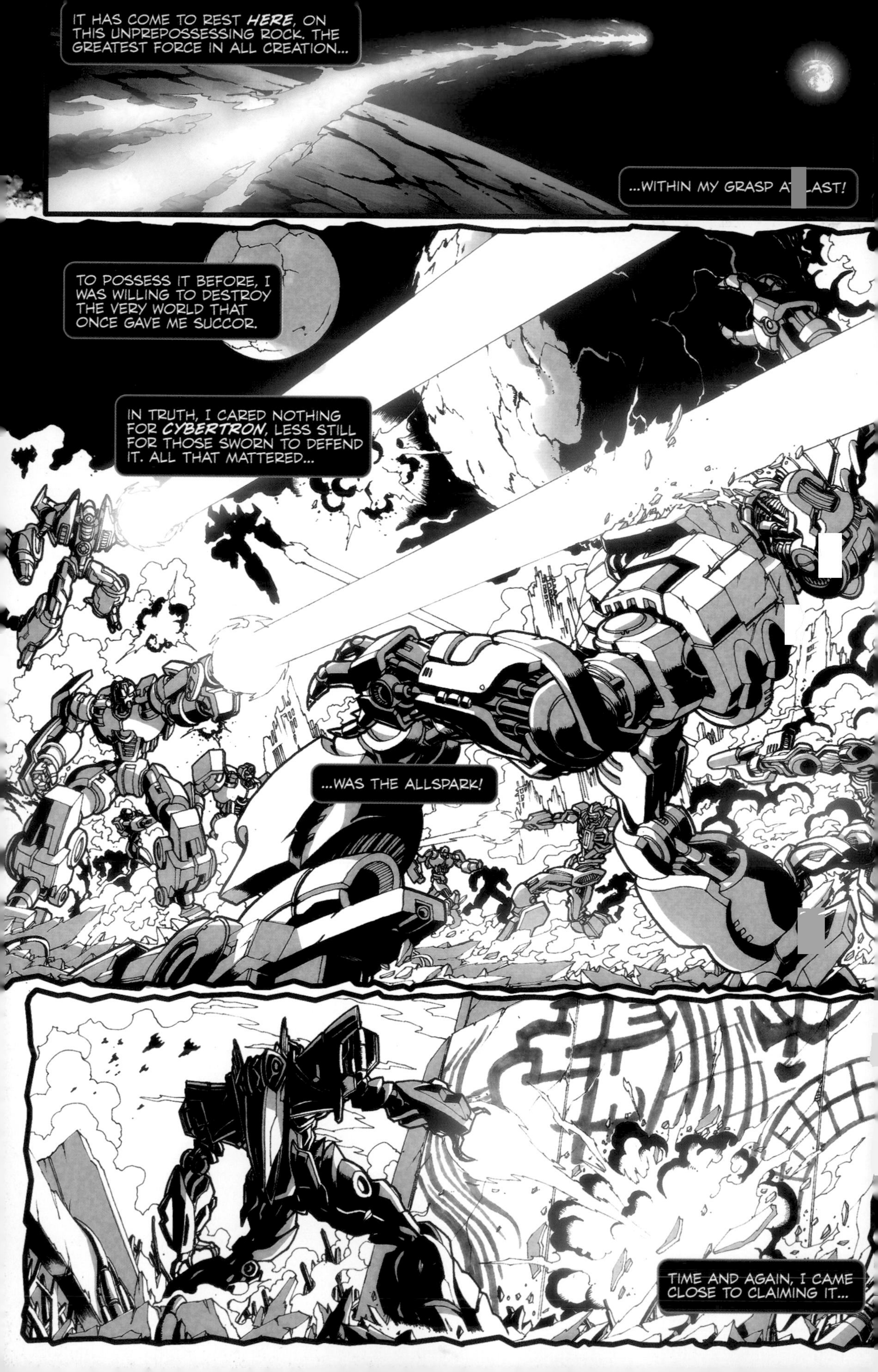
IT HAS COME TO REST HERE, ON THIS UNPREPOSSESSING ROCK. THE GREATEST FORCE IN ALL CREATION...
...WITHIN MY GRASP AT LAST!
TO POSSESS IT BEFORE, I WAS WILLING TO DESTROY THE VERY WORLD THAT ONCE GAVE ME SUCCOR.
IN TRUTH, I CARED NOTHING FOR CYBERTRON, LESS STILL FOR THOSE SWORN TO DEFEND IT. ALL THAT MATTERED...
...WAS THE ALLSPARK!
TIME AND AGAIN, I CAME CLOSE TO CLAIMING IT...

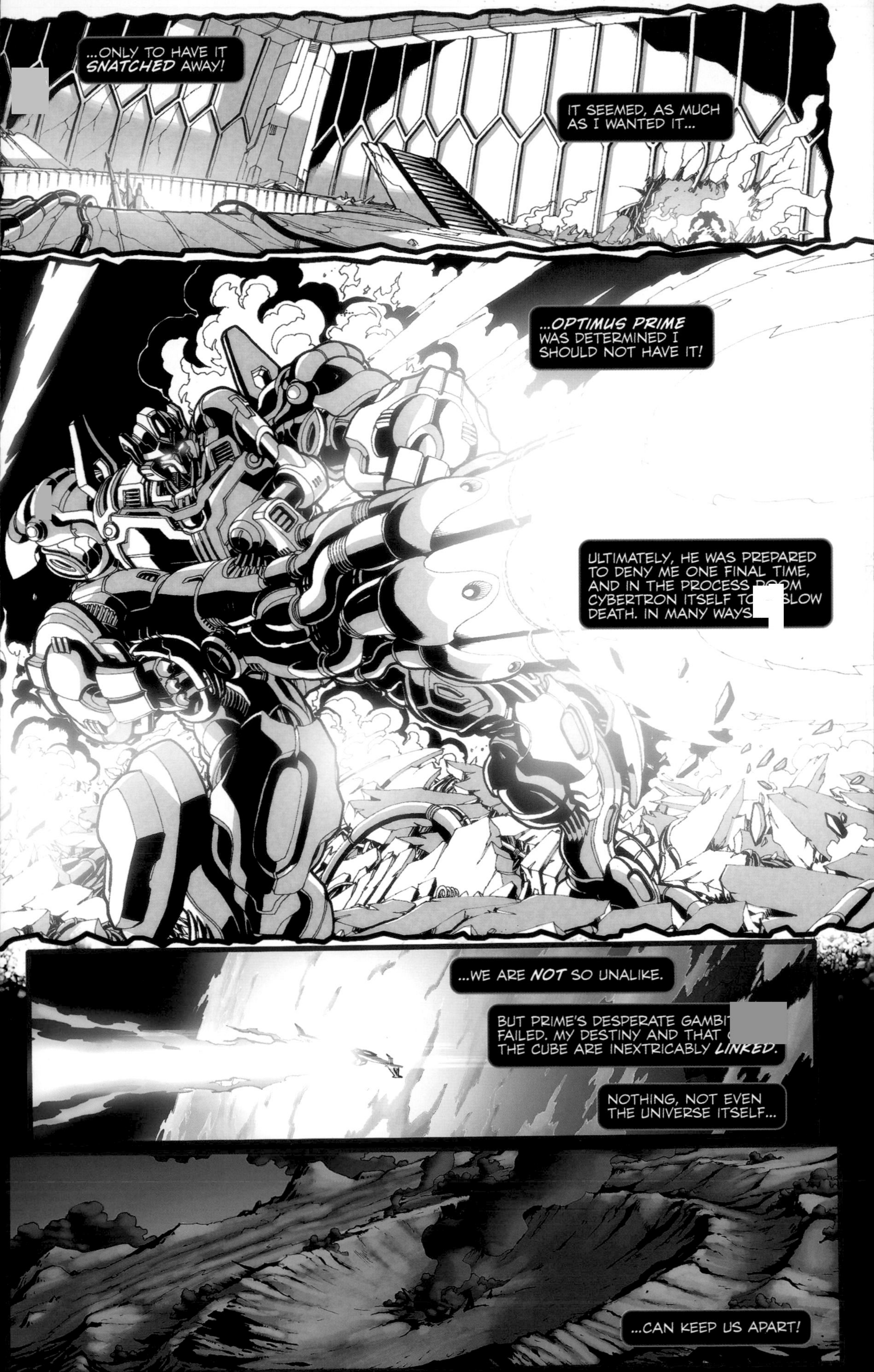

...ONLY TO HAVE IT *SNATCHED* AWAY!
IT SEEMED, AS MUCH AS I WANTED IT...
...*OPTIMUS PRIME* WAS DETERMINED I SHOULD NOT HAVE IT!
ULTIMATELY, HE WAS PREPARED TO DENY ME ONE FINAL TIME, AND IN THE PROCESS DOOM CYBERTRON ITSELF TO SLOW DEATH. IN MANY WAYS
...WE ARE *NOT* SO UNALIKE.
BUT PRIME'S DESPERATE GAMBIT FAILED. MY DESTINY AND THAT THE CUBE ARE INEXTRICABLY *LINKED*.
NOTHING, NOT EVEN THE UNIVERSE ITSELF...
...CAN KEEP US APART!

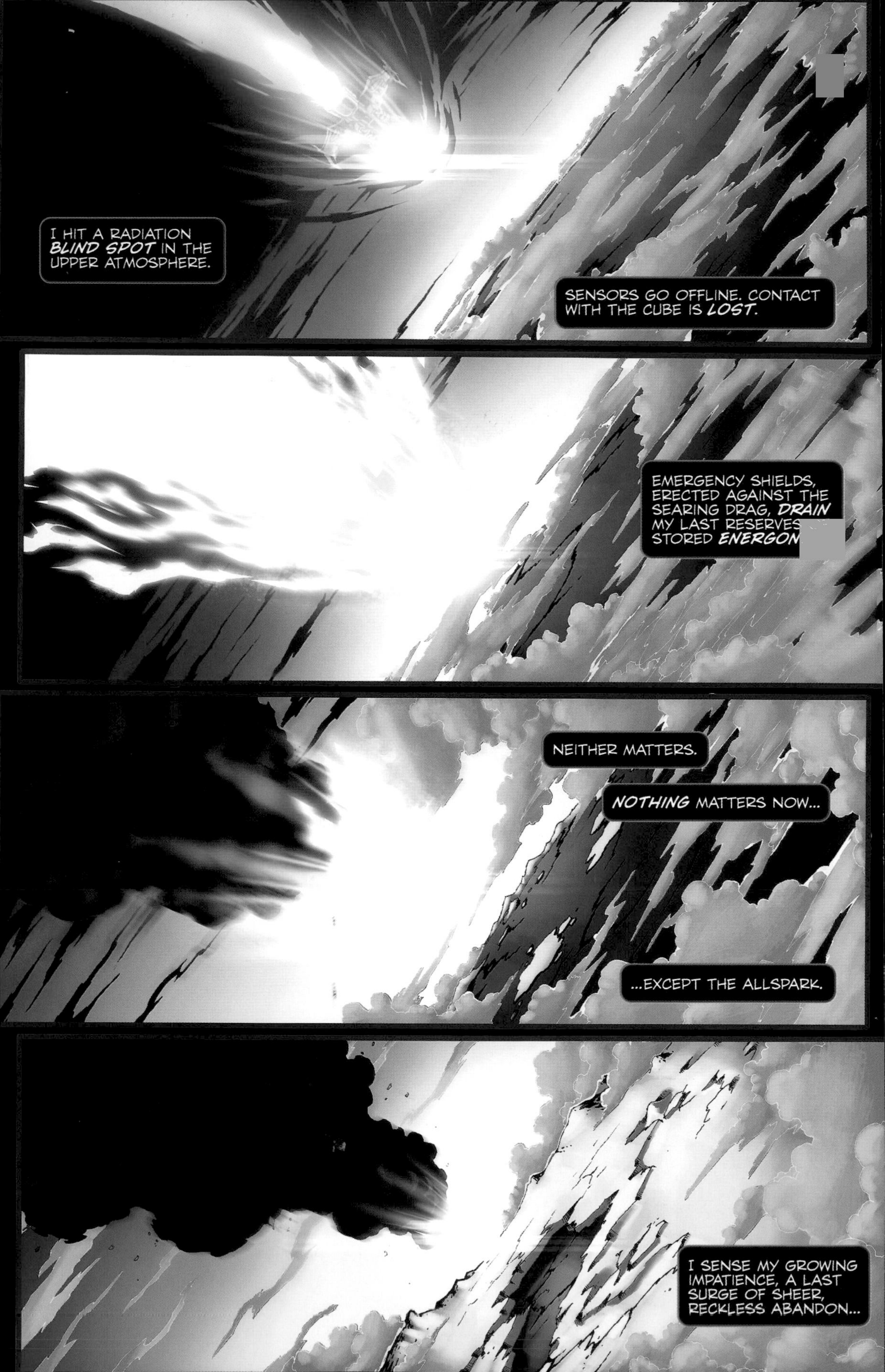

I HIT A RADIATION *BLIND SPOT* IN THE UPPER ATMOSPHERE.
SENSORS GO OFFLINE. CONTACT WITH THE CUBE IS *LOST*.
EMERGENCY SHIELDS, ERECTED AGAINST THE SEARING DRAG, *DRAIN* MY LAST RESERVES
STORED *ENERGON*
NEITHER MATTERS.
NOTHING MATTERS NOW...
...EXCEPT THE ALLSPARK.
I SENSE MY GROWING IMPATIENCE, A LAST SURGE OF SHEER, RECKLESS ABANDON...

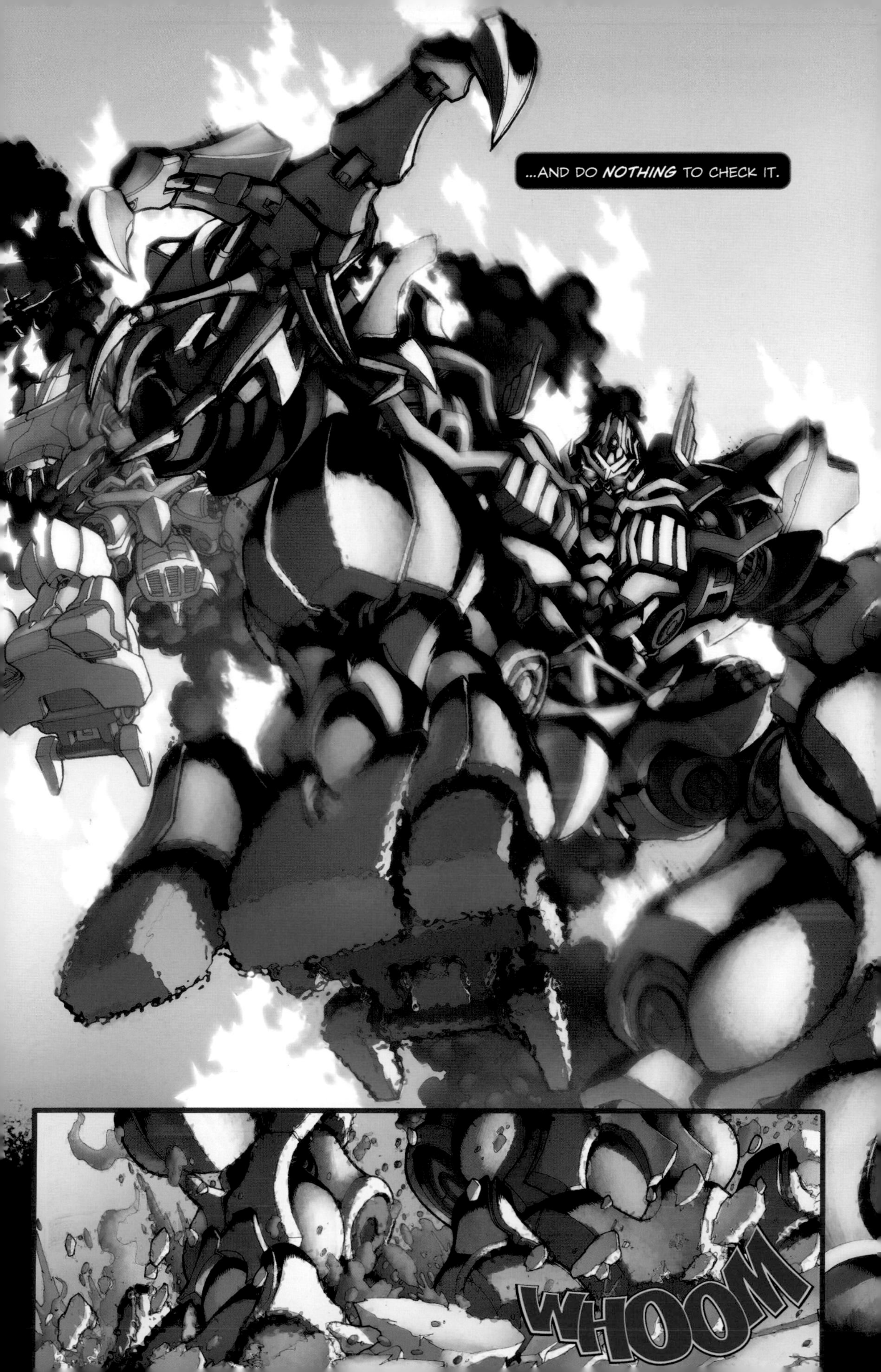
...AND DO NOTHING TO CHECK IT.
WHOOM

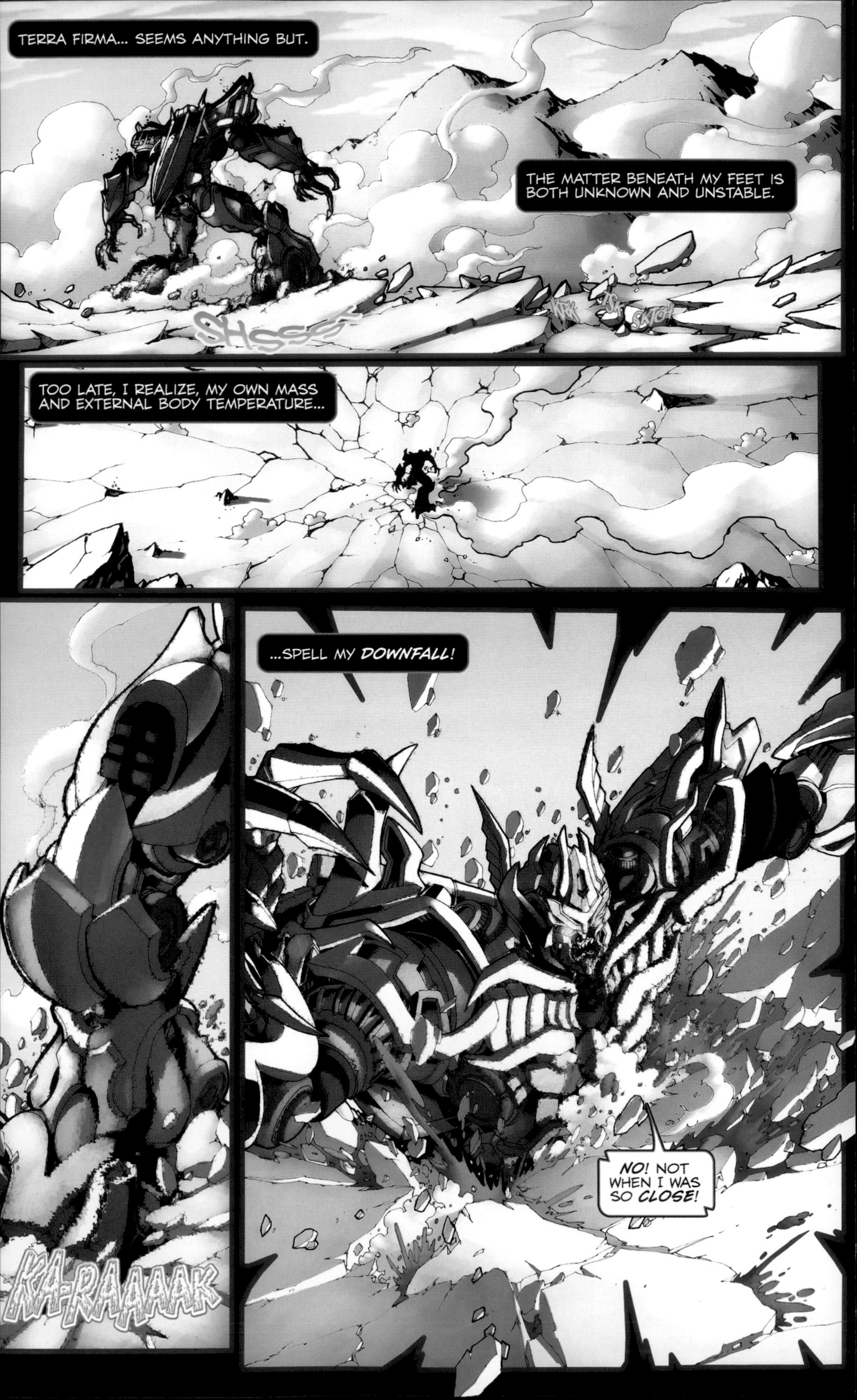

TERRA FIRMA... SEEMS ANYTHING BUT.
THE MATTER BENEATH MY FEET IS BOTH UNKNOWN AND UNSTABLE.
SHSSST
KRK
TSK
SKTCH
TOO LATE, I REALIZE, MY OWN MASS AND EXTERNAL BODY TEMPERATURE...
KA-RAAAAK
...SPELL MY *DOWNFALL*!
NO! NOT WHEN I WAS SO *CLOSE*!

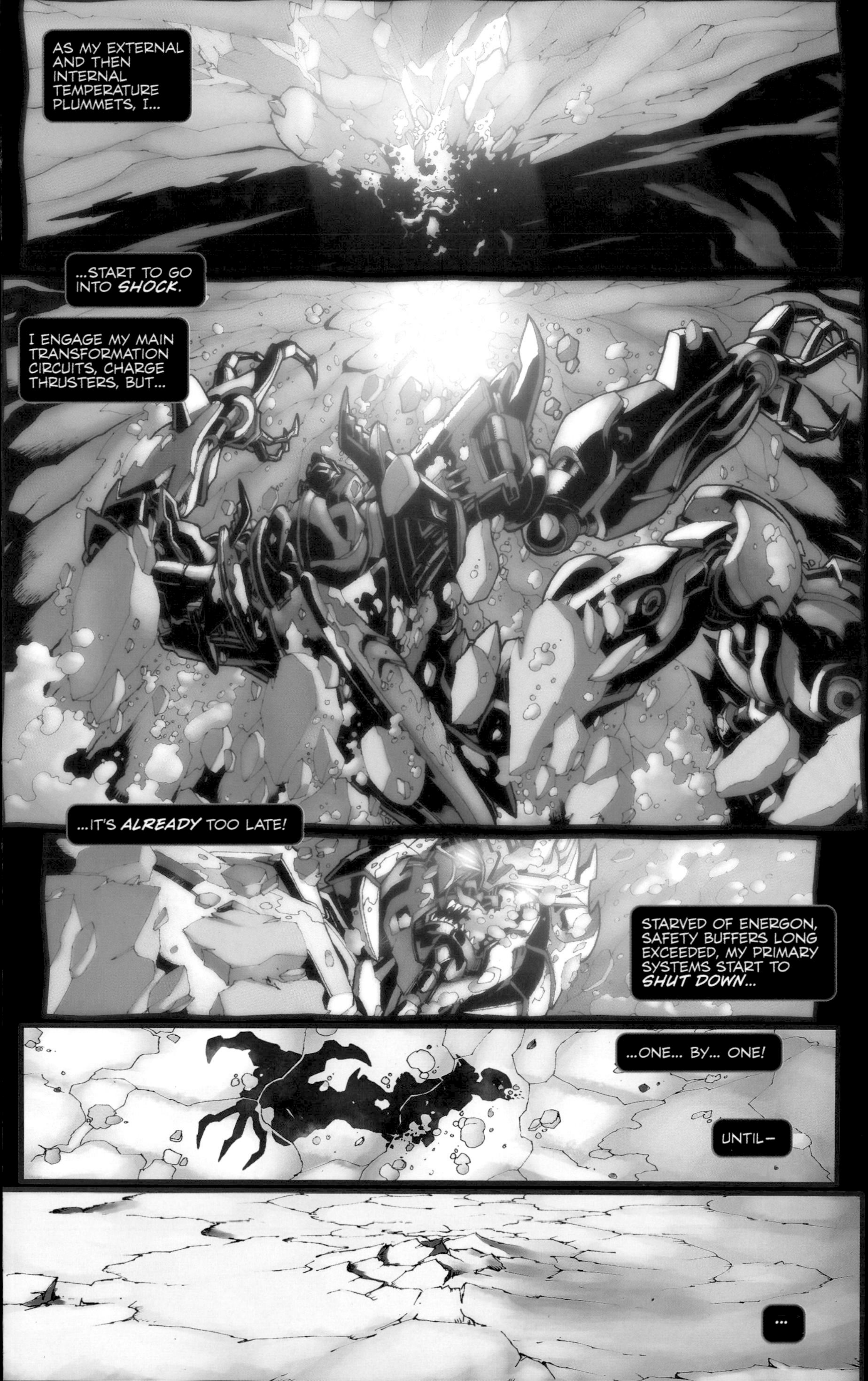
AS MY EXTERNAL AND THEN INTERNAL TEMPERATURE PLUMMETS, I...
...START TO GO INTO SHOCK.
I ENGAGE MY MAIN TRANSFORMATION CIRCUITS, CHARGE THRUSTERS, BUT...
...IT'S ALREADY TOO LATE!
STARVED OF ENERGON, SAFETY BUFFERS LONG EXCEEDED, MY PRIMARY SYSTEMS START TO SHUT DOWN...
...ONE... BY... ONE!
UNTIL—
...

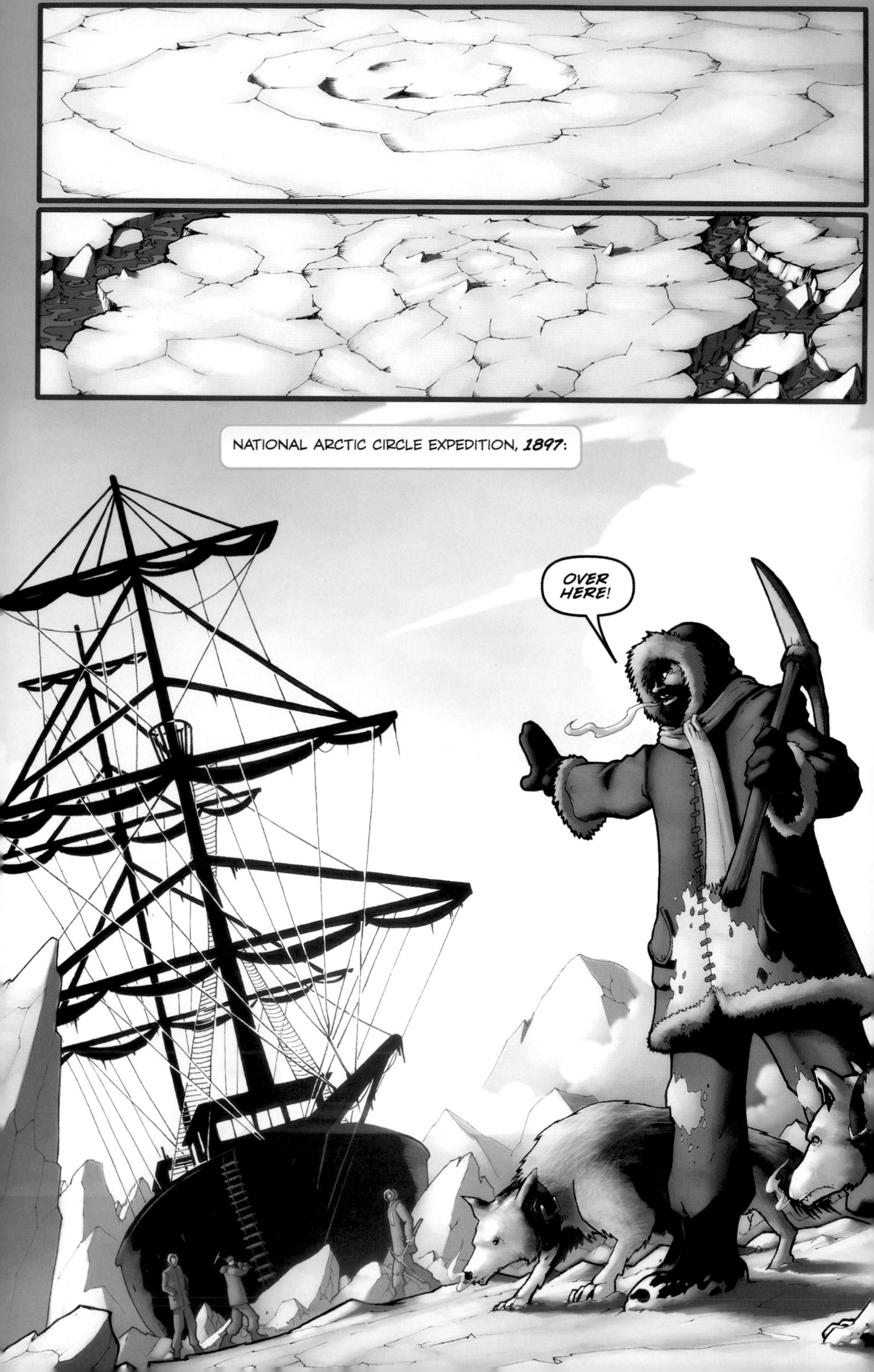
NATIONAL ARCTIC CIRCLE EXPEDITION, 1897:
OVER HERE!

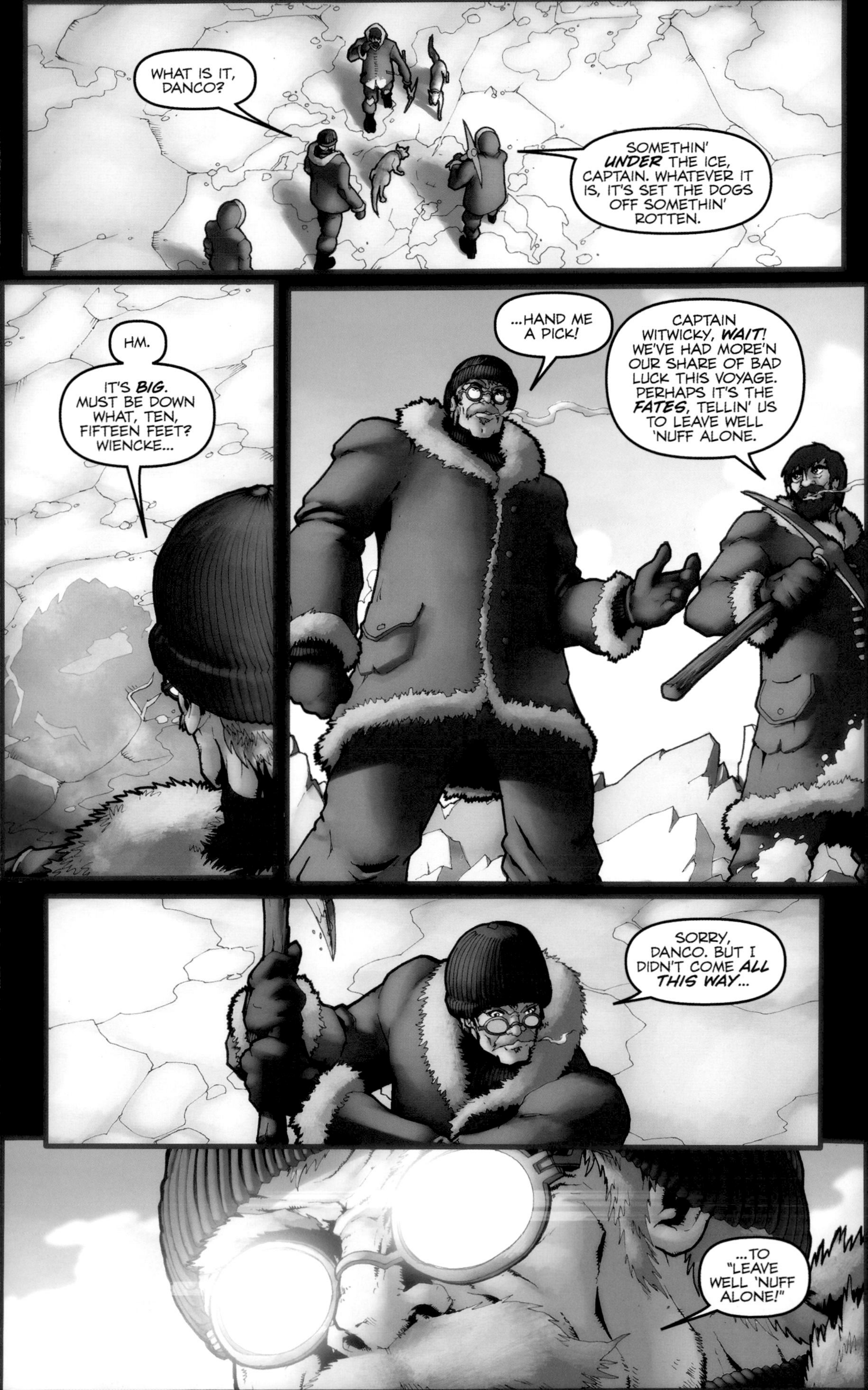
WHAT IS IT, DANCO?
SOMETHIN' UNDER THE ICE, CAPTAIN. WHATEVER IT IS, IT'S SET THE DOGS OFF SOMETHIN' ROTTEN.
HM.
IT'S BIG. MUST BE DOWN WHAT, TEN, FIFTEEN FEET? WIENCKE...
...HAND ME A PICK!
CAPTAIN WITWICKY, WAIT! WE'VE HAD MORE'N OUR SHARE OF BAD LUCK THIS VOYAGE. PERHAPS IT'S THE FATES, TELLIN' US TO LEAVE WELL 'NUFF ALONE.
SORRY, DANCO. BUT I DIDN'T COME ALL THIS WAY...
...TO "LEAVE WELL 'NUFF ALONE!"

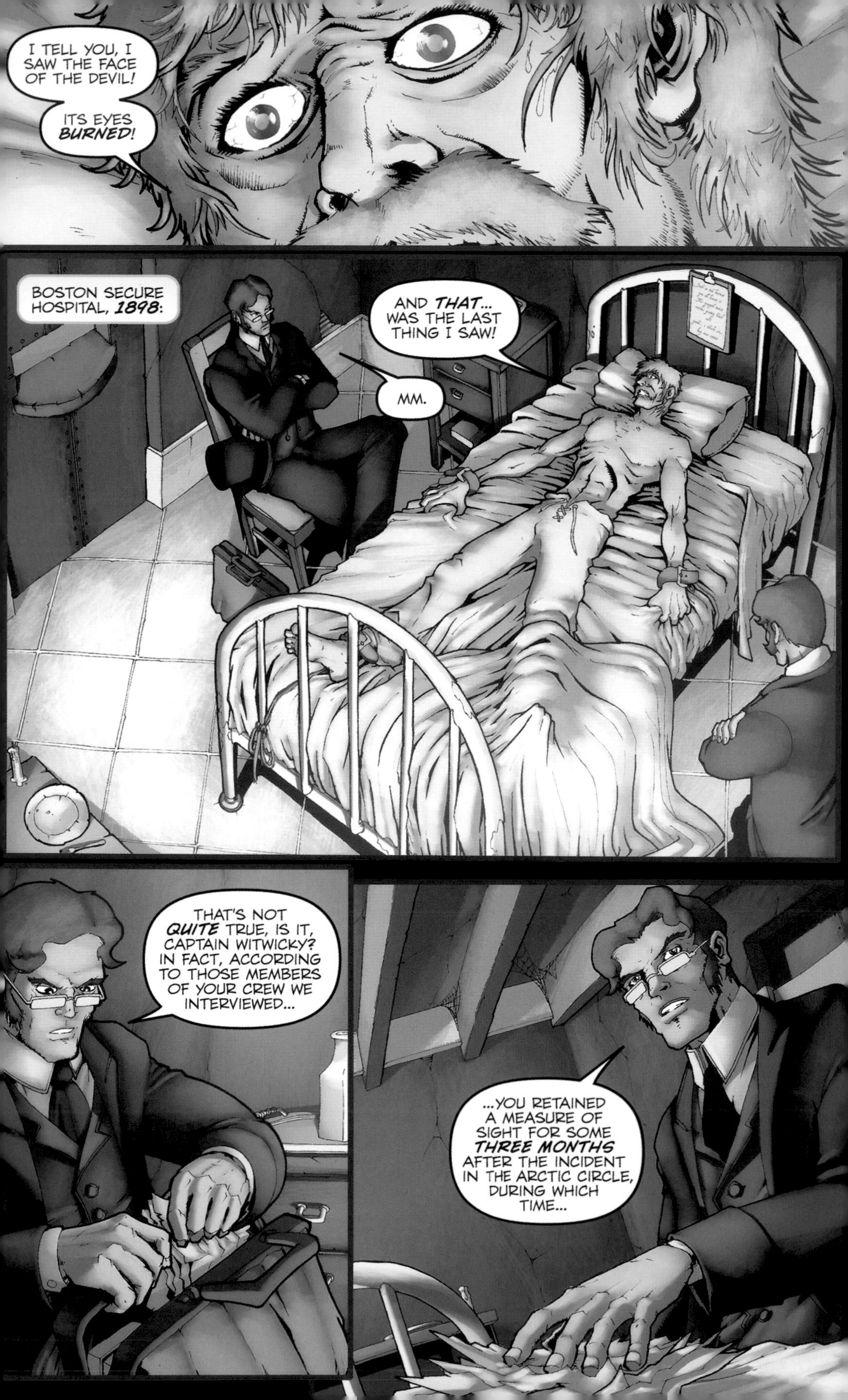
I TELL YOU, I SAW THE FACE OF THE DEVIL!
ITS EYES **BURNED**!
BOSTON SECURE HOSPITAL, **1898**:
AND **THAT**... WAS THE LAST THING I SAW!
MM.
THAT'S NOT **QUITE** TRUE, IS IT, CAPTAIN WITWICKY? IN FACT, ACCORDING TO THOSE MEMBERS OF YOUR CREW WE INTERVIEWED...
...YOU RETAINED A MEASURE OF SIGHT FOR SOME **THREE MONTHS** AFTER THE INCIDENT IN THE ARCTIC CIRCLE, DURING WHICH TIME...

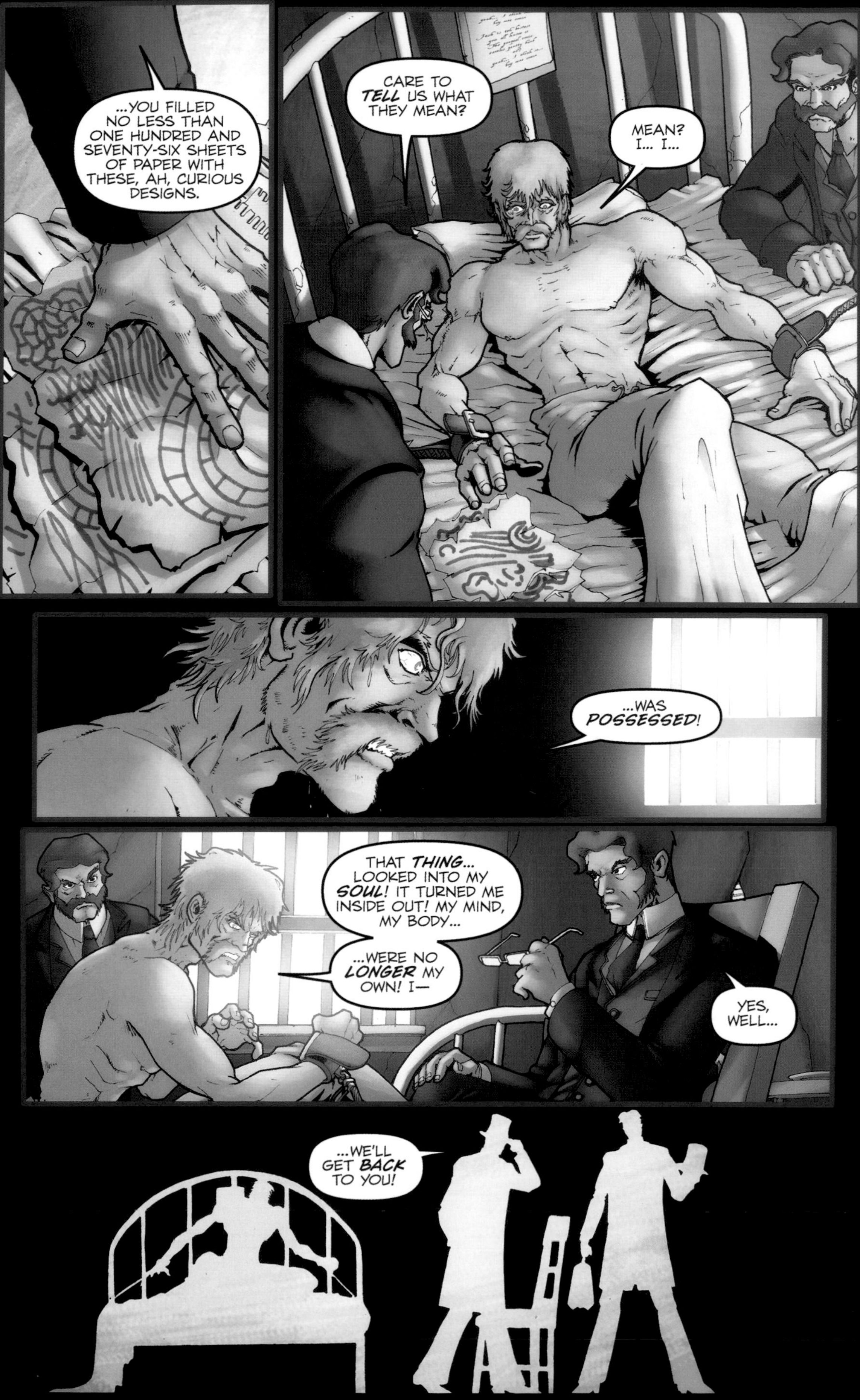
...YOU FILLED NO LESS THAN ONE HUNDRED AND SEVENTY-SIX SHEETS OF PAPER WITH THESE, AH, CURIOUS DESIGNS.
CARE TO TELL US WHAT THEY MEAN?
MEAN? I... I...
...WAS POSSESSED!
THAT THING... LOOKED INTO MY SOUL! IT TURNED ME INSIDE OUT! MY MIND, MY BODY...
...WERE NO LONGER MY OWN! I—
YES, WELL...
...WE'LL GET BACK TO YOU!

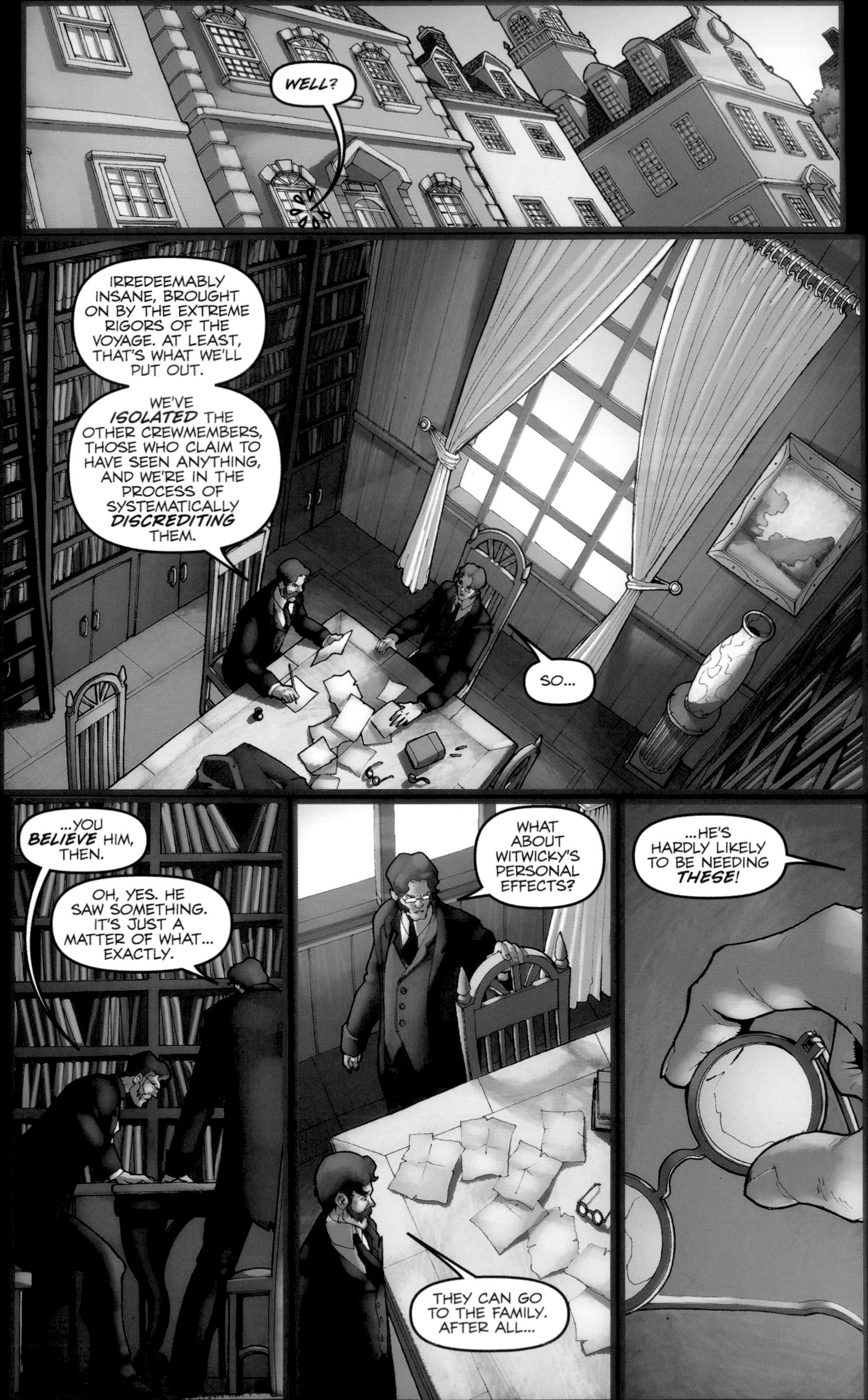
WELL?
IRREDEEMABLY INSANE, BROUGHT ON BY THE EXTREME RIGORS OF THE VOYAGE. AT LEAST, THAT'S WHAT WE'LL PUT OUT.
WE'VE ISOLATED THE OTHER CREWMEMBERS, THOSE WHO CLAIM TO HAVE SEEN ANYTHING, AND WE'RE IN THE PROCESS OF SYSTEMATICALLY DISCREDITING THEM.
SO...
...YOU BELIEVE HIM, THEN.
OH, YES. HE SAW SOMETHING. IT'S JUST A MATTER OF WHAT... EXACTLY.
WHAT ABOUT WITWICKY'S PERSONAL EFFECTS?
THEY CAN GO TO THE FAMILY. AFTER ALL...
...HE'S HARDLY LIKELY TO BE NEEDING THESE!

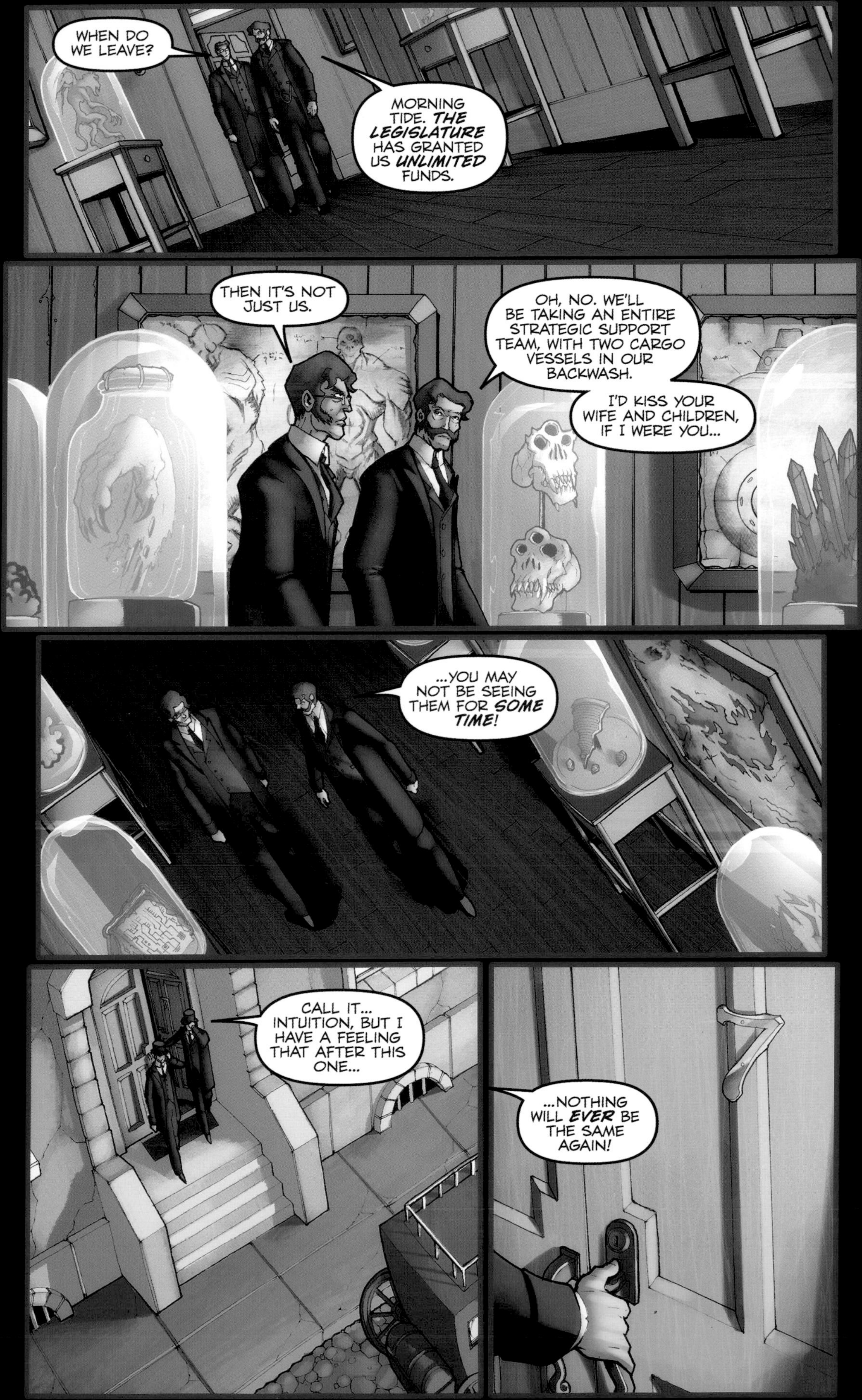
WHEN DO WE LEAVE?
MORNING TIDE. THE LEGISLATURE HAS GRANTED US UNLIMITED FUNDS.
THEN IT'S NOT JUST US.
OH, NO. WE'LL BE TAKING AN ENTIRE STRATEGIC SUPPORT TEAM, WITH TWO CARGO VESSELS IN OUR BACKWASH.
I'D KISS YOUR WIFE AND CHILDREN, IF I WERE YOU...
...YOU MAY NOT BE SEEING THEM FOR SOME TIME!
CALL IT... INTUITION, BUT I HAVE A FEELING THAT AFTER THIS ONE...
...NOTHING WILL EVER BE THE SAME AGAIN!

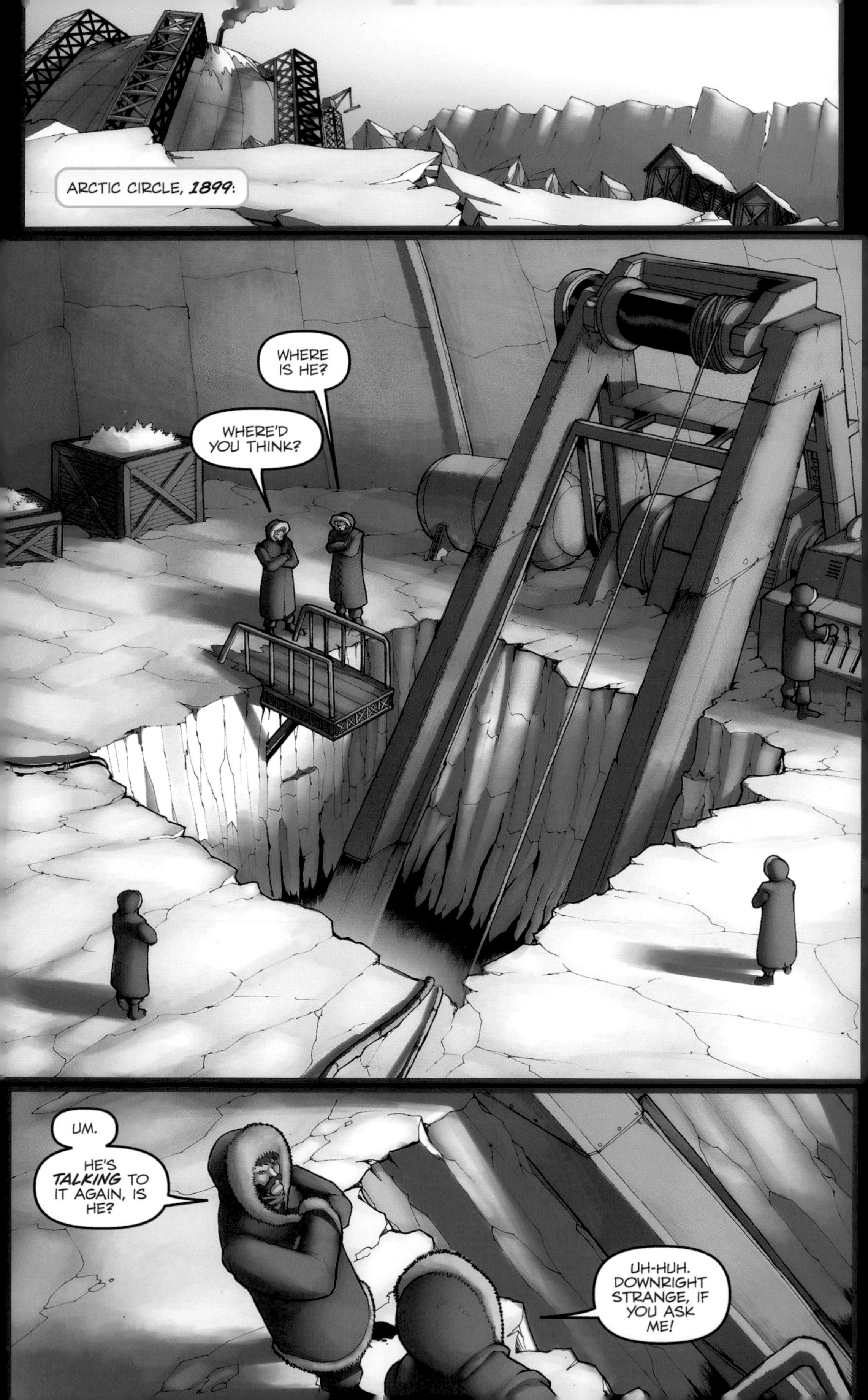
ARCTIC CIRCLE, 1899:
WHERE IS HE?
WHERE'D YOU THINK?
UM.
HE'S TALKING TO IT AGAIN, IS HE?
UH-HUH. DOWNRIGHT STRANGE, IF YOU ASK ME!

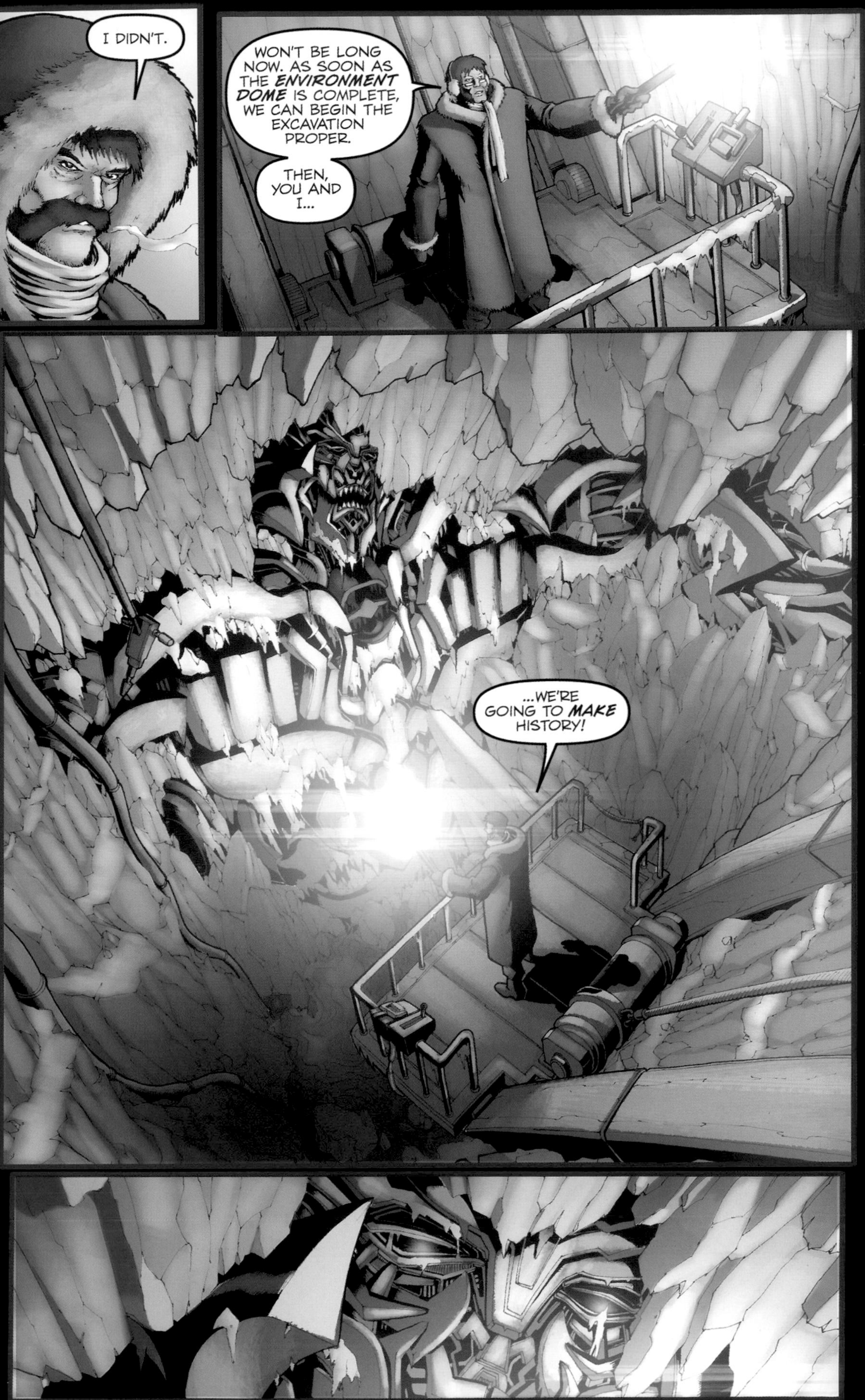
I DIDN'T.
WON'T BE LONG NOW. AS SOON AS THE ENVIRONMENT DOME IS COMPLETE, WE CAN BEGIN THE EXCAVATION PROPER.
THEN, YOU AND I...
...WE'RE GOING TO MAKE HISTORY!

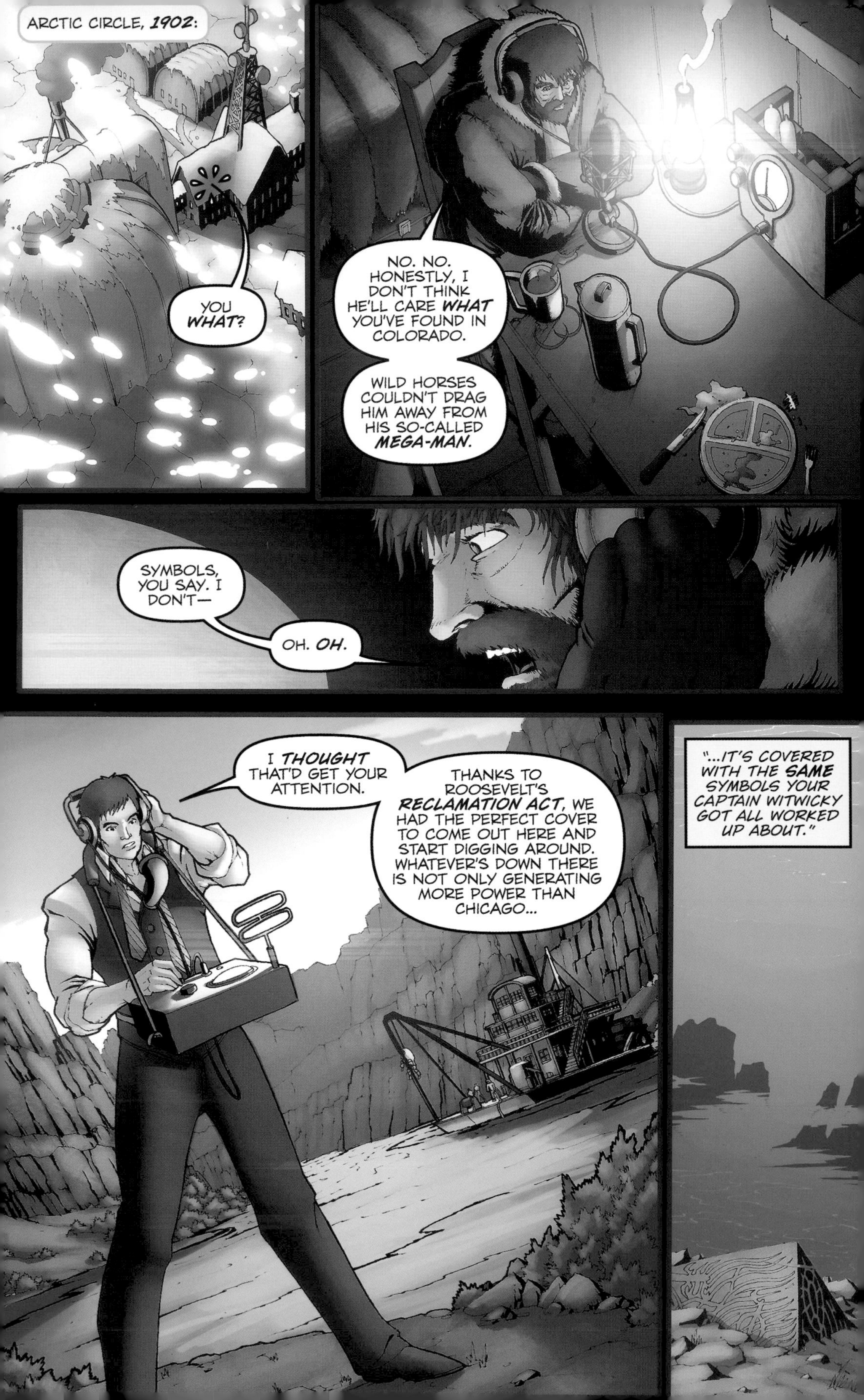
ARCTIC CIRCLE, 1902:
YOU WHAT?
NO. NO. HONESTLY, I DON'T THINK HE'LL CARE WHAT YOU'VE FOUND IN COLORADO.
WILD HORSES COULDN'T DRAG HIM AWAY FROM HIS SO-CALLED MEGA-MAN.
SYMBOLS, YOU SAY. I DON'T—
OH. OH.
I THOUGHT THAT'D GET YOUR ATTENTION.
THANKS TO ROOSEVELT'S RECLAMATION ACT, WE HAD THE PERFECT COVER TO COME OUT HERE AND START DIGGING AROUND. WHATEVER'S DOWN THERE IS NOT ONLY GENERATING MORE POWER THAN CHICAGO...
"...IT'S COVERED WITH THE SAME SYMBOLS YOUR CAPTAIN WITWICKY GOT ALL WORKED UP ABOUT."

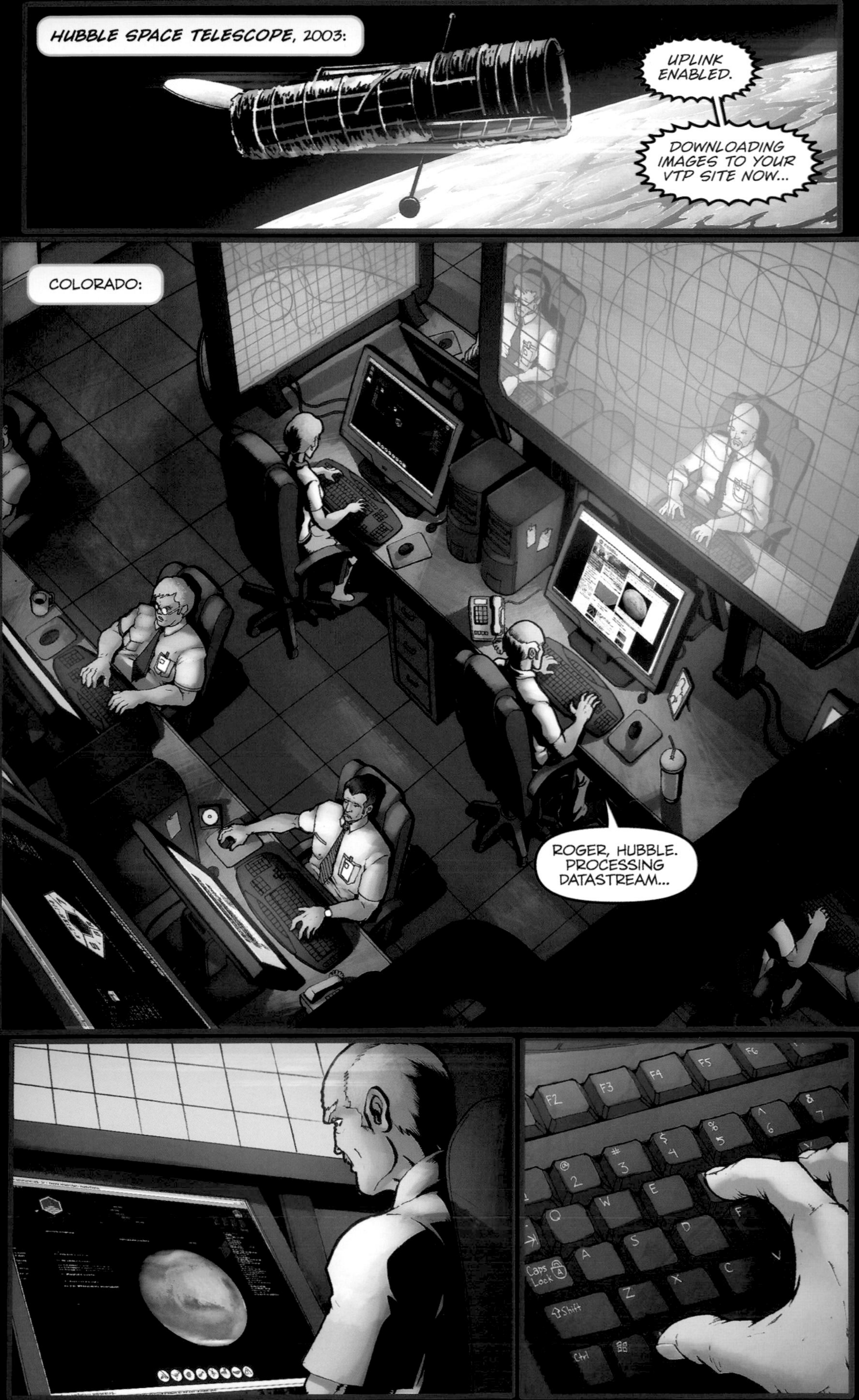
HUBBLE SPACE TELESCOPE, 2003:
UPLINK ENABLED.
DOWNLOADING IMAGES TO YOUR VTP SITE NOW...
COLORADO:
ROGER, HUBBLE. PROCESSING DATASTREAM...

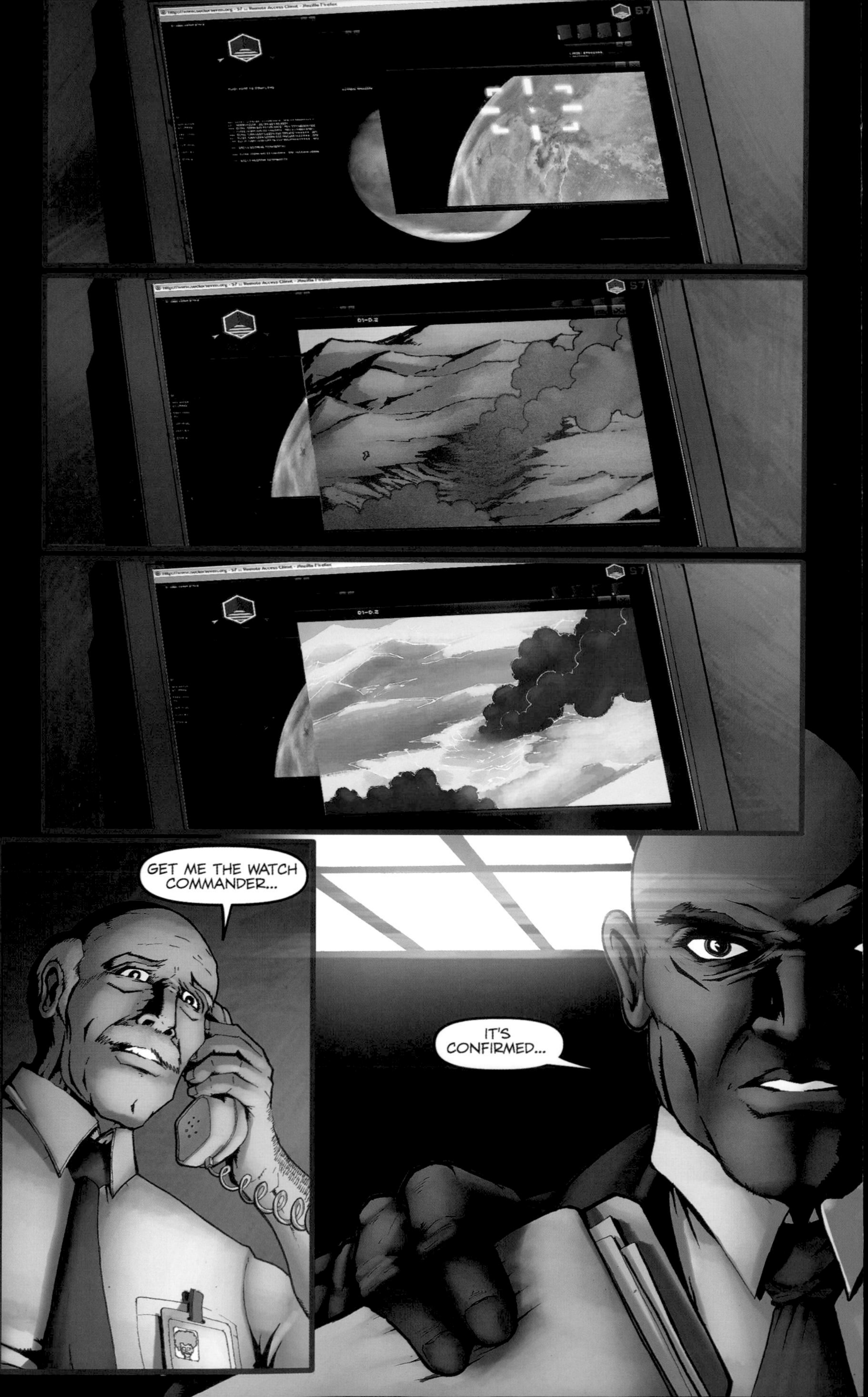
GET ME THE WATCH COMMANDER...
IT'S CONFIRMED...

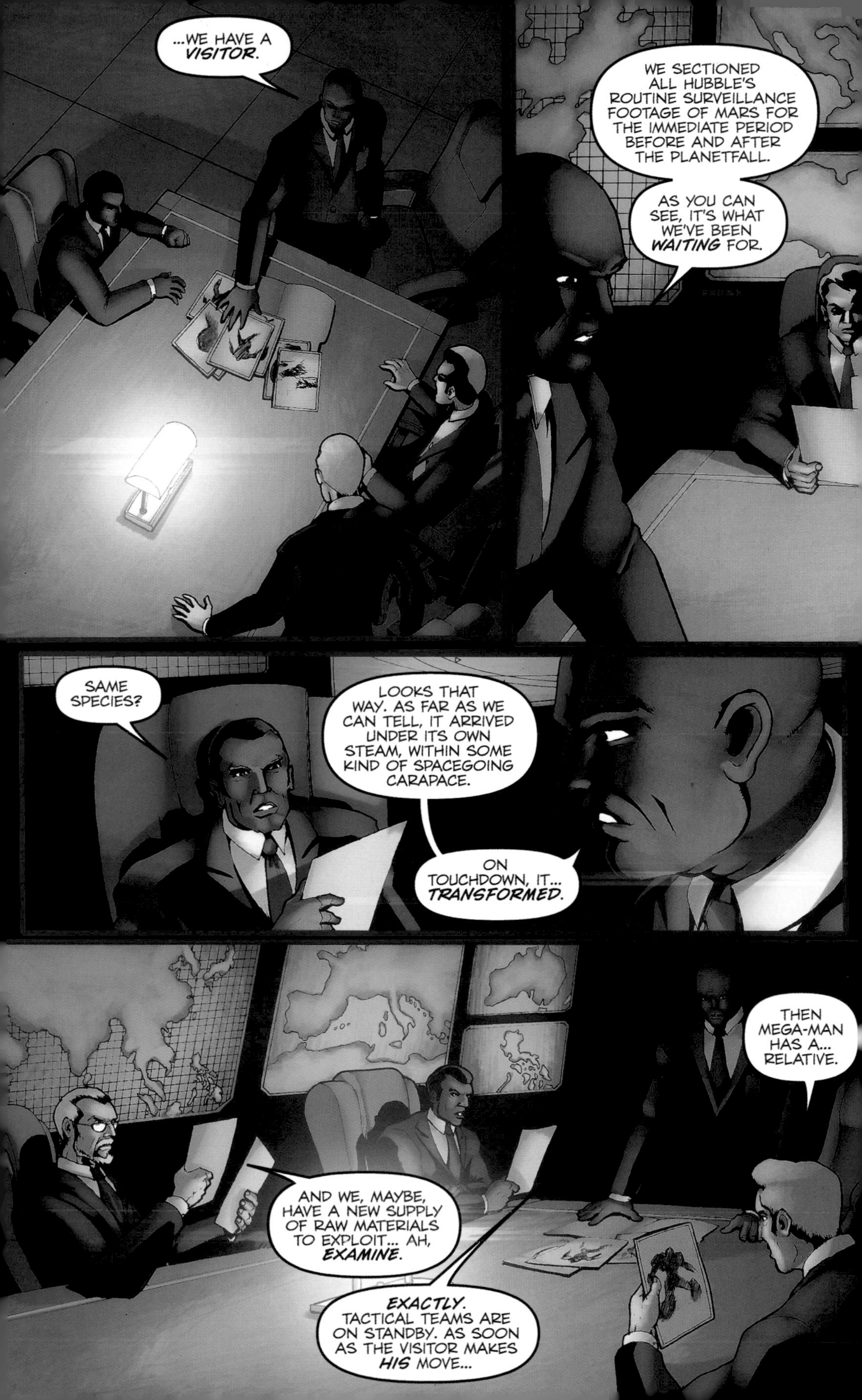
...WE HAVE A VISITOR.
WE SECTIONED ALL HUBBLE'S ROUTINE SURVEILLANCE FOOTAGE OF MARS FOR THE IMMEDIATE PERIOD BEFORE AND AFTER THE PLANETFALL.
AS YOU CAN SEE, IT'S WHAT WE'VE BEEN WAITING FOR.
SAME SPECIES?
LOOKS THAT WAY. AS FAR AS WE CAN TELL, IT ARRIVED UNDER ITS OWN STEAM, WITHIN SOME KIND OF SPACEGOING CARAPACE.
ON TOUCHDOWN, IT... TRANSFORMED.
THEN MEGA-MAN HAS A... RELATIVE.
AND WE, MAYBE, HAVE A NEW SUPPLY OF RAW MATERIALS TO EXPLOIT... AH, EXAMINE.
EXACTLY. TACTICAL TEAMS ARE ON STANDBY. AS SOON AS THE VISITOR MAKES HIS MOVE...

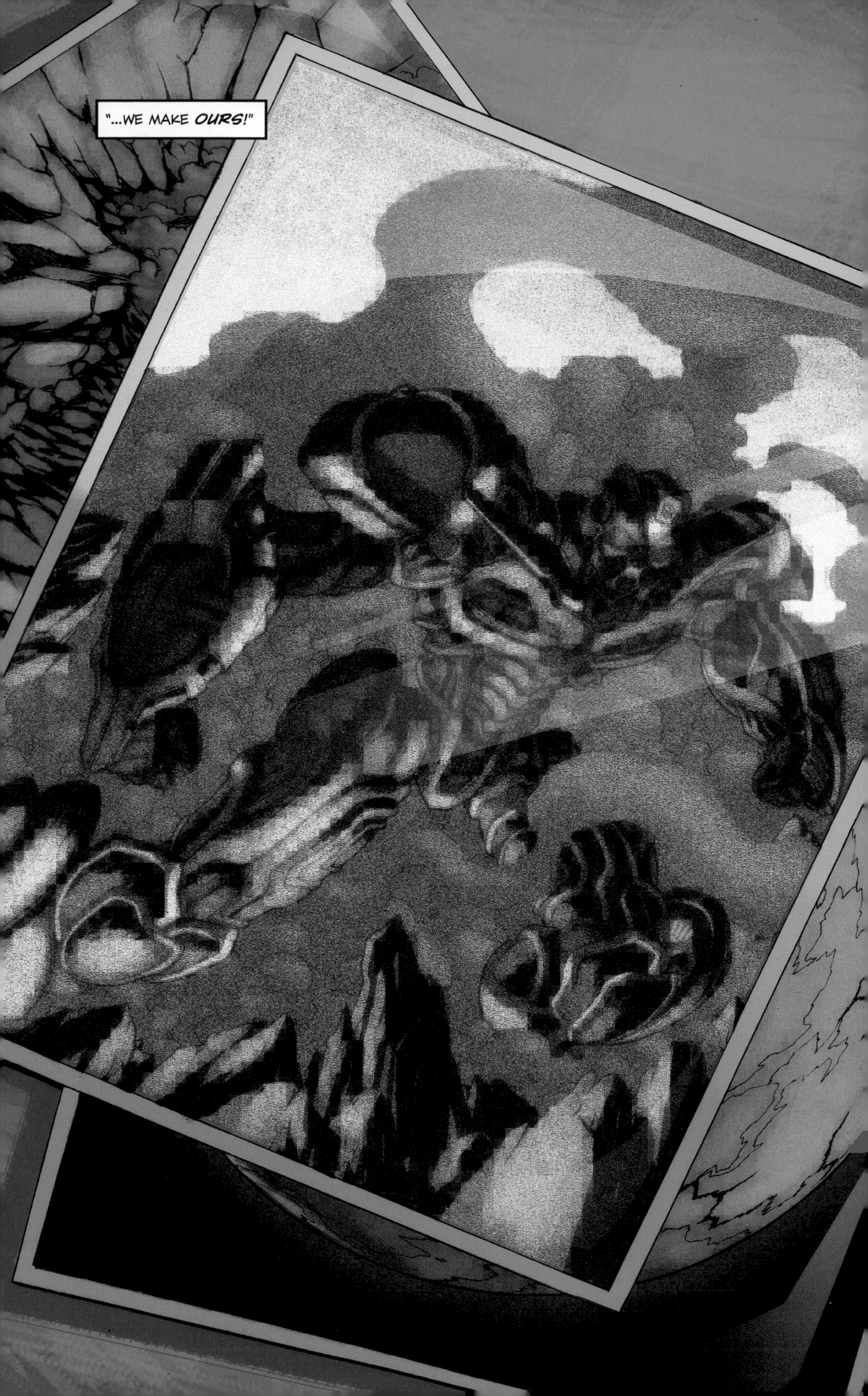
"...WE MAKE OURS!"

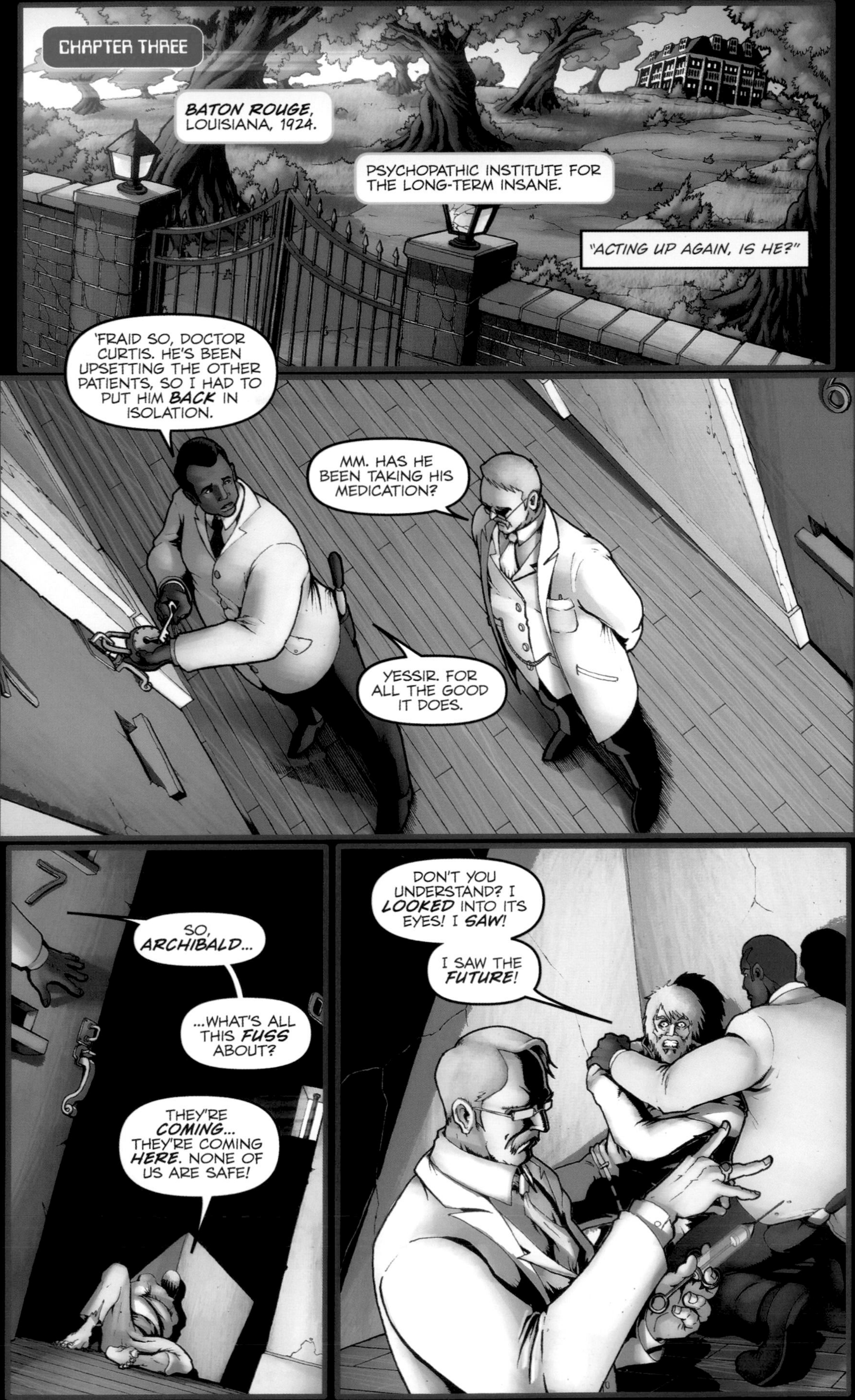
CHAPTER THREE
BATON ROUGE, LOUISIANA, 1924.
PSYCHOPATHIC INSTITUTE FOR THE LONG-TERM INSANE.
"ACTING UP AGAIN, IS HE?"
'FRAID SO, DOCTOR CURTIS. HE'S BEEN UPSETTING THE OTHER PATIENTS, SO I HAD TO PUT HIM BACK IN ISOLATION.
MM. HAS HE BEEN TAKING HIS MEDICATION?
YESSIR. FOR ALL THE GOOD IT DOES.
SO, ARCHIBALD...
...WHAT'S ALL THIS FUSS ABOUT?
THEY'RE COMING... THEY'RE COMING HERE. NONE OF US ARE SAFE!
DON'T YOU UNDERSTAND? I LOOKED INTO ITS EYES! I SAW!
I SAW THE FUTURE!

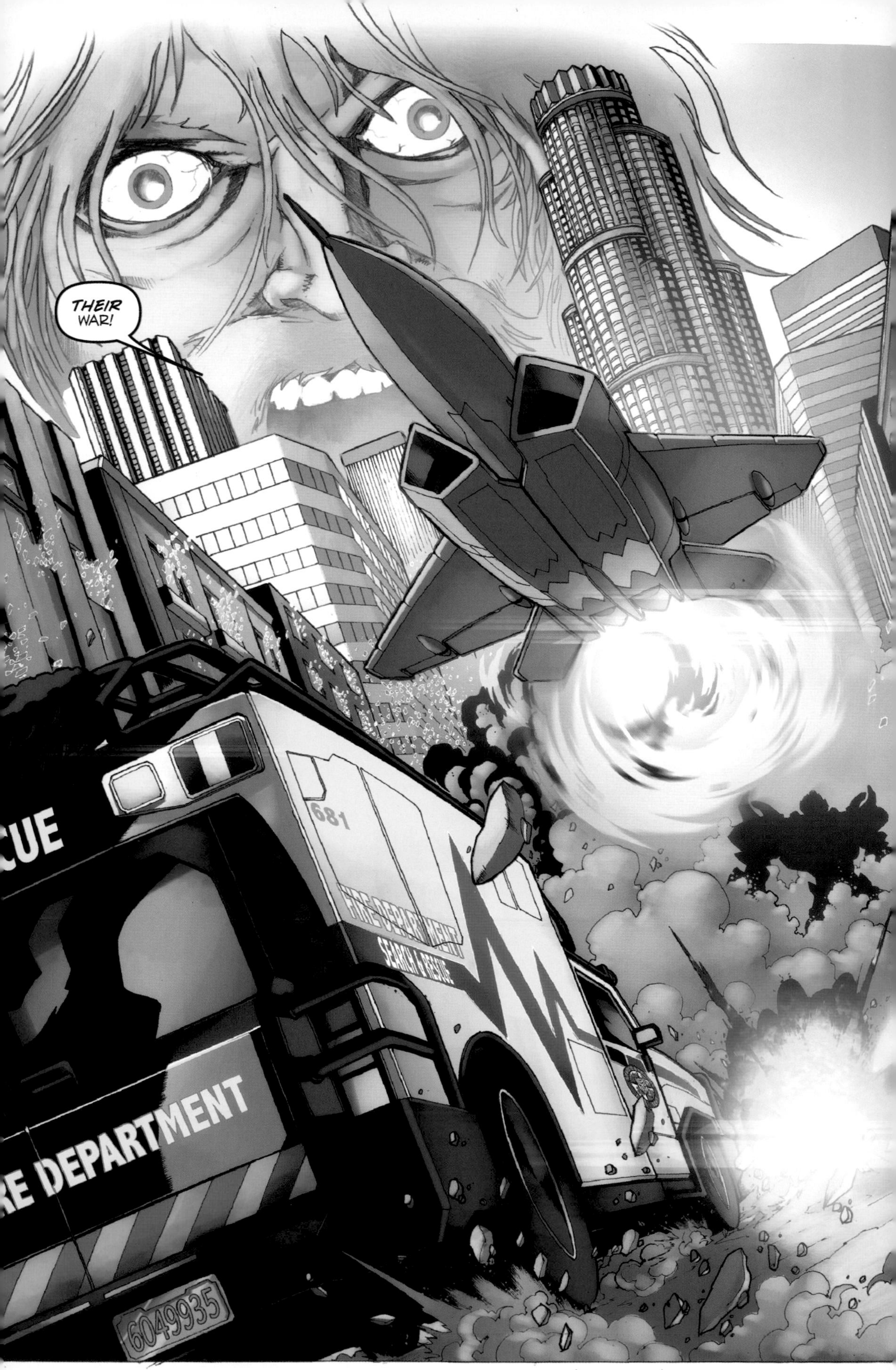
THEIR WAR!
CUE
681
RE DEPARTMENT
6049935

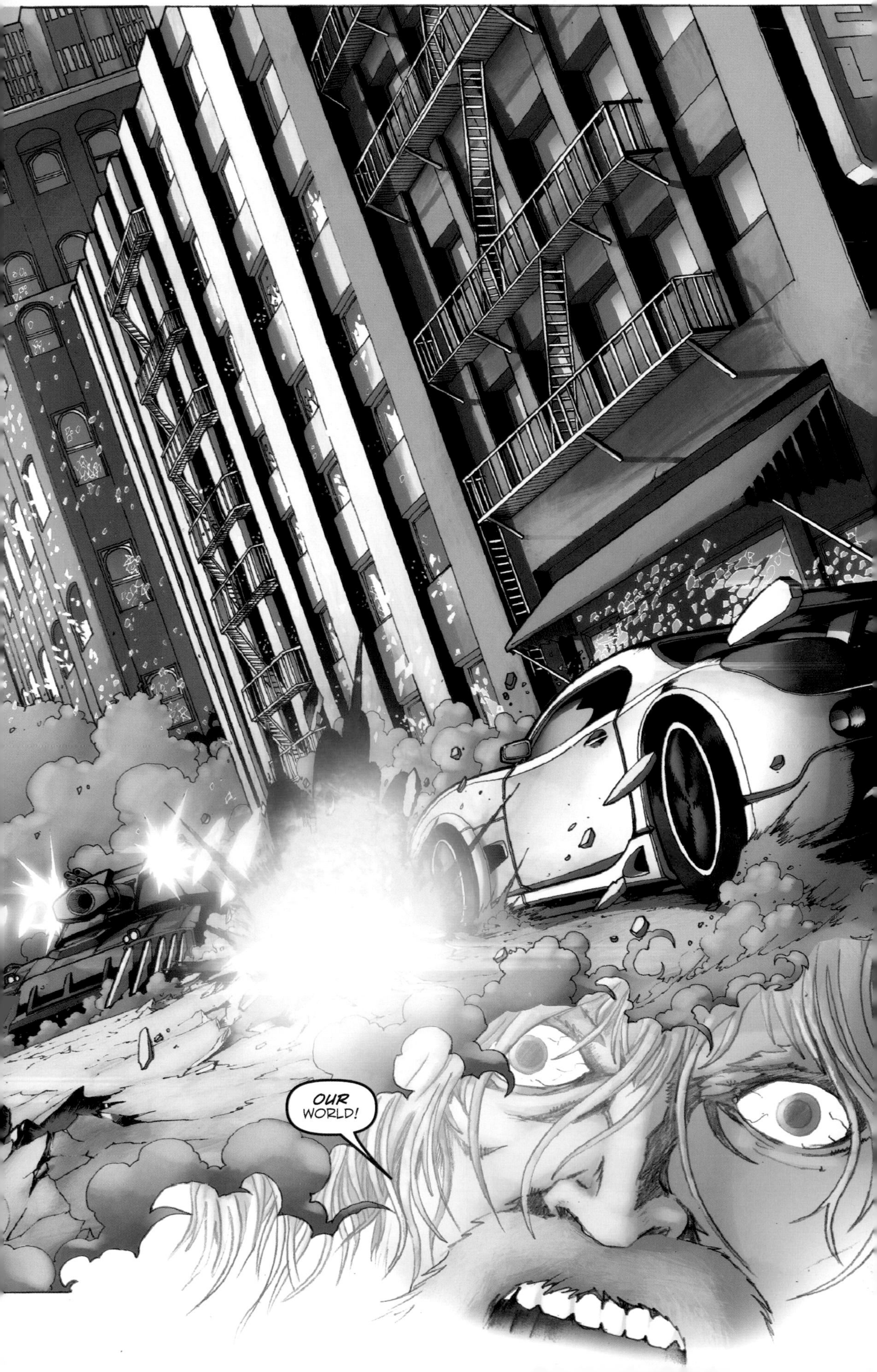
OUR WORLD!

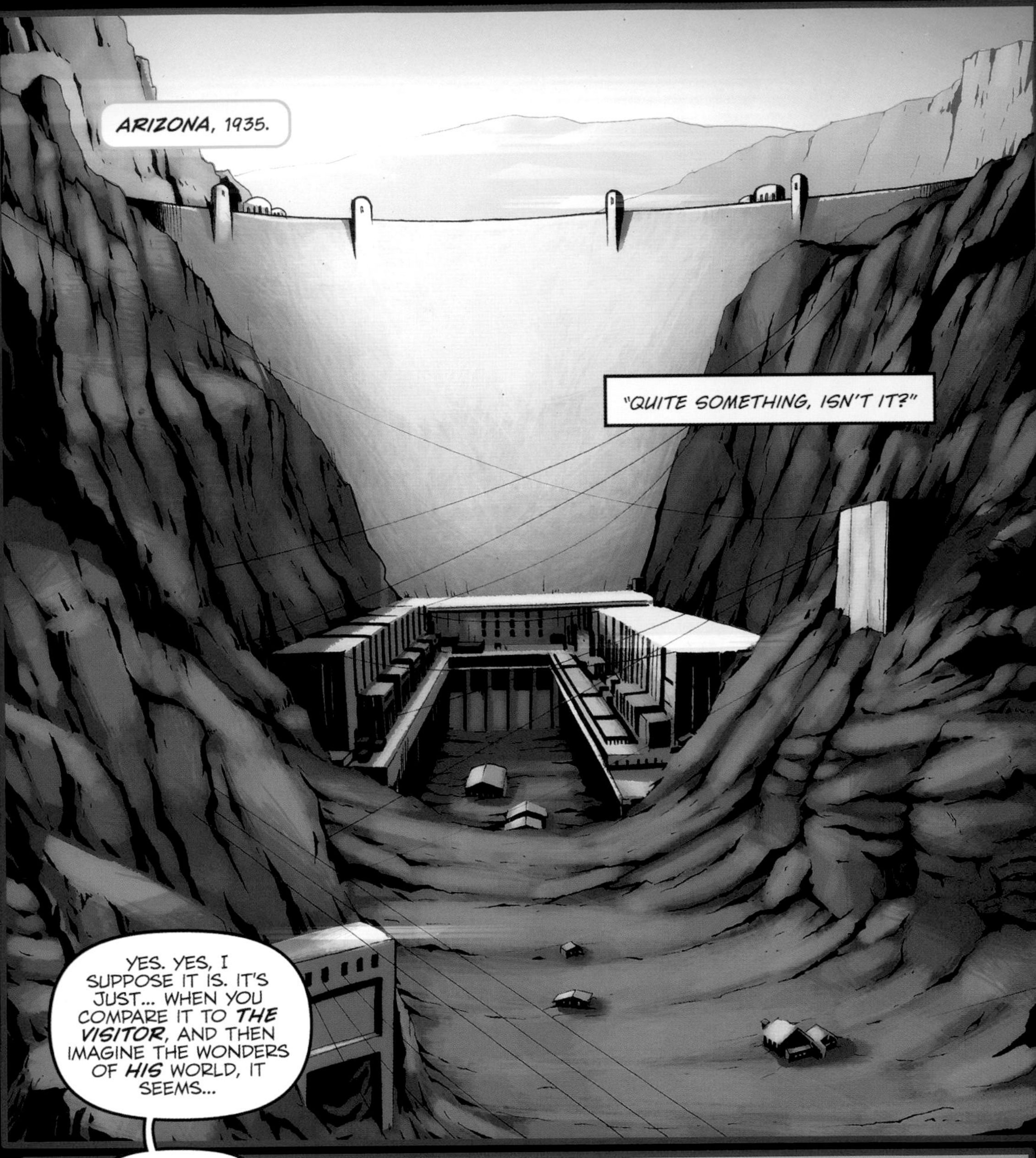
ARIZONA, 1935.
"QUITE SOMETHING, ISN'T IT?"
YES. YES, I SUPPOSE IT IS. IT'S JUST... WHEN YOU COMPARE IT TO THE VISITOR, AND THEN IMAGINE THE WONDERS OF HIS WORLD, IT SEEMS...

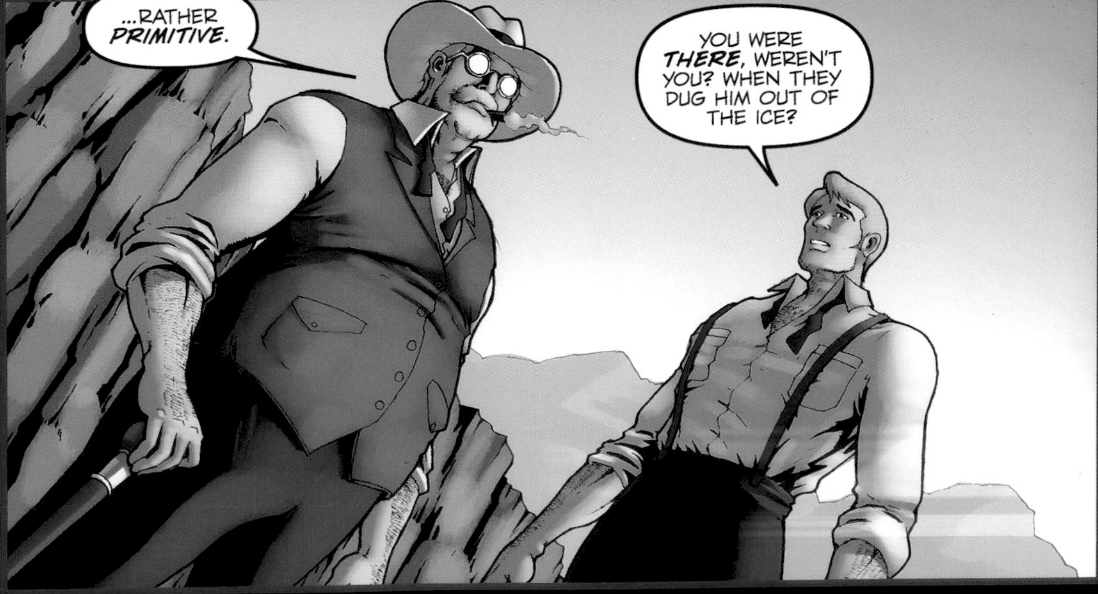
...RATHER PRIMITIVE.
YOU WERE THERE, WEREN'T YOU? WHEN THEY DUG HIM OUT OF THE ICE?

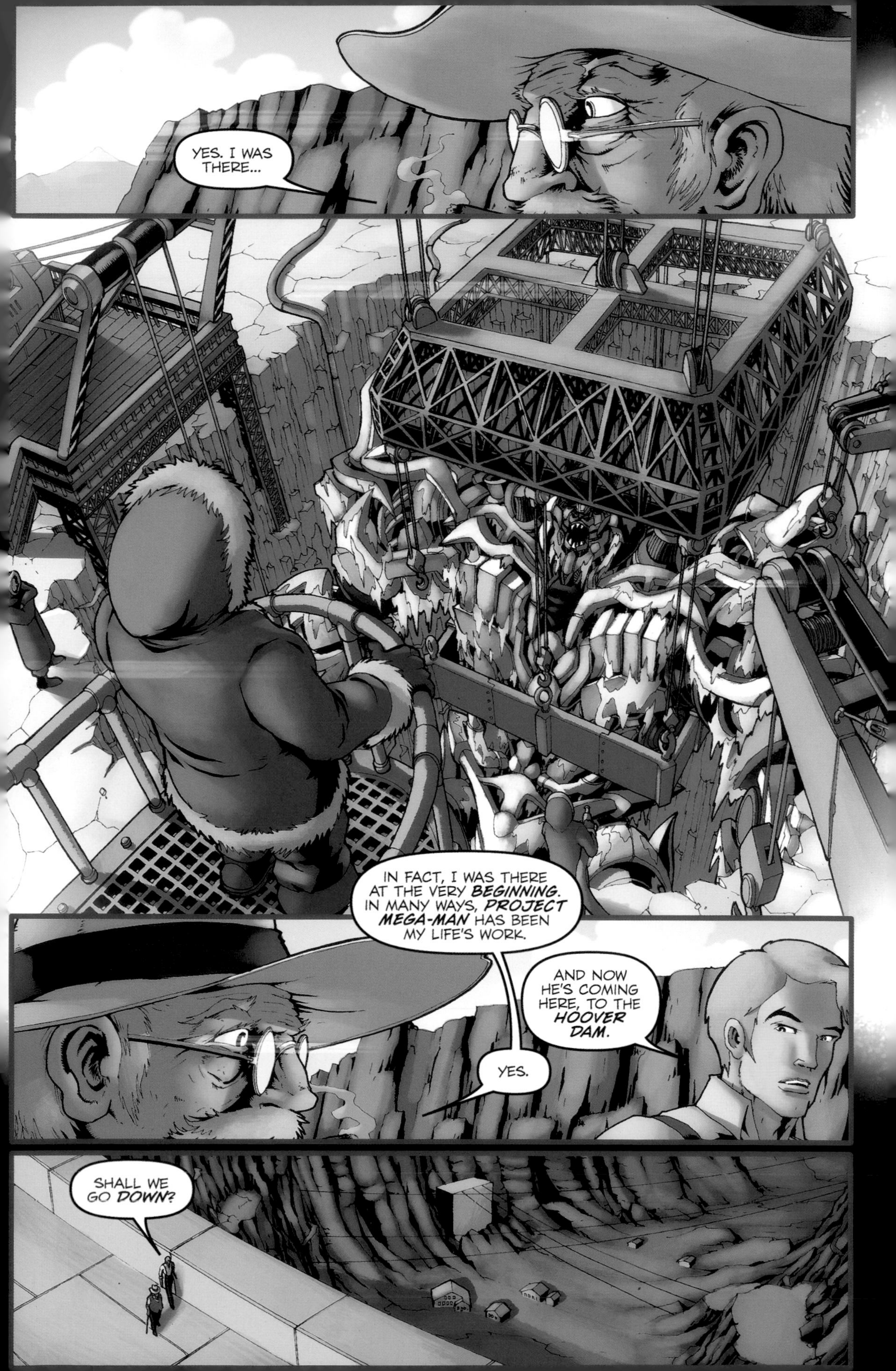
YES. I WAS THERE...
IN FACT, I WAS THERE AT THE VERY *BEGINNING*. IN MANY WAYS, ***PROJECT MEGA-MAN*** HAS BEEN MY LIFE'S WORK.
AND NOW HE'S COMING HERE, TO THE ***HOOVER DAM***.
YES.
SHALL WE GO *DOWN*?

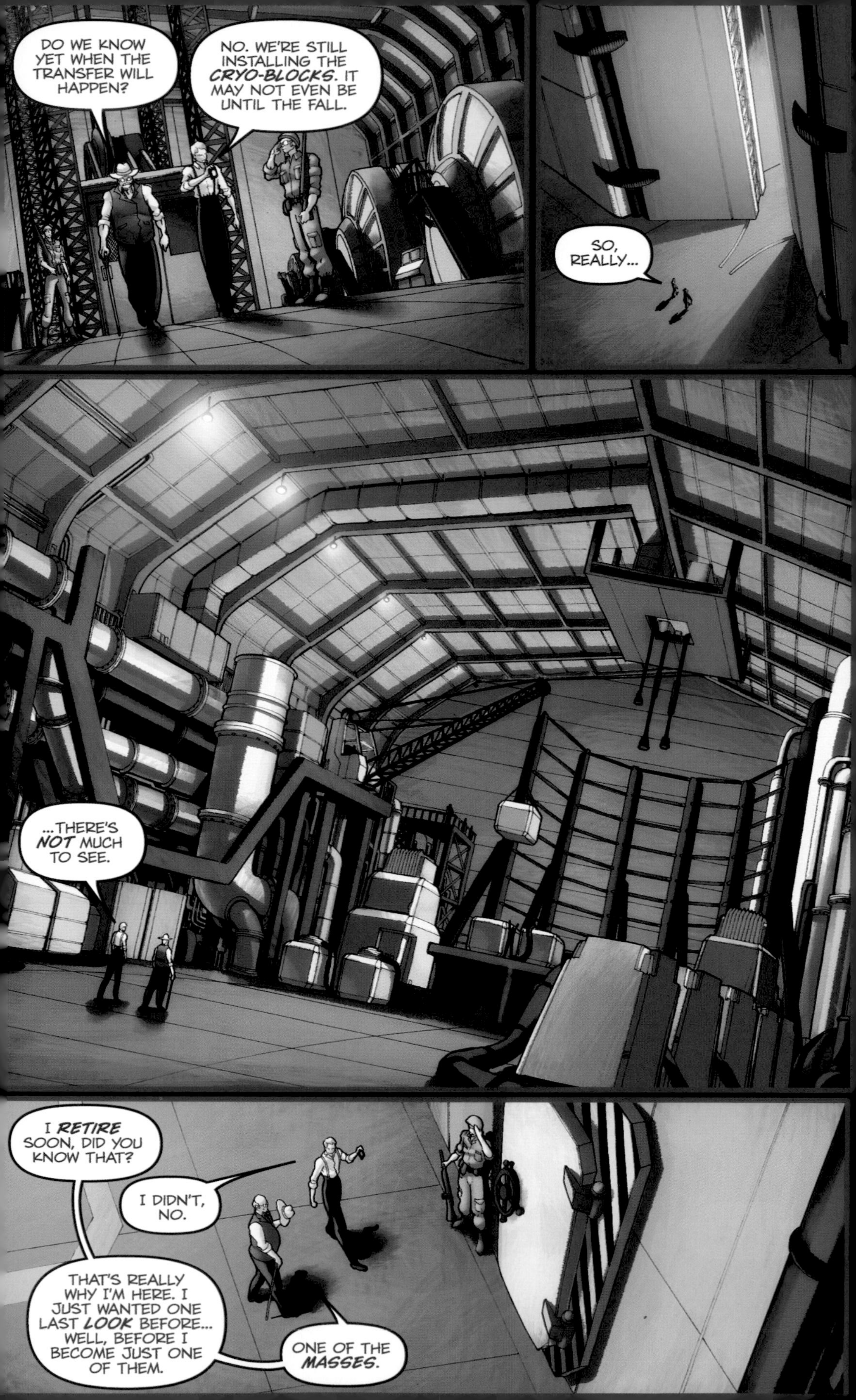
DO WE KNOW YET WHEN THE TRANSFER WILL HAPPEN?
NO. WE'RE STILL INSTALLING THE CRYO-BLOCKS. IT MAY NOT EVEN BE UNTIL THE FALL.
SO, REALLY...
...THERE'S NOT MUCH TO SEE.
I RETIRE SOON, DID YOU KNOW THAT?
I DIDN'T, NO.
THAT'S REALLY WHY I'M HERE. I JUST WANTED ONE LAST LOOK BEFORE... WELL, BEFORE I BECOME JUST ONE OF THEM.
ONE OF THE MASSES.

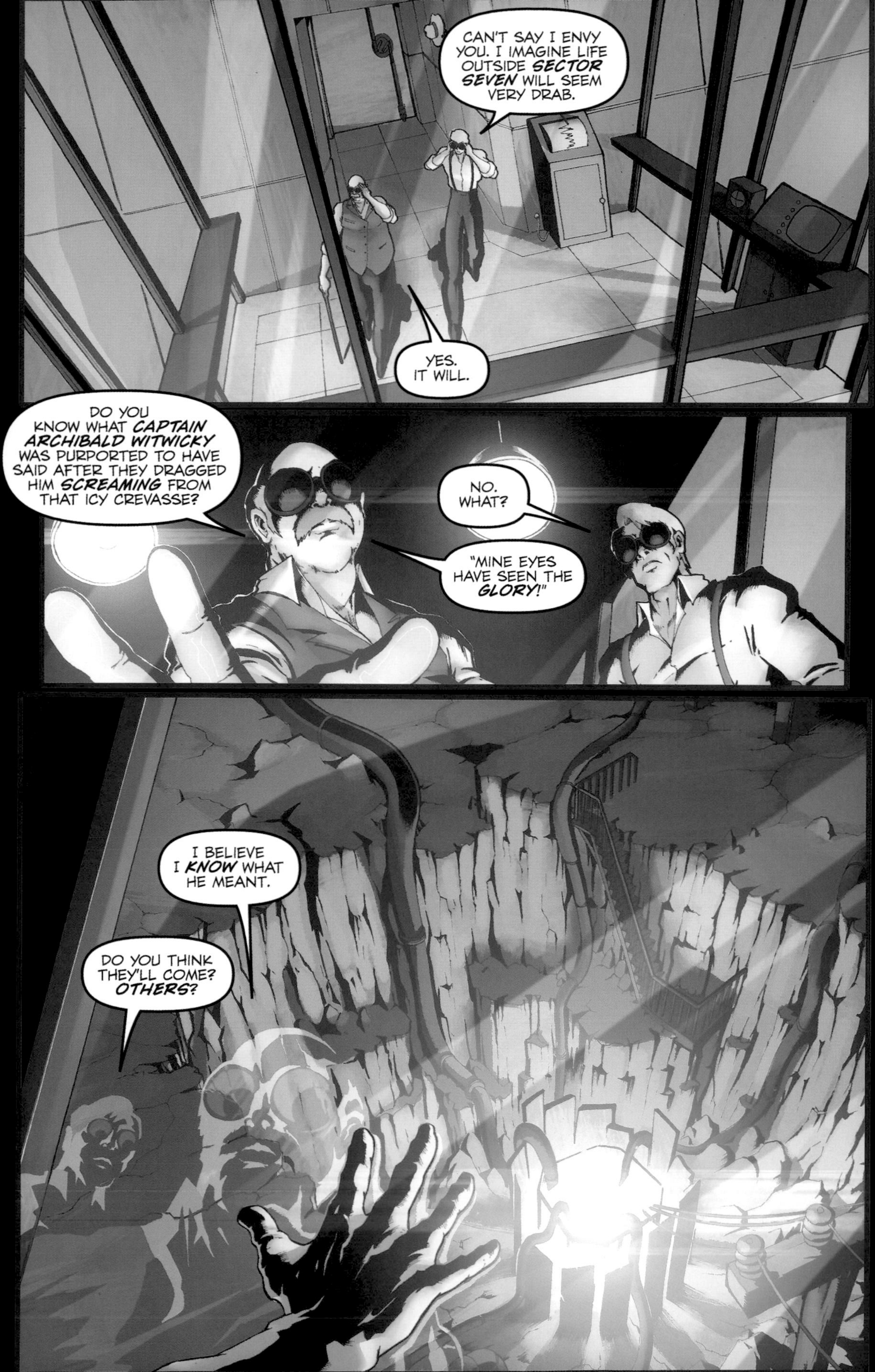
CAN'T SAY I ENVY YOU. I IMAGINE LIFE OUTSIDE **SECTOR SEVEN** WILL SEEM VERY DRAB.
YES. IT WILL.
DO YOU KNOW WHAT **CAPTAIN ARCHIBALD WITWICKY** WAS PURPORTED TO HAVE SAID AFTER THEY DRAGGED HIM **SCREAMING** FROM THAT ICY CREVASSE?
NO. WHAT?
"MINE EYES HAVE SEEN THE **GLORY**!"
I BELIEVE I **KNOW** WHAT HE MEANT.
DO YOU THINK THEY'LL COME? **OTHERS**?

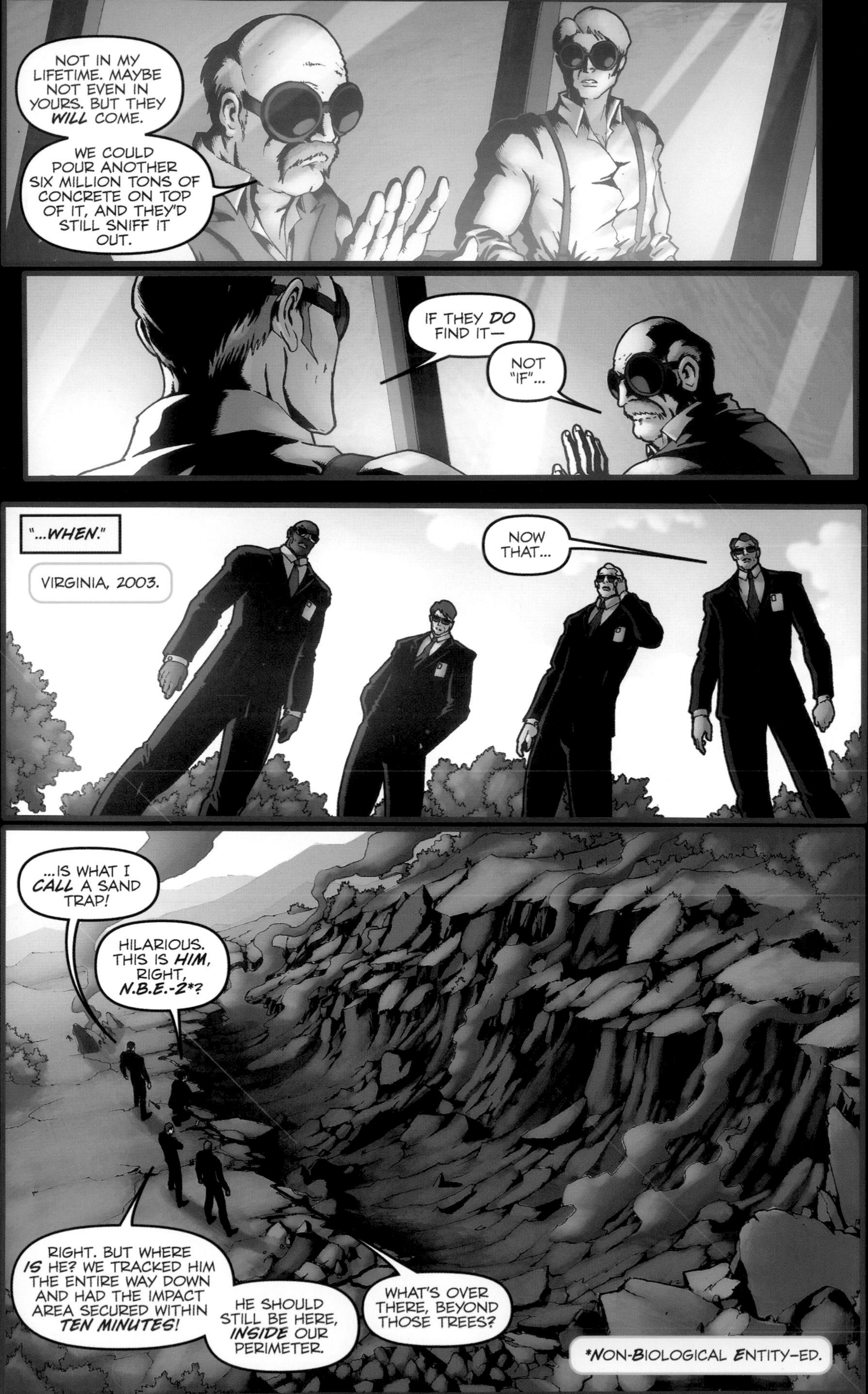
NOT IN MY LIFETIME. MAYBE NOT EVEN IN YOURS. BUT THEY WILL COME.
WE COULD POUR ANOTHER SIX MILLION TONS OF CONCRETE ON TOP OF IT, AND THEY'D STILL SNIFF IT OUT.
IF THEY DO FIND IT—
NOT "IF"...
"...WHEN."
VIRGINIA, 2003.
NOW THAT...
...IS WHAT I CALL A SAND TRAP!
HILARIOUS. THIS IS HIM, RIGHT, N.B.E.-2*?
RIGHT. BUT WHERE IS HE? WE TRACKED HIM THE ENTIRE WAY DOWN AND HAD THE IMPACT AREA SECURED WITHIN TEN MINUTES!
HE SHOULD STILL BE HERE, INSIDE OUR PERIMETER.
WHAT'S OVER THERE, BEYOND THOSE TREES?
*NON-BIOLOGICAL ENTITY–ED.

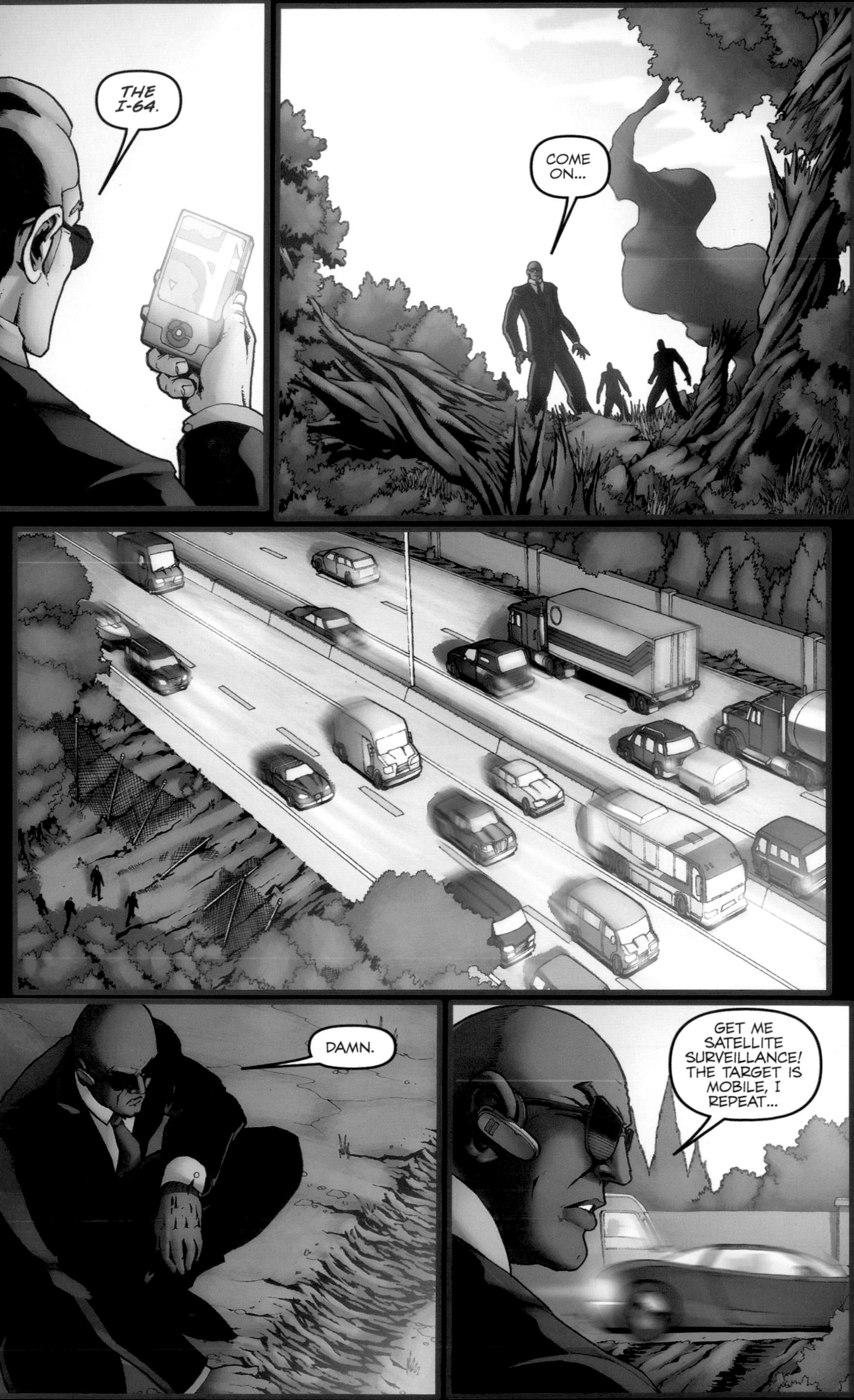
THE I-64.
COME ON...
DAMN.
GET ME SATELLITE SURVEILLANCE! THE TARGET IS MOBILE, I REPEAT...

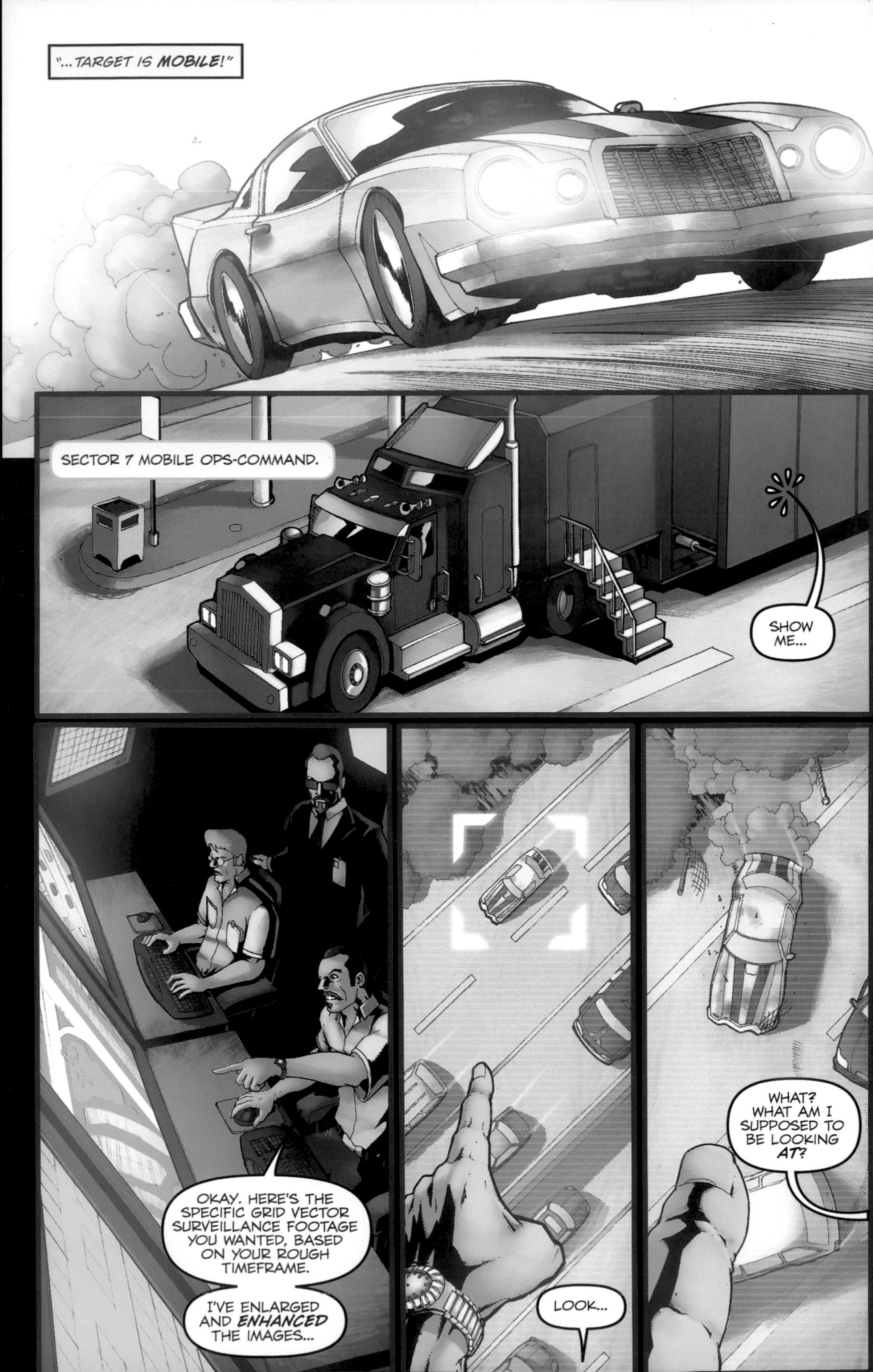
"...TARGET IS MOBILE!"
SECTOR 7 MOBILE OPS-COMMAND.
SHOW ME...
OKAY. HERE'S THE SPECIFIC GRID VECTOR SURVEILLANCE FOOTAGE YOU WANTED, BASED ON YOUR ROUGH TIMEFRAME.
I'VE ENLARGED AND ENHANCED THE IMAGES...
LOOK...
WHAT? WHAT AM I SUPPOSED TO BE LOOKING AT?

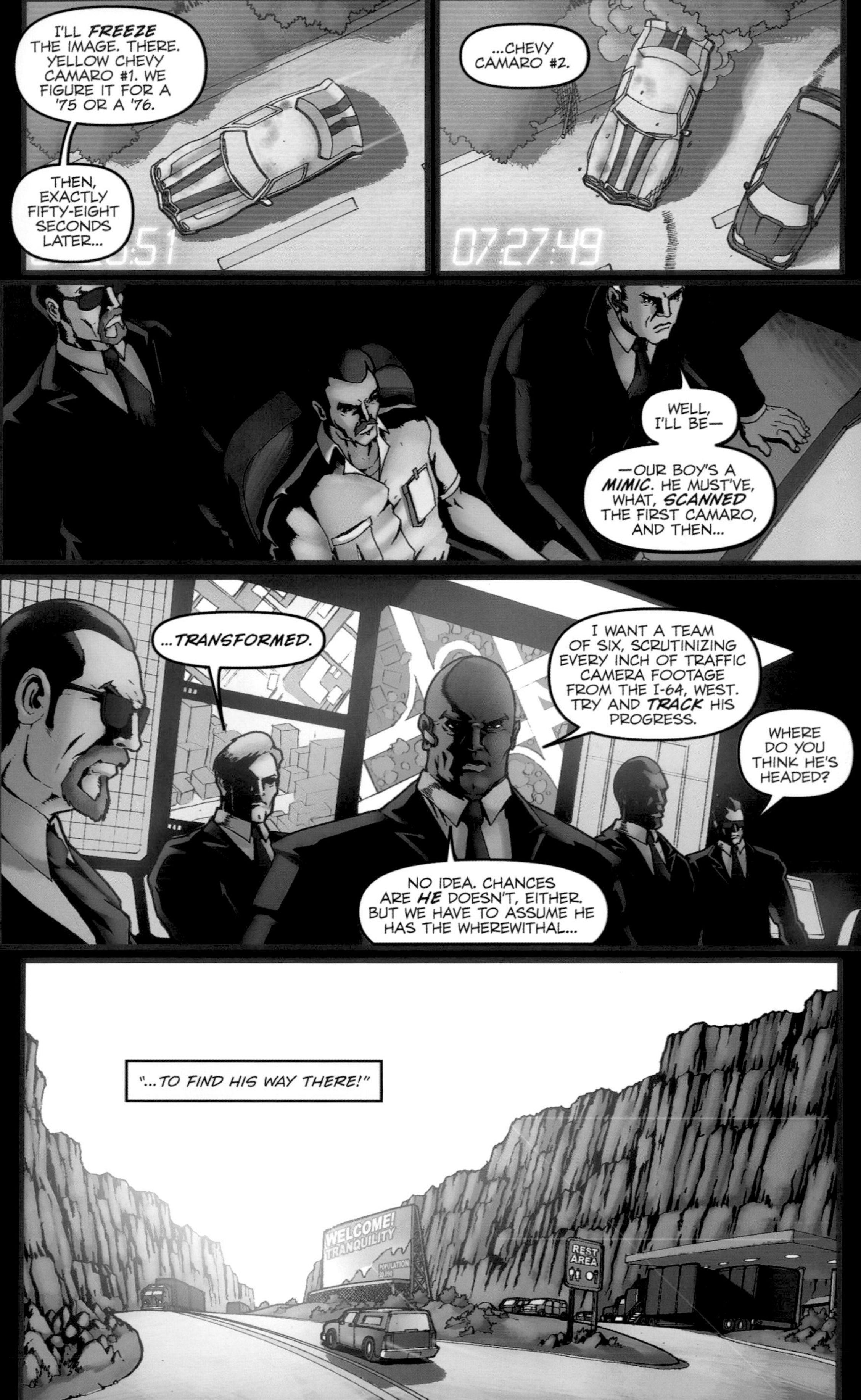
I'LL FREEZE THE IMAGE. THERE. YELLOW CHEVY CAMARO #1. WE FIGURE IT FOR A '75 OR A '76.
THEN, EXACTLY FIFTY-EIGHT SECONDS LATER...
...CHEVY CAMARO #2.
07:27:49
WELL, I'LL BE—
—OUR BOY'S A MIMIC. HE MUST'VE, WHAT, SCANNED THE FIRST CAMARO, AND THEN...
...TRANSFORMED.
I WANT A TEAM OF SIX, SCRUTINIZING EVERY INCH OF TRAFFIC CAMERA FOOTAGE FROM THE I-64, WEST. TRY AND TRACK HIS PROGRESS.
WHERE DO YOU THINK HE'S HEADED?
NO IDEA. CHANCES ARE HE DOESN'T, EITHER. BUT WE HAVE TO ASSUME HE HAS THE WHEREWITHAL...
"...TO FIND HIS WAY THERE!"
WELCOME! TRANQUILITY
REST AREA

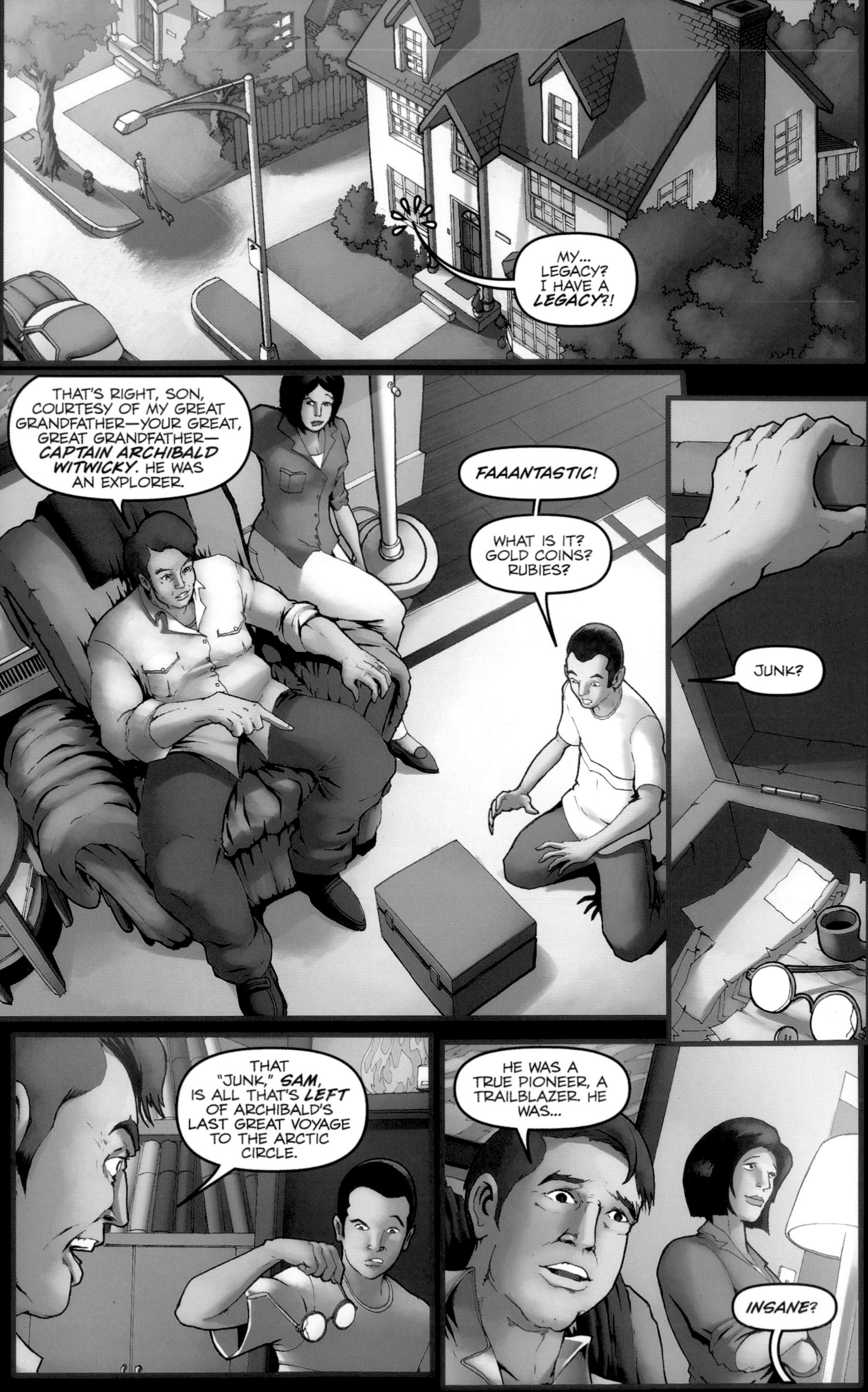
MY... LEGACY? I HAVE A LEGACY?!
THAT'S RIGHT, SON, COURTESY OF MY GREAT GRANDFATHER—YOUR GREAT, GREAT GRANDFATHER—CAPTAIN ARCHIBALD WITWICKY. HE WAS AN EXPLORER.
FAAANTASTIC!
WHAT IS IT? GOLD COINS? RUBIES?
JUNK?
THAT "JUNK," SAM, IS ALL THAT'S LEFT OF ARCHIBALD'S LAST GREAT VOYAGE TO THE ARCTIC CIRCLE.
HE WAS A TRUE PIONEER, A TRAILBLAZER. HE WAS...
INSANE?

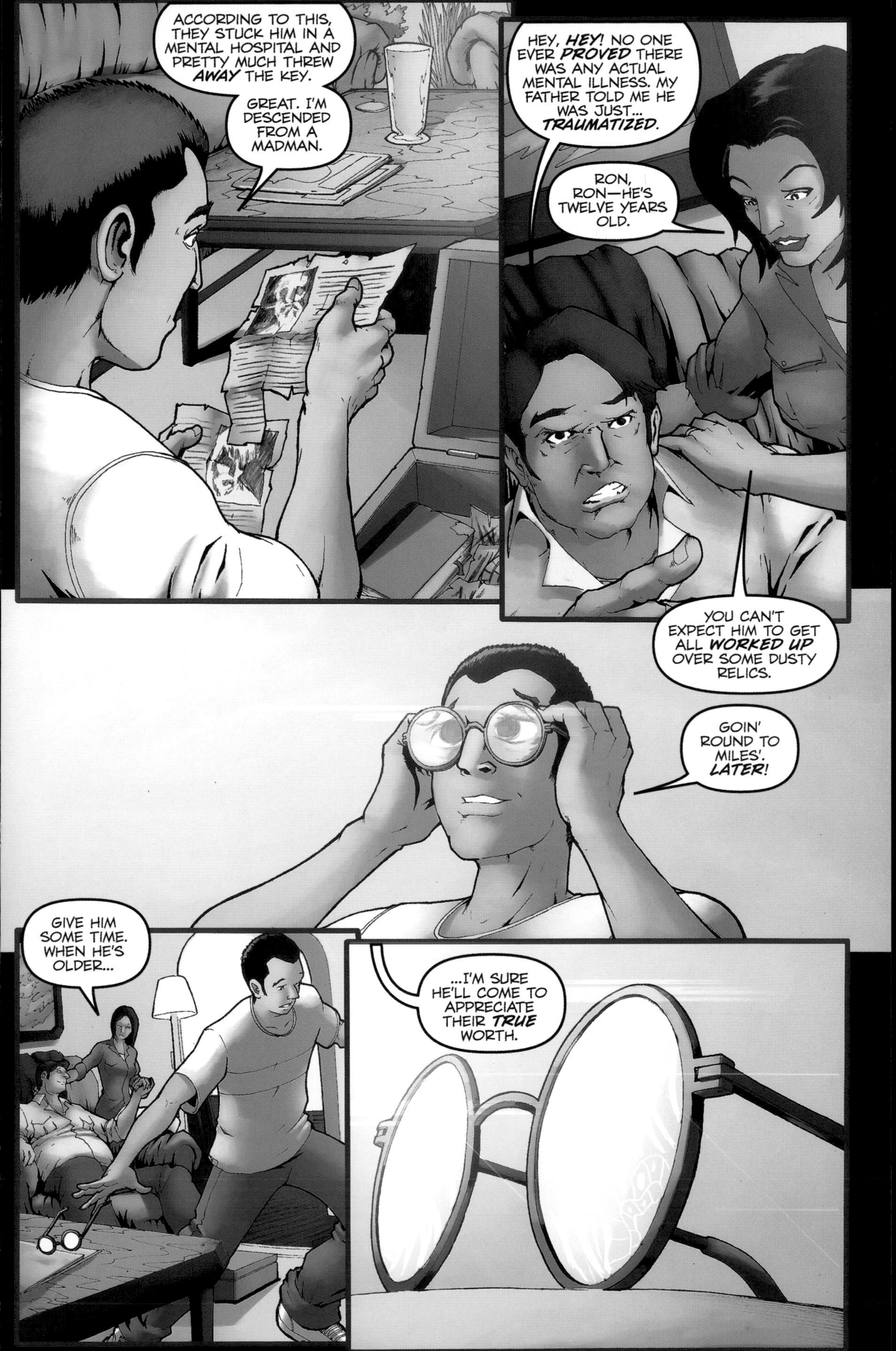
ACCORDING TO THIS, THEY STUCK HIM IN A MENTAL HOSPITAL AND PRETTY MUCH THREW AWAY THE KEY.
GREAT. I'M DESCENDED FROM A MADMAN.
HEY, HEY! NO ONE EVER PROVED THERE WAS ANY ACTUAL MENTAL ILLNESS. MY FATHER TOLD ME HE WAS JUST... TRAUMATIZED.
RON, RON—HE'S TWELVE YEARS OLD.
YOU CAN'T EXPECT HIM TO GET ALL WORKED UP OVER SOME DUSTY RELICS.
GOIN' ROUND TO MILES'. LATER!
GIVE HIM SOME TIME. WHEN HE'S OLDER...
...I'M SURE HE'LL COME TO APPRECIATE THEIR TRUE WORTH.

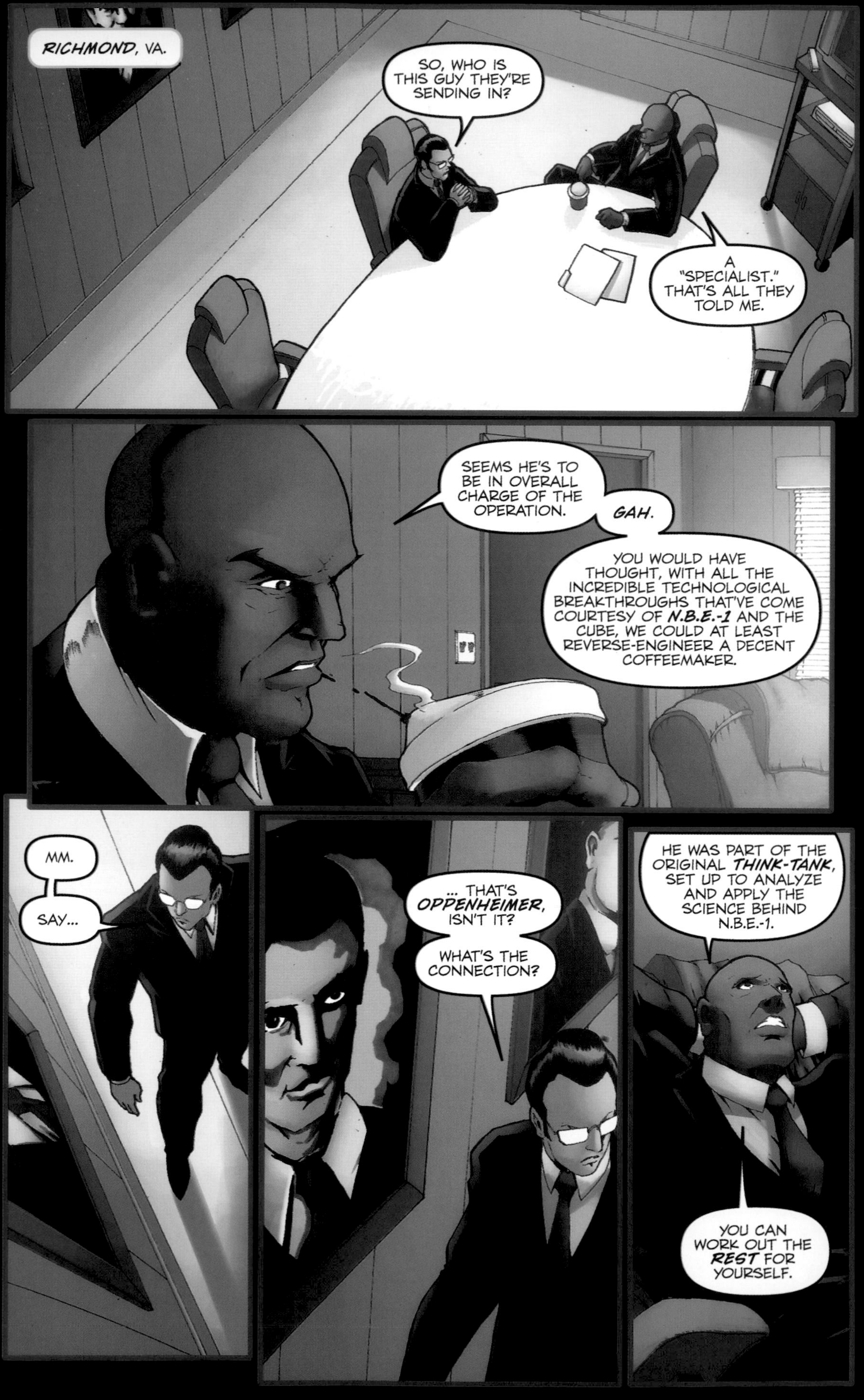
RICHMOND, VA.
SO, WHO IS THIS GUY THEY'RE SENDING IN?
A "SPECIALIST." THAT'S ALL THEY TOLD ME.
SEEMS HE'S TO BE IN OVERALL CHARGE OF THE OPERATION.
GAH.
YOU WOULD HAVE THOUGHT, WITH ALL THE INCREDIBLE TECHNOLOGICAL BREAKTHROUGHS THAT'VE COME COURTESY OF N.B.E.-1 AND THE CUBE, WE COULD AT LEAST REVERSE-ENGINEER A DECENT COFFEEMAKER.
MM.
SAY...
... THAT'S OPPENHEIMER, ISN'T IT?
WHAT'S THE CONNECTION?
HE WAS PART OF THE ORIGINAL THINK-TANK, SET UP TO ANALYZE AND APPLY THE SCIENCE BEHIND N.B.E.-1.
YOU CAN WORK OUT THE REST FOR YOURSELF.

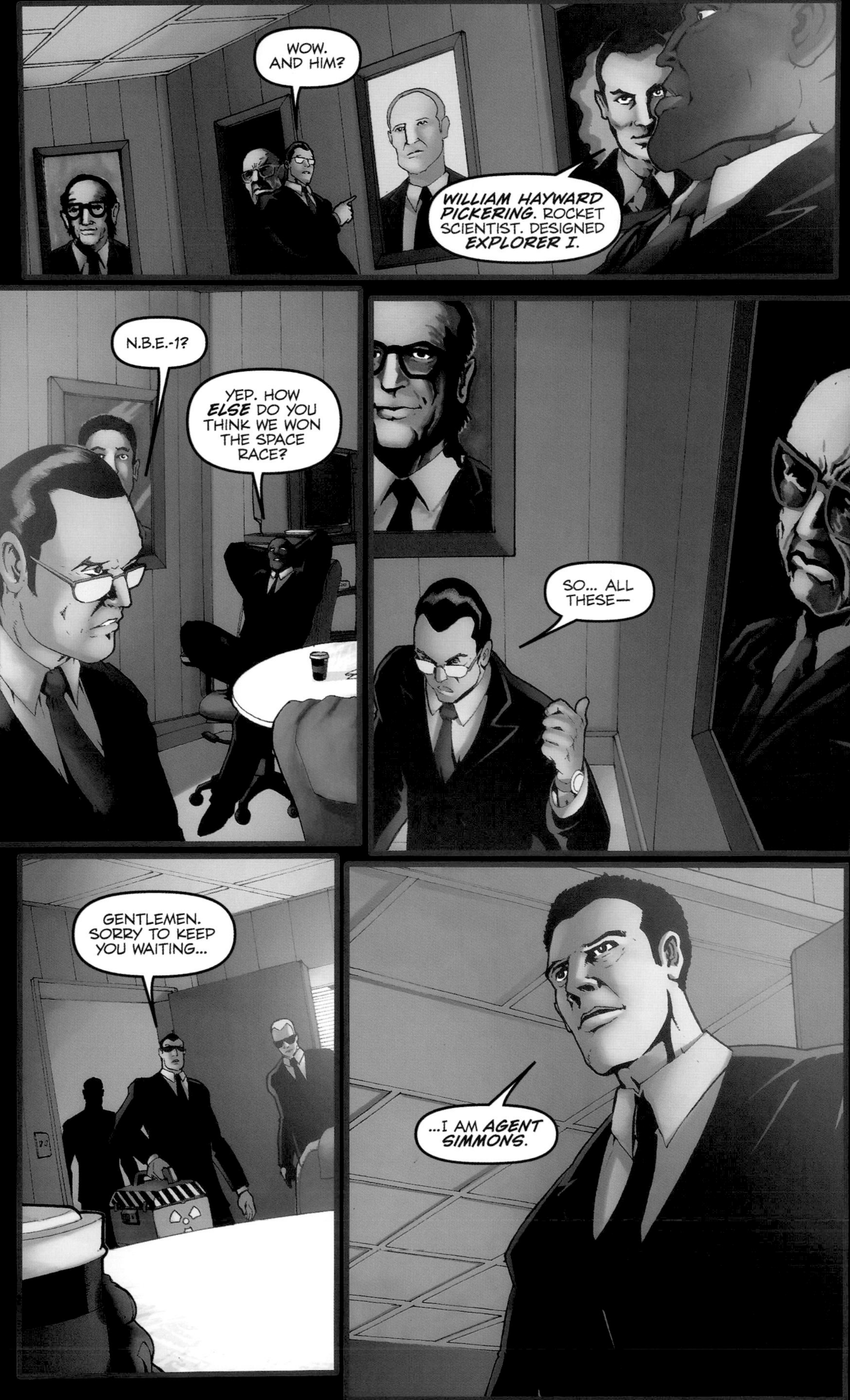
WOW. AND HIM?
WILLIAM HAYWARD PICKERING. ROCKET SCIENTIST. DESIGNED EXPLORER I.
N.B.E.-1?
YEP. HOW ELSE DO YOU THINK WE WON THE SPACE RACE?
SO... ALL THESE—
GENTLEMEN. SORRY TO KEEP YOU WAITING...
...I AM AGENT SIMMONS.

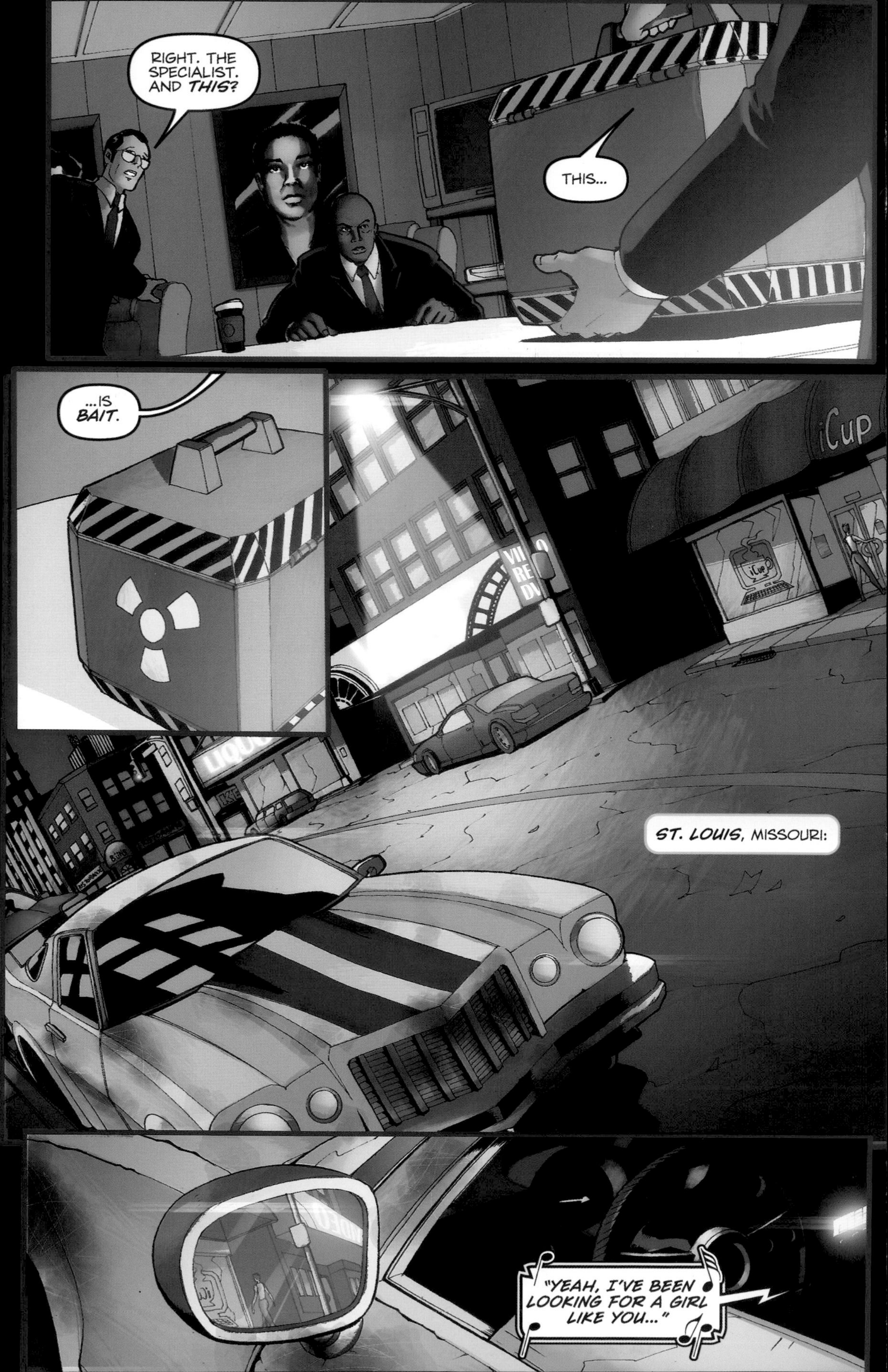
RIGHT. THE SPECIALIST. AND *THIS*?
THIS...
...IS *BAIT*.
iCup
LIQUO
ST. LOUIS, MISSOURI:
"YEAH, I'VE BEEN LOOKING FOR A GIRL LIKE YOU..."

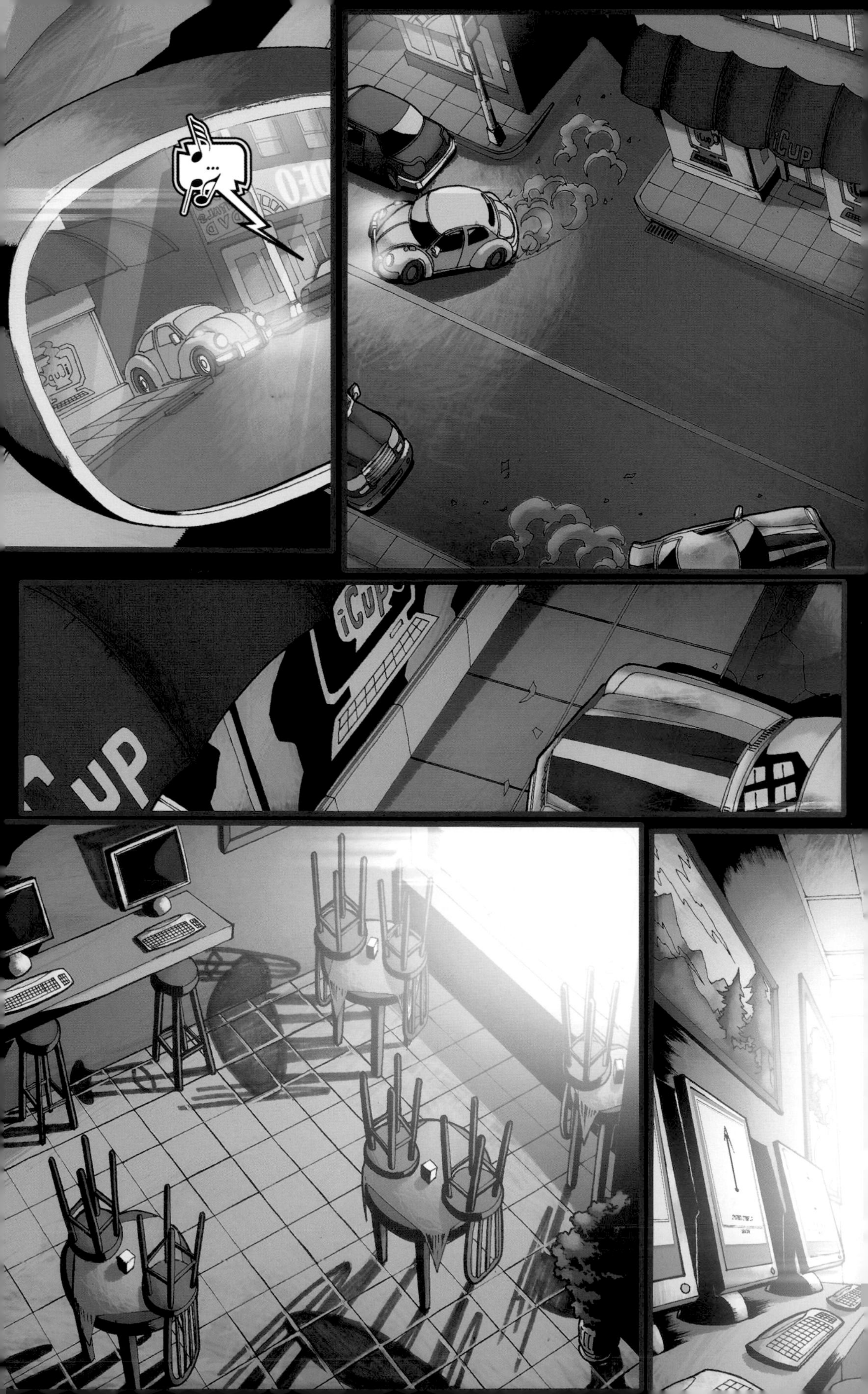
...
iCup
iCup

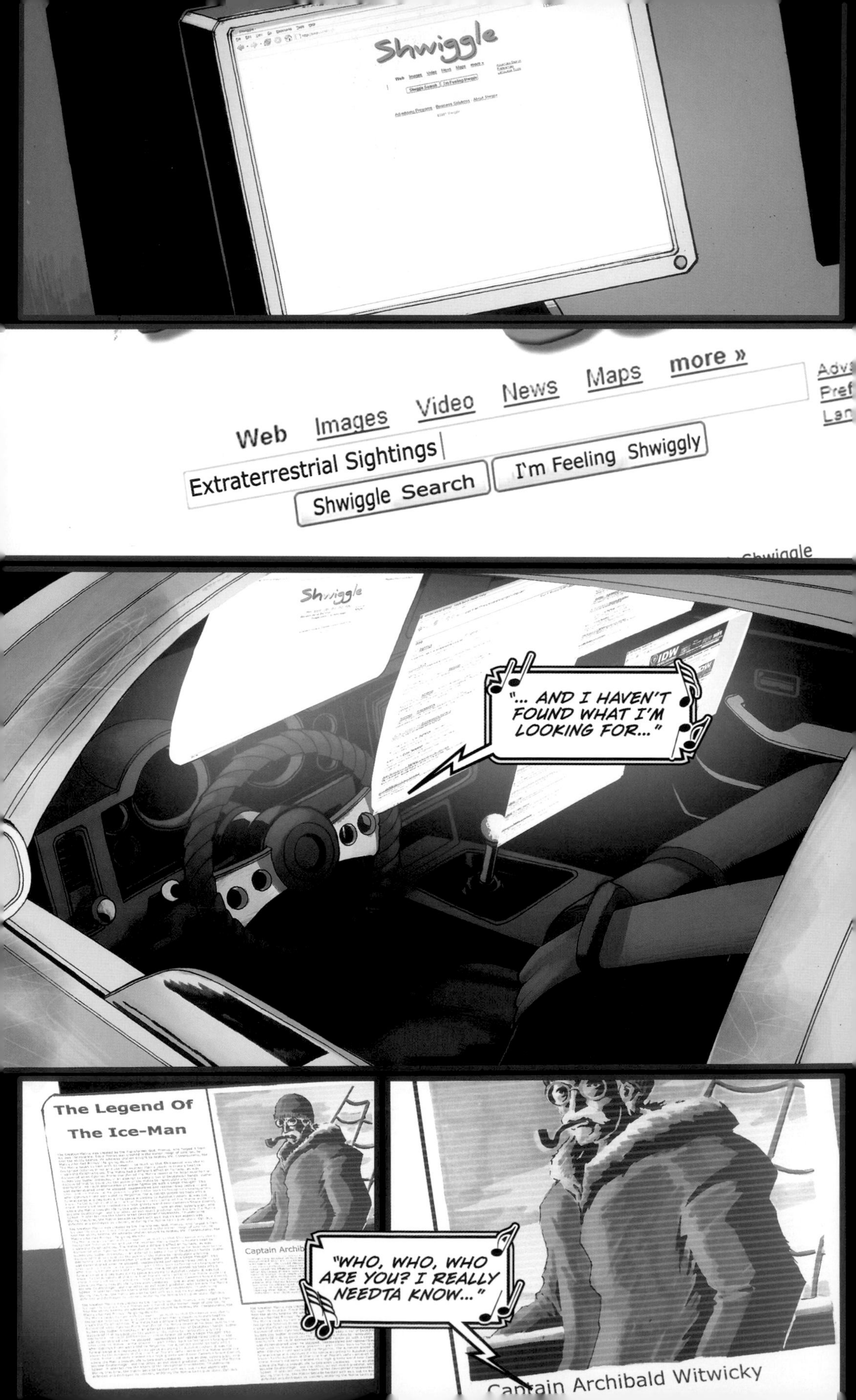
Shwiggle
Web Images Video News Maps more »
Extraterrestrial Sightings
Shwiggle Search
I'm Feeling Shwiggly
Shwiggle
"... AND I HAVEN'T FOUND WHAT I'M LOOKING FOR..."
The Legend Of The Ice-Man
"WHO, WHO, WHO ARE YOU? I REALLY NEEDTA KNOW..."
Captain Archibald Witwicky

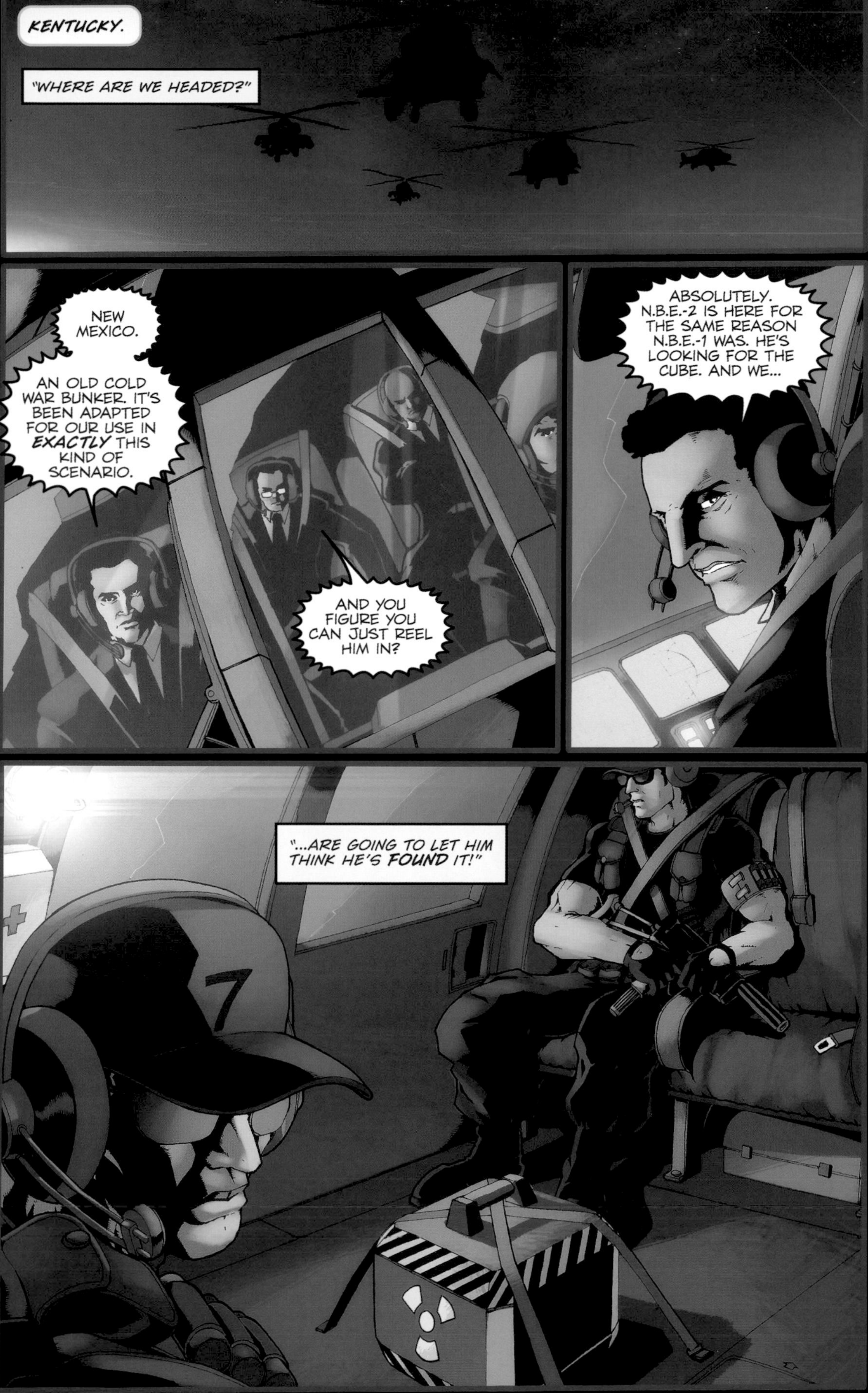
KENTUCKY.
"WHERE ARE WE HEADED?"
NEW MEXICO.
AN OLD COLD WAR BUNKER. IT'S BEEN ADAPTED FOR OUR USE IN EXACTLY THIS KIND OF SCENARIO.
AND YOU FIGURE YOU CAN JUST REEL HIM IN?
ABSOLUTELY. N.B.E.-2 IS HERE FOR THE SAME REASON N.B.E.-1 WAS. HE'S LOOKING FOR THE CUBE. AND WE...
"...ARE GOING TO LET HIM THINK HE'S FOUND IT!"

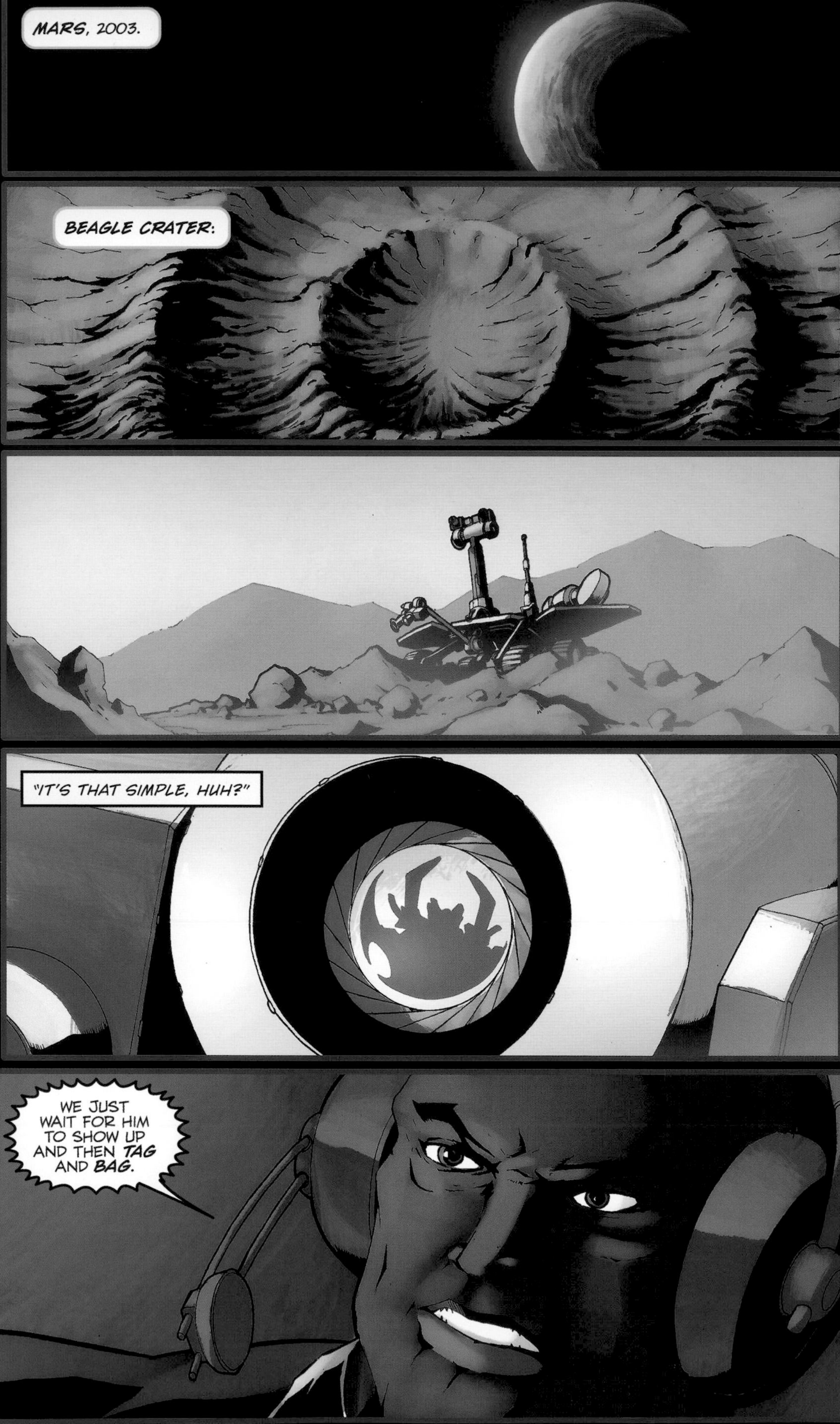
MARS, 2003.
BEAGLE CRATER:
"IT'S THAT SIMPLE, HUH?"
WE JUST WAIT FOR HIM TO SHOW UP AND THEN TAG AND BAG.

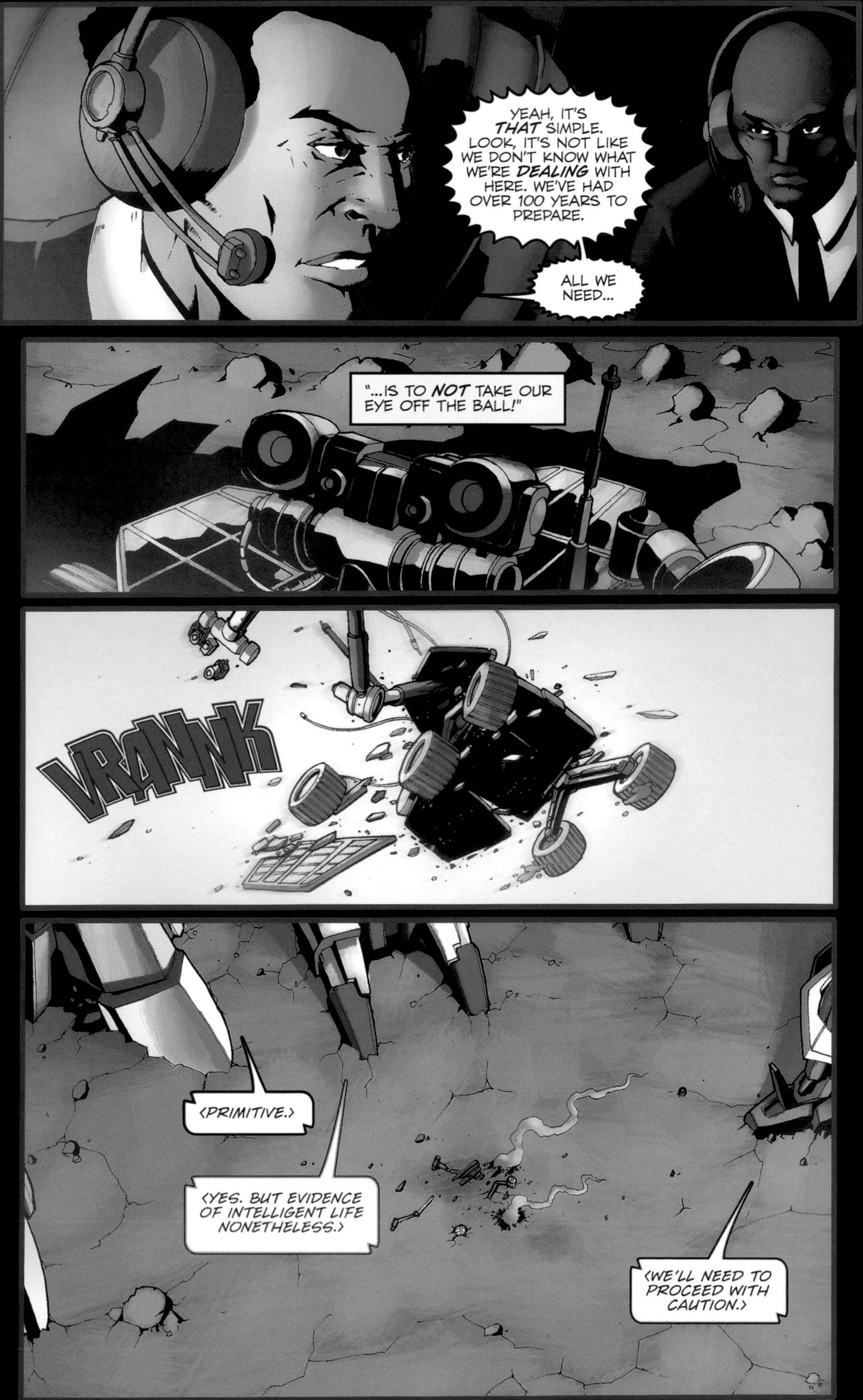
YEAH, IT'S *THAT* SIMPLE. LOOK, IT'S NOT LIKE WE DON'T KNOW WHAT WE'RE *DEALING* WITH HERE. WE'VE HAD OVER 100 YEARS TO PREPARE.
ALL WE NEED...
"...IS TO *NOT* TAKE OUR EYE OFF THE BALL!"
VRANNK
‹PRIMITIVE.›
‹YES. BUT EVIDENCE OF INTELLIGENT LIFE NONETHELESS.›
‹WE'LL NEED TO PROCEED WITH CAUTION.›

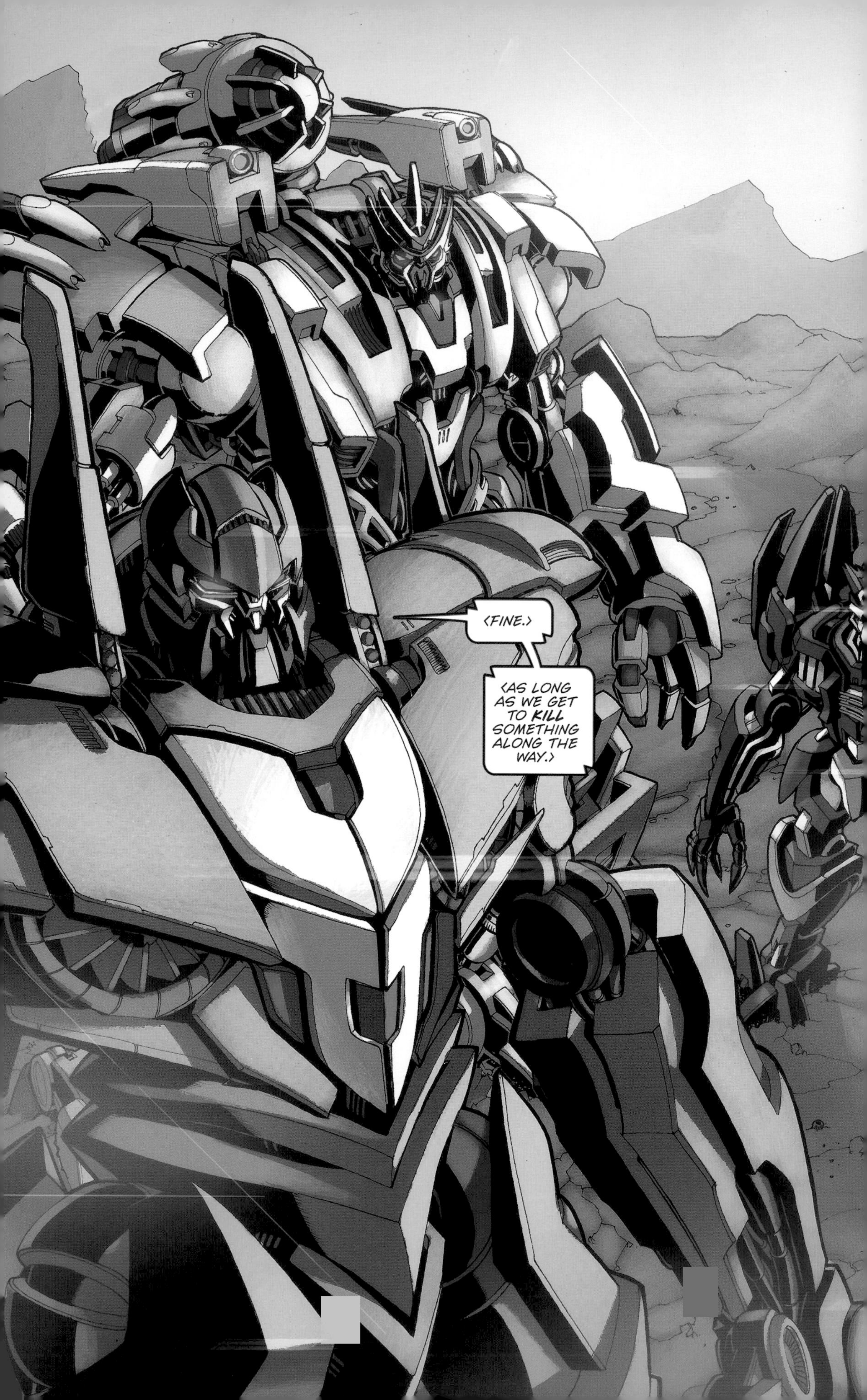
<FINE.>
<AS LONG AS WE GET TO KILL SOMETHING ALONG THE WAY.>

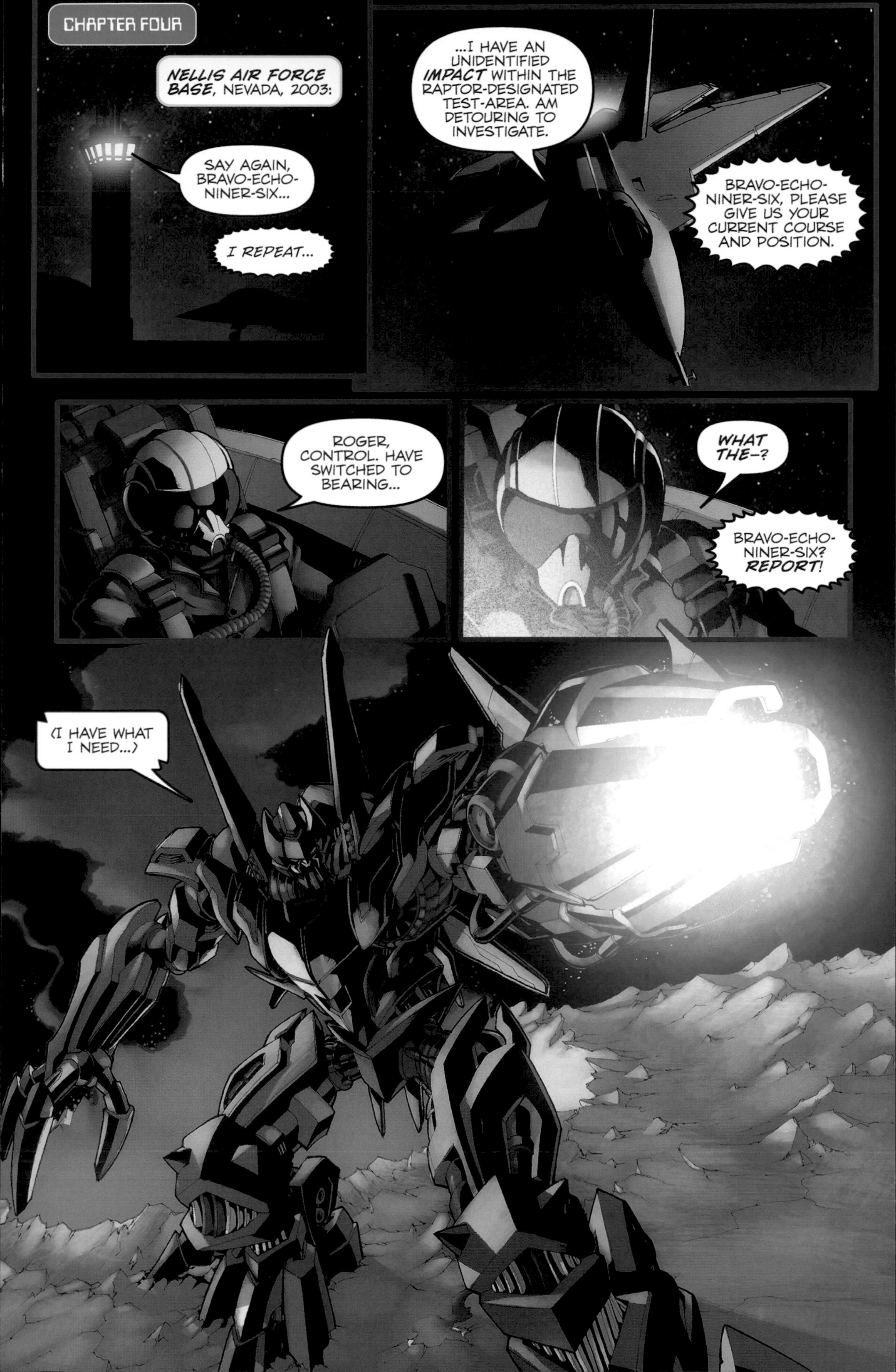
CHAPTER FOUR
NELLIS AIR FORCE BASE, NEVADA, 2003:
SAY AGAIN, BRAVO-ECHO-NINER-SIX...
I REPEAT...
...I HAVE AN UNIDENTIFIED IMPACT WITHIN THE RAPTOR-DESIGNATED TEST-AREA. AM DETOURING TO INVESTIGATE.
BRAVO-ECHO-NINER-SIX, PLEASE GIVE US YOUR CURRENT COURSE AND POSITION.
ROGER, CONTROL. HAVE SWITCHED TO BEARING...
WHAT THE–?
BRAVO-ECHO-NINER-SIX? REPORT!
(I HAVE WHAT I NEED...)

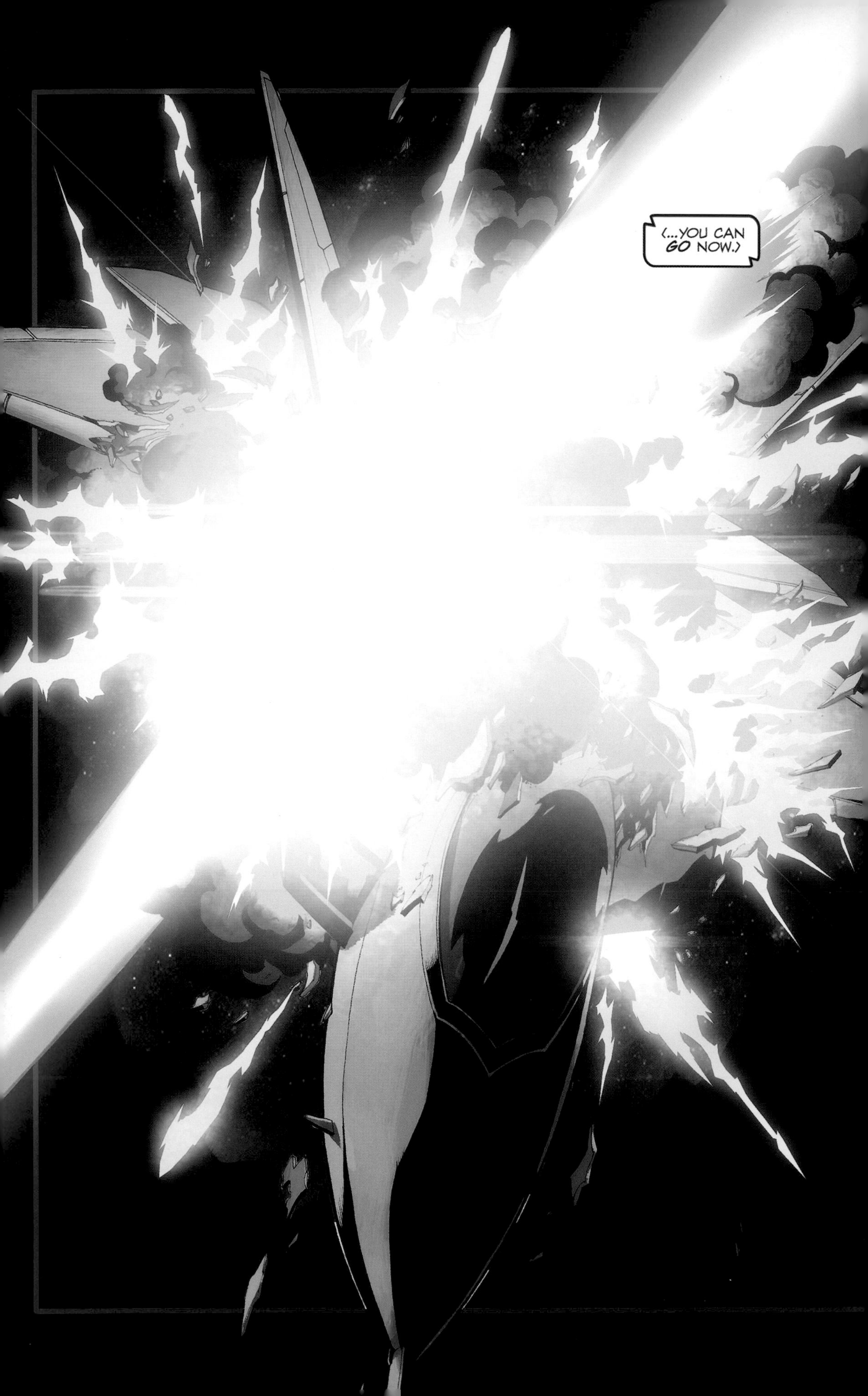
(...YOU CAN GO NOW.)

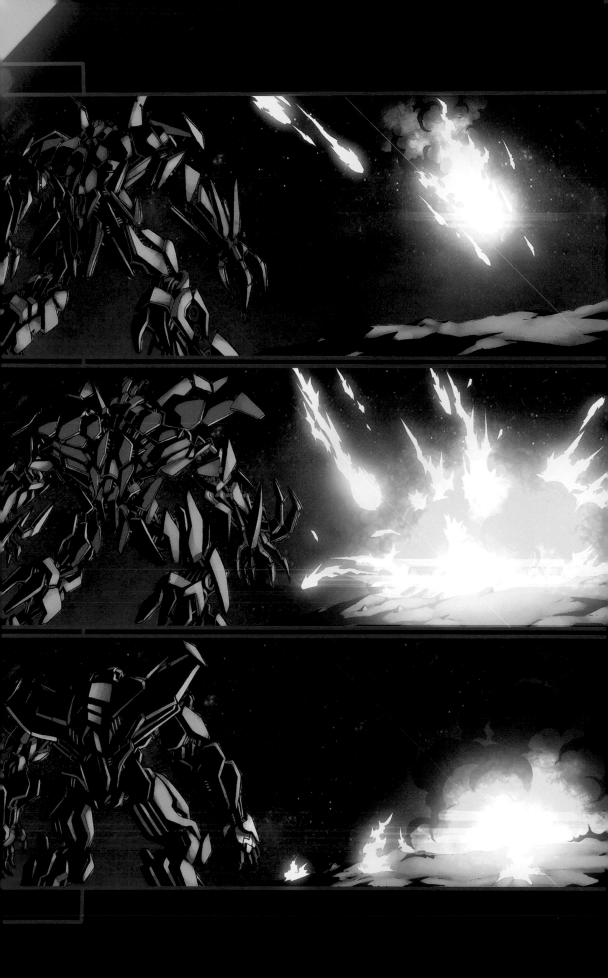

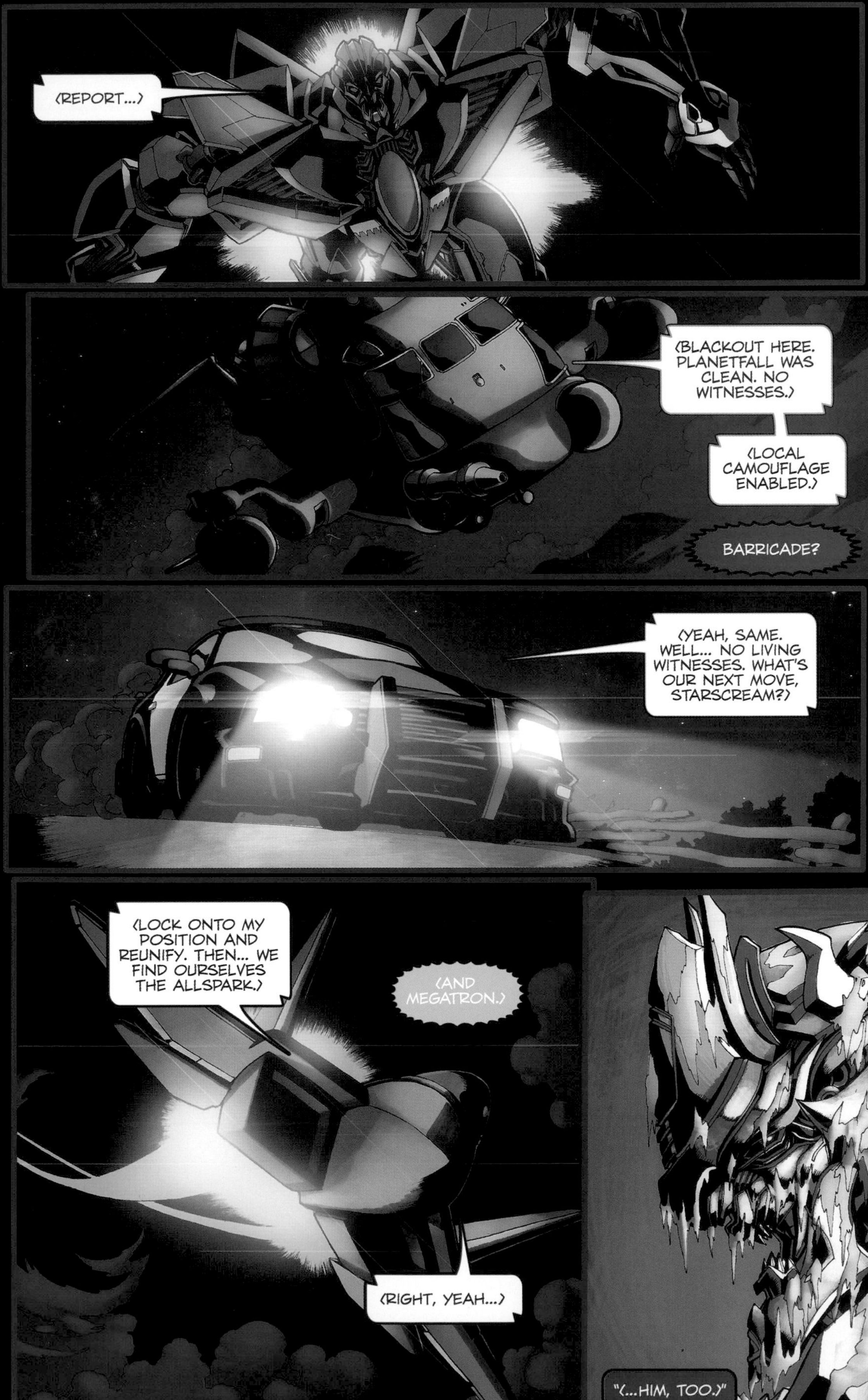

‹REPORT...›
‹BLACKOUT HERE. PLANETFALL WAS CLEAN. NO WITNESSES.›
‹LOCAL CAMOUFLAGE ENABLED.›
BARRICADE?
‹YEAH, SAME. WELL... NO LIVING WITNESSES. WHAT'S OUR NEXT MOVE, STARSCREAM?›
‹LOCK ONTO MY POSITION AND REUNIFY. THEN... WE FIND OURSELVES THE ALLSPARK.›
‹AND MEGATRON.›
‹RIGHT, YEAH...›
"‹...HIM, TOO.›"

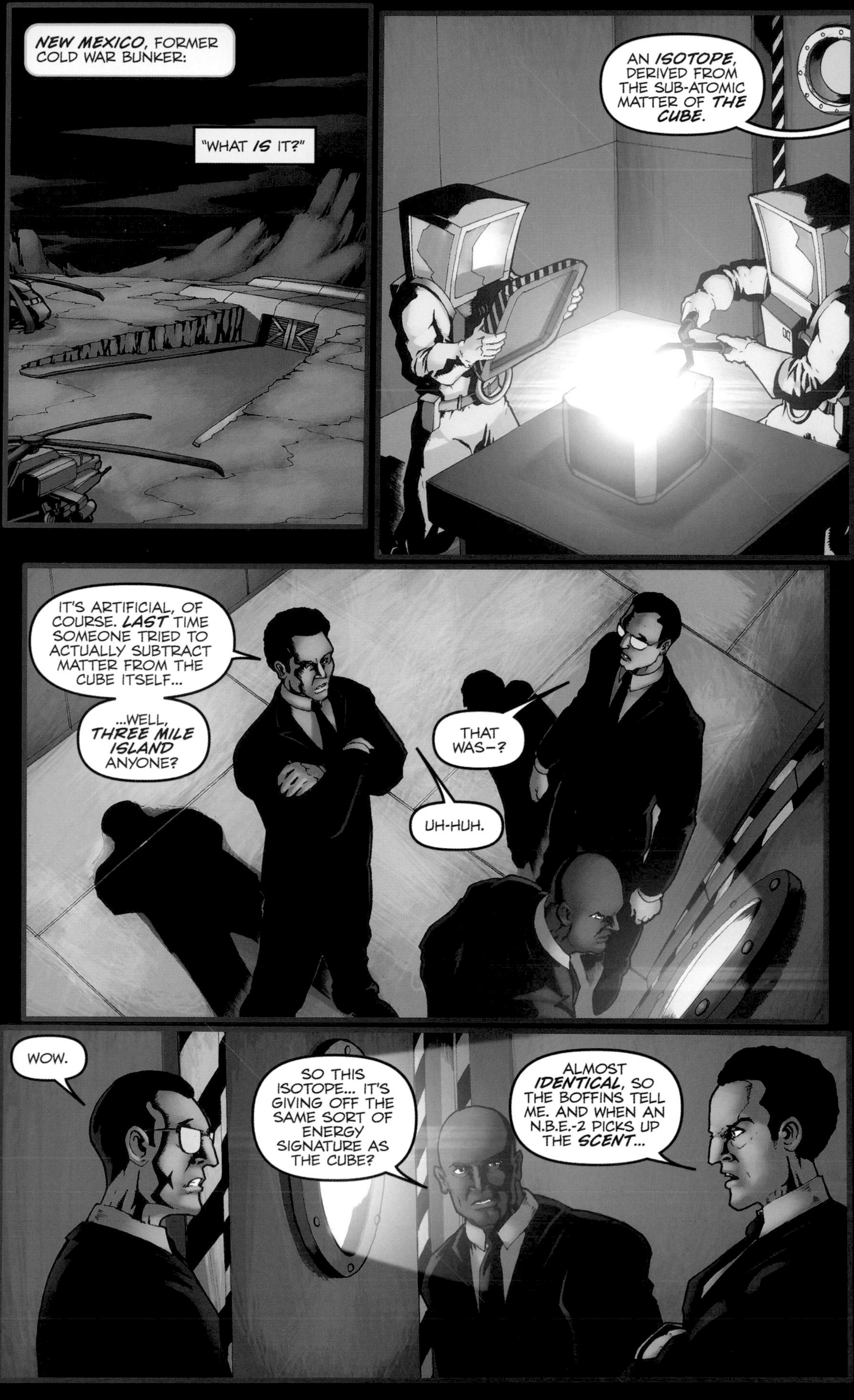
NEW MEXICO, FORMER COLD WAR BUNKER:
"WHAT IS IT?"
AN ISOTOPE, DERIVED FROM THE SUB-ATOMIC MATTER OF THE CUBE.
IT'S ARTIFICIAL, OF COURSE. LAST TIME SOMEONE TRIED TO ACTUALLY SUBTRACT MATTER FROM THE CUBE ITSELF...
...WELL, THREE MILE ISLAND ANYONE?
THAT WAS--?
UH-HUH.
WOW.
SO THIS ISOTOPE... IT'S GIVING OFF THE SAME SORT OF ENERGY SIGNATURE AS THE CUBE?
ALMOST IDENTICAL, SO THE BOFFINS TELL ME. AND WHEN AN N.B.E.-2 PICKS UP THE SCENT...

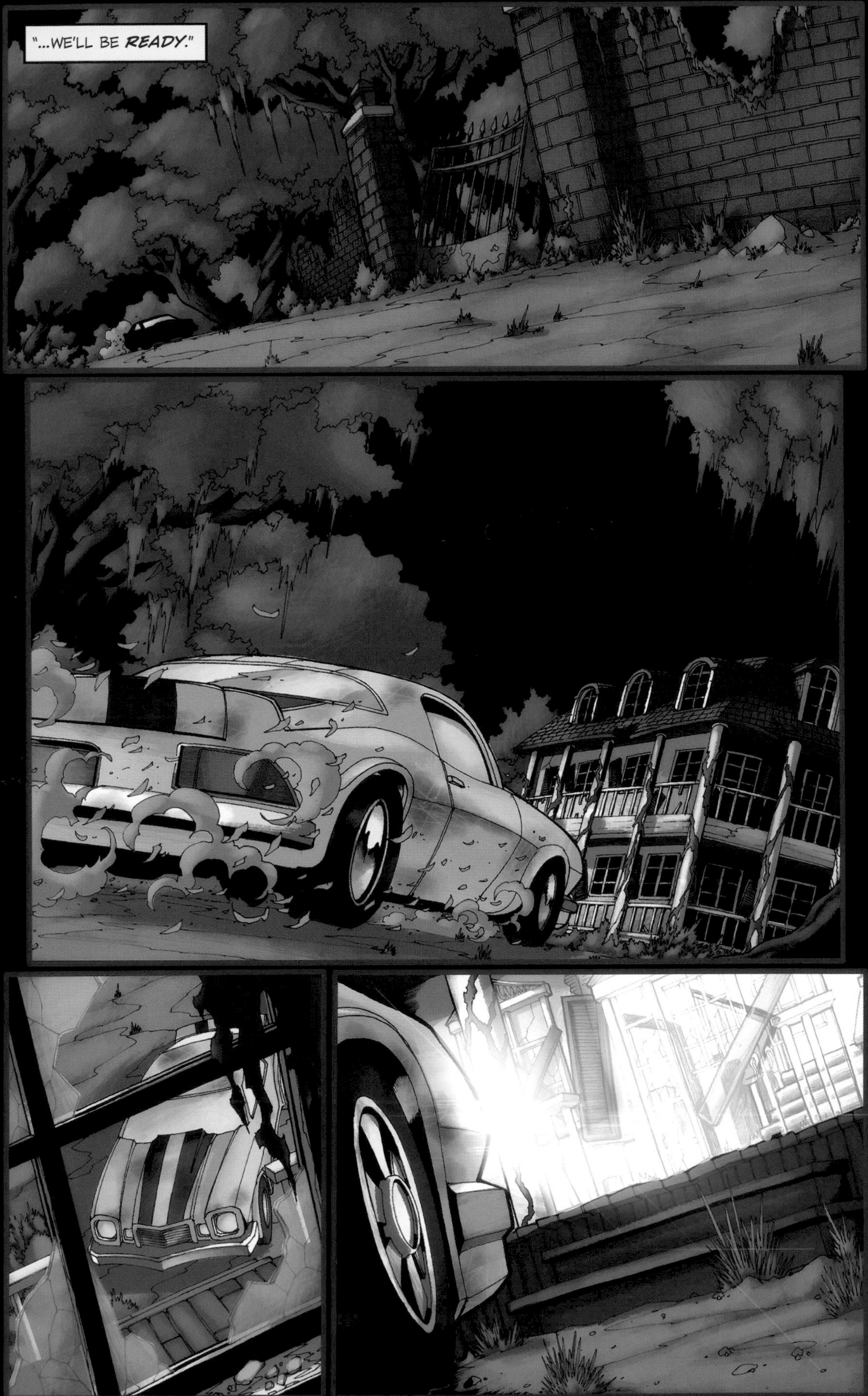
"...WE'LL BE READY."

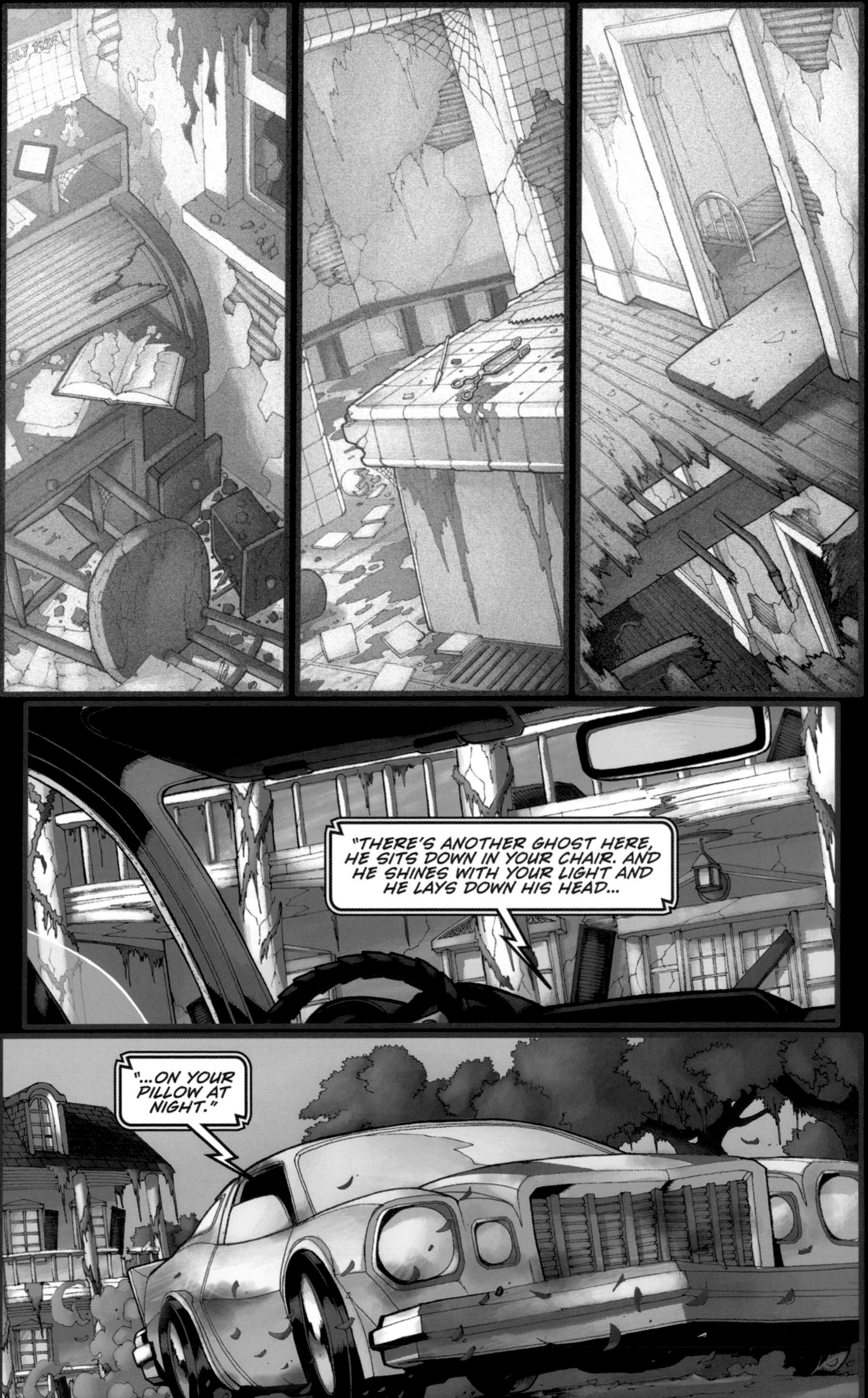
"THERE'S ANOTHER GHOST HERE, HE SITS DOWN IN YOUR CHAIR. AND HE SHINES WITH YOUR LIGHT AND HE LAYS DOWN HIS HEAD...
"...ON YOUR PILLOW AT NIGHT."

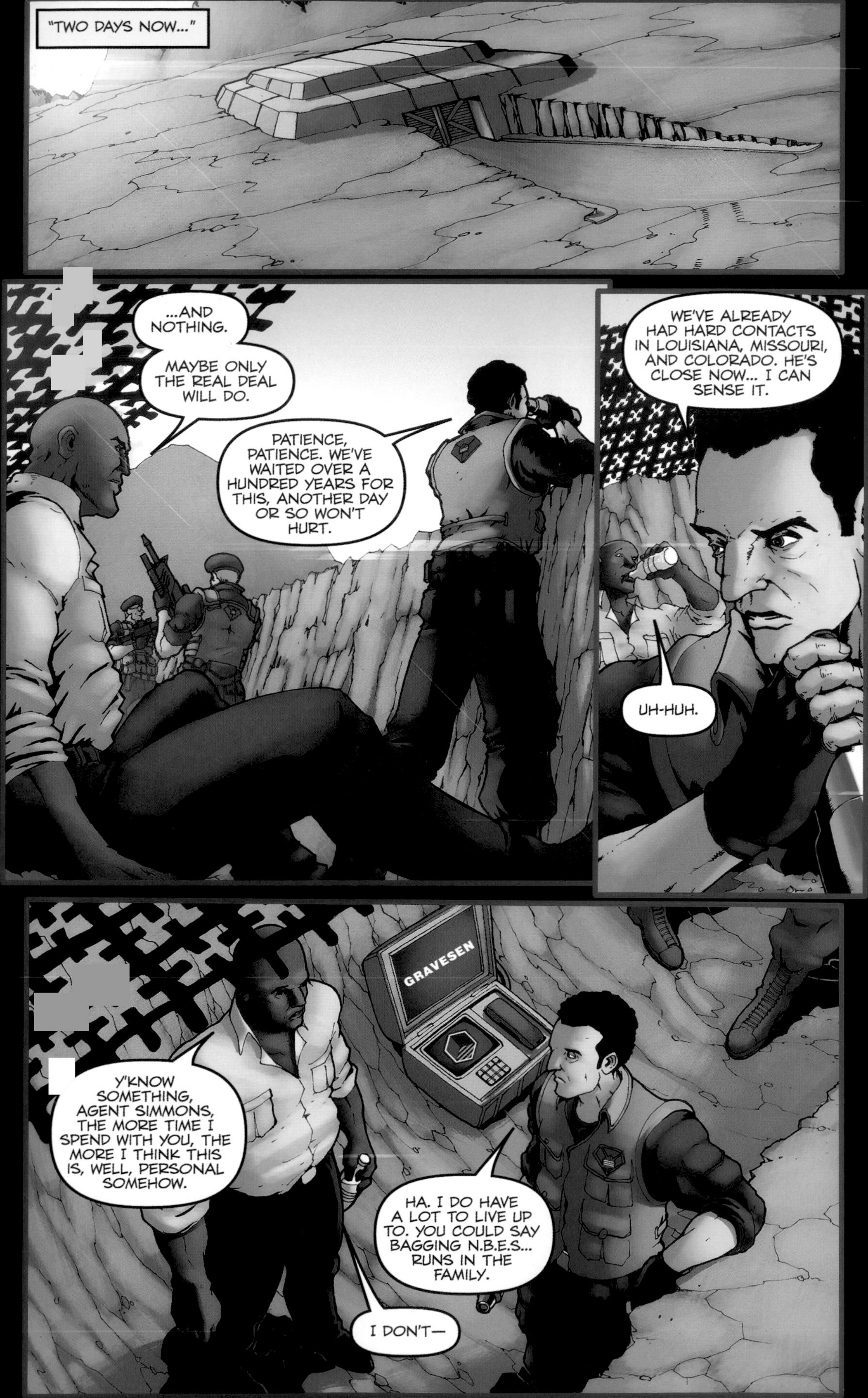
"TWO DAYS NOW..."
...AND NOTHING.
MAYBE ONLY THE REAL DEAL WILL DO.
PATIENCE, PATIENCE. WE'VE WAITED OVER A HUNDRED YEARS FOR THIS, ANOTHER DAY OR SO WON'T HURT.
WE'VE ALREADY HAD HARD CONTACTS IN LOUISIANA, MISSOURI, AND COLORADO. HE'S CLOSE NOW... I CAN SENSE IT.
UH-HUH.
GRAVESEN
Y'KNOW SOMETHING, AGENT SIMMONS, THE MORE TIME I SPEND WITH YOU, THE MORE I THINK THIS IS, WELL, PERSONAL SOMEHOW.
HA. I DO HAVE A LOT TO LIVE UP TO. YOU COULD SAY BAGGING N.B.E.S... RUNS IN THE FAMILY.
I DON'T—

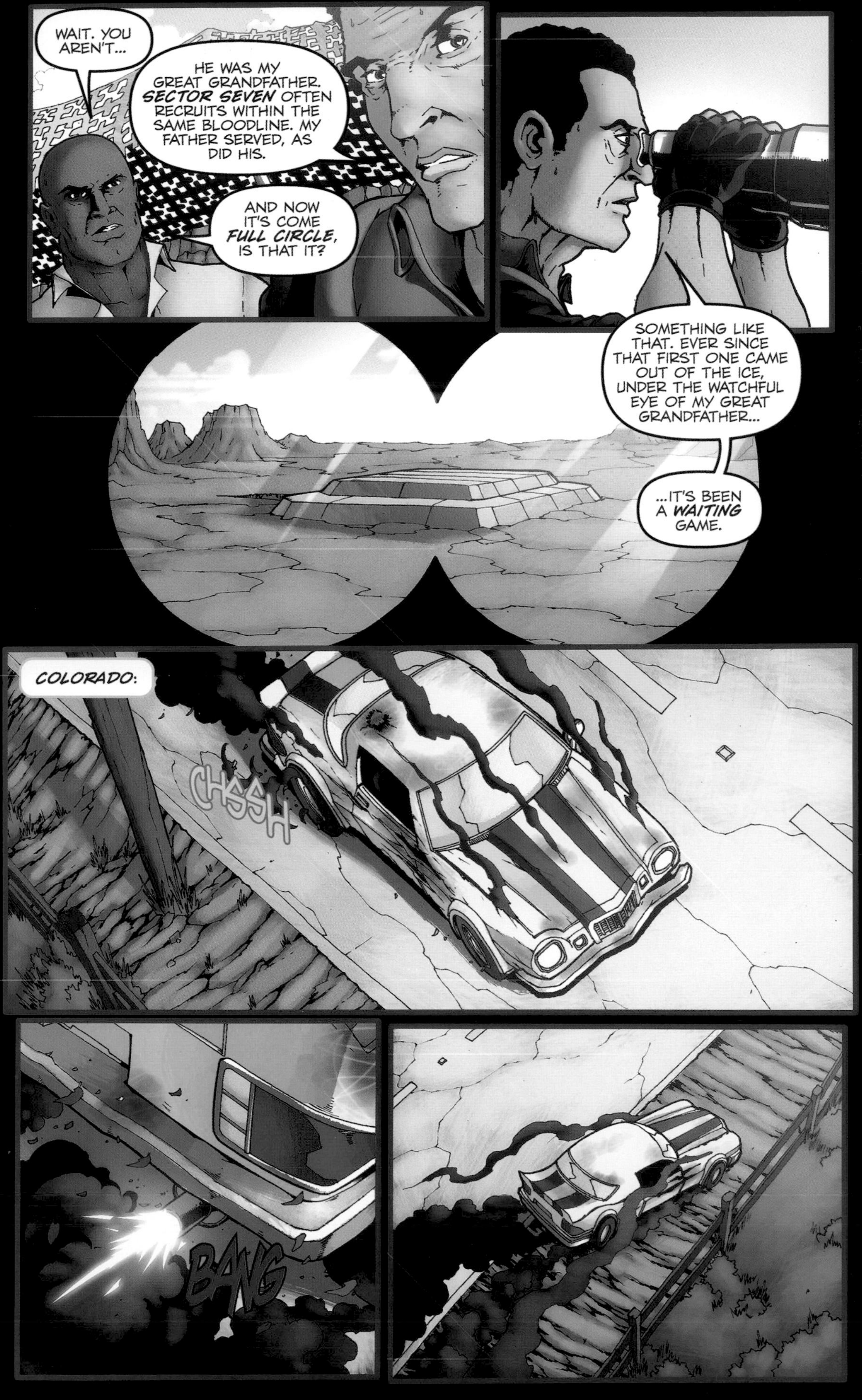
WAIT. YOU AREN'T...
HE WAS MY GREAT GRANDFATHER. SECTOR SEVEN OFTEN RECRUITS WITHIN THE SAME BLOODLINE. MY FATHER SERVED, AS DID HIS.
AND NOW IT'S COME FULL CIRCLE, IS THAT IT?
SOMETHING LIKE THAT. EVER SINCE THAT FIRST ONE CAME OUT OF THE ICE, UNDER THE WATCHFUL EYE OF MY GREAT GRANDFATHER...
...IT'S BEEN A WAITING GAME.
COLORADO:
CHSSH
BANG

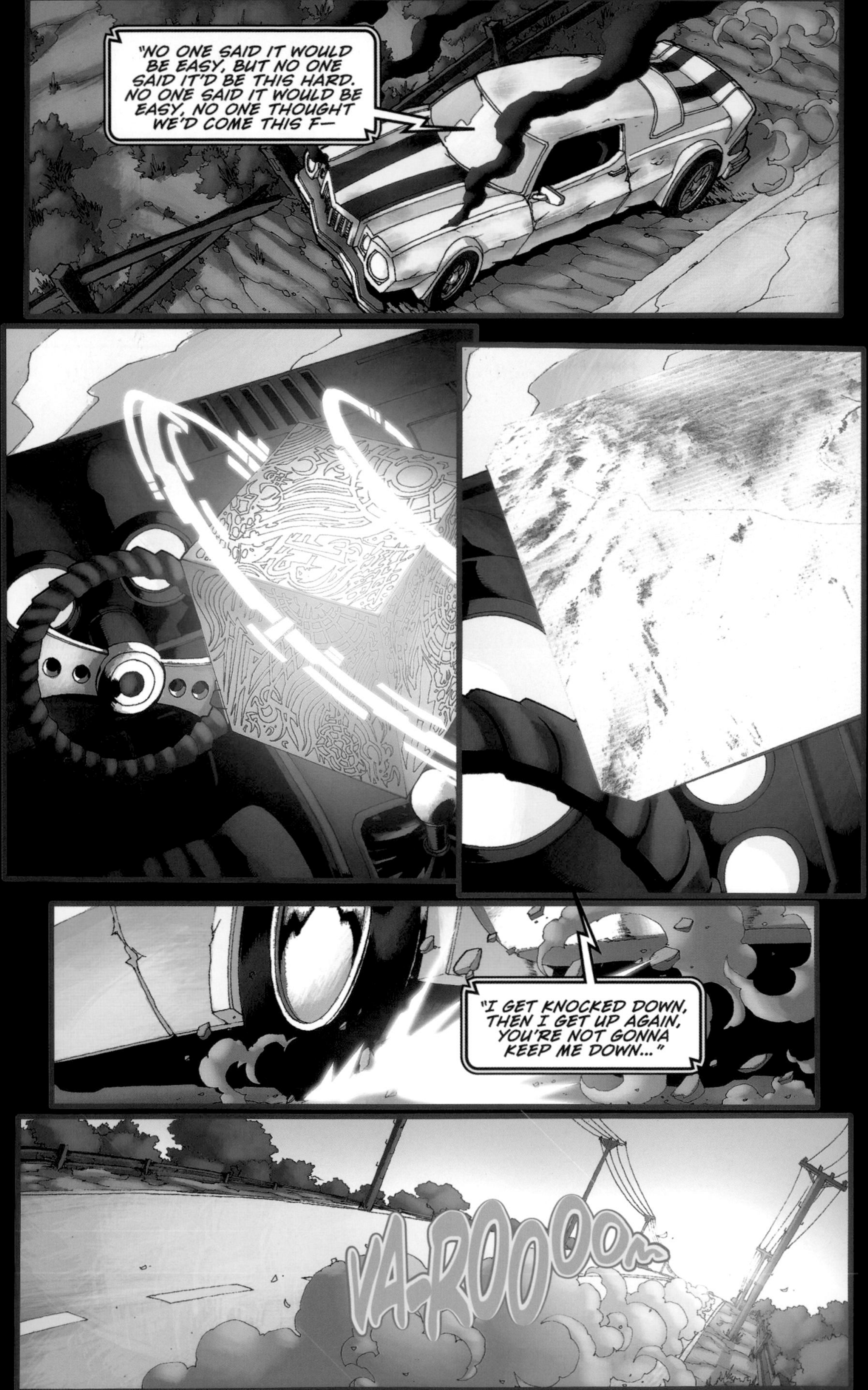
"NO ONE SAID IT WOULD BE EASY, BUT NO ONE SAID IT'D BE THIS HARD. NO ONE SAID IT WOULD BE EASY, NO ONE THOUGHT WE'D COME THIS F—
"I GET KNOCKED DOWN, THEN I GET UP AGAIN, YOU'RE NOT GONNA KEEP ME DOWN..."
VA-ROOOOOm

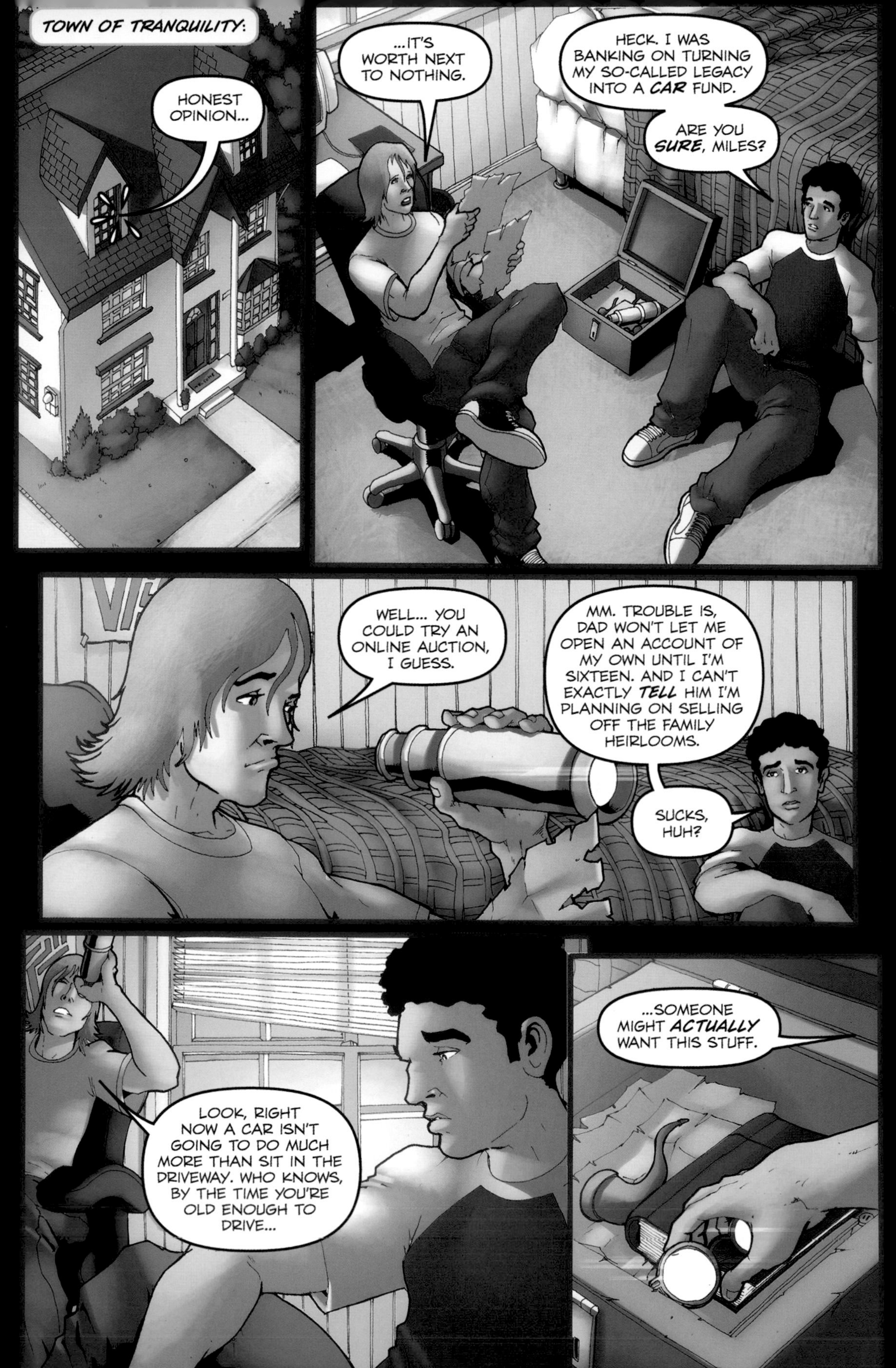
TOWN OF TRANQUILITY:
HONEST OPINION...
...IT'S WORTH NEXT TO NOTHING.
HECK. I WAS BANKING ON TURNING MY SO-CALLED LEGACY INTO A CAR FUND.
ARE YOU SURE, MILES?
WELL... YOU COULD TRY AN ONLINE AUCTION, I GUESS.
MM. TROUBLE IS, DAD WON'T LET ME OPEN AN ACCOUNT OF MY OWN UNTIL I'M SIXTEEN. AND I CAN'T EXACTLY TELL HIM I'M PLANNING ON SELLING OFF THE FAMILY HEIRLOOMS.
SUCKS, HUH?
LOOK, RIGHT NOW A CAR ISN'T GOING TO DO MUCH MORE THAN SIT IN THE DRIVEWAY. WHO KNOWS, BY THE TIME YOU'RE OLD ENOUGH TO DRIVE...
...SOMEONE MIGHT ACTUALLY WANT THIS STUFF.

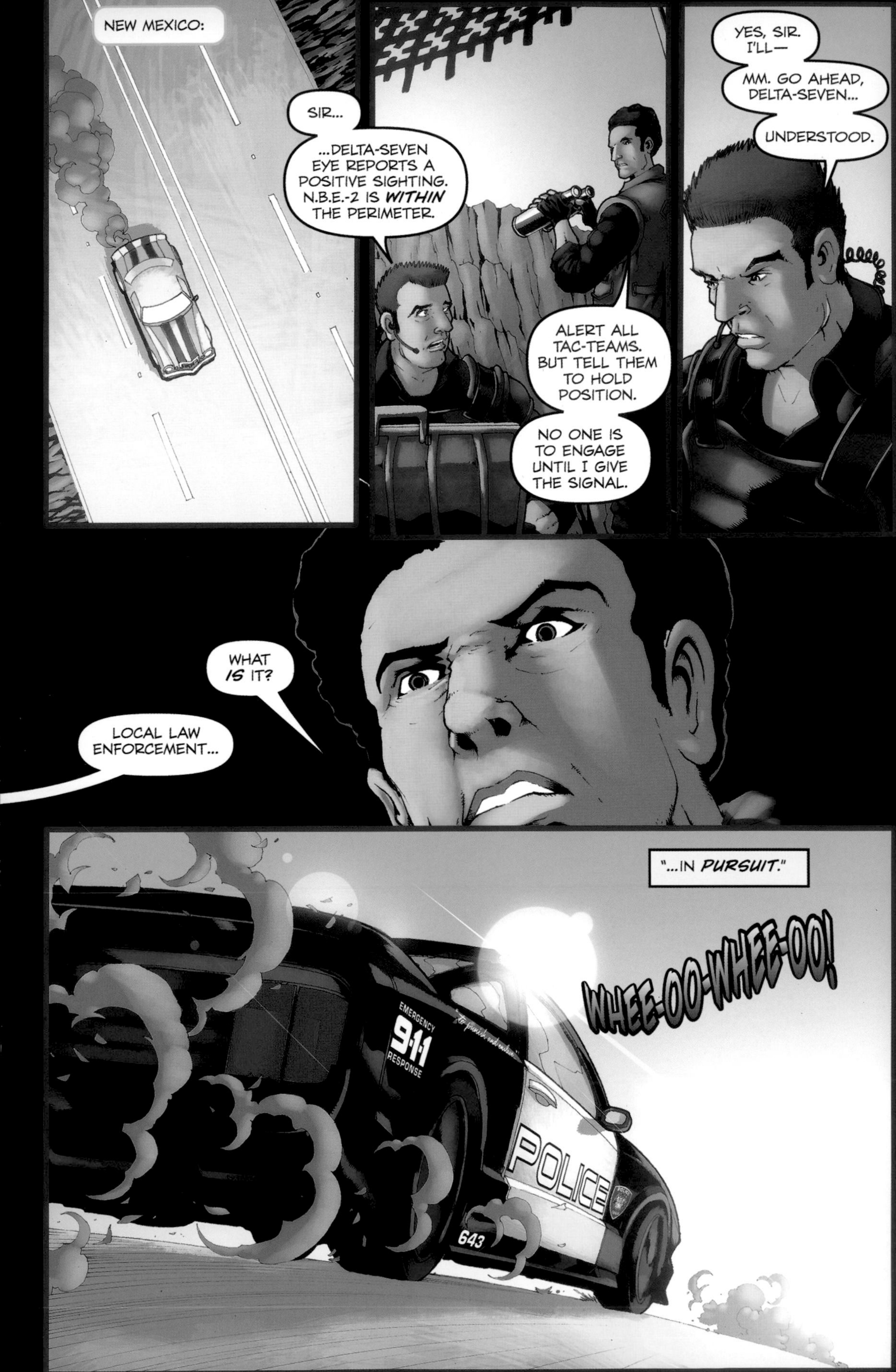
NEW MEXICO:
SIR...
...DELTA-SEVEN EYE REPORTS A POSITIVE SIGHTING. N.B.E.-2 IS WITHIN THE PERIMETER.
ALERT ALL TAC-TEAMS. BUT TELL THEM TO HOLD POSITION.
NO ONE IS TO ENGAGE UNTIL I GIVE THE SIGNAL.
YES, SIR. I'LL—
MM. GO AHEAD, DELTA-SEVEN...
UNDERSTOOD.
WHAT IS IT?
LOCAL LAW ENFORCEMENT...
"...IN PURSUIT."
WHEE-OO-WHEE-OO!
EMERGENCY 9-1-1 RESPONSE
POLICE
643

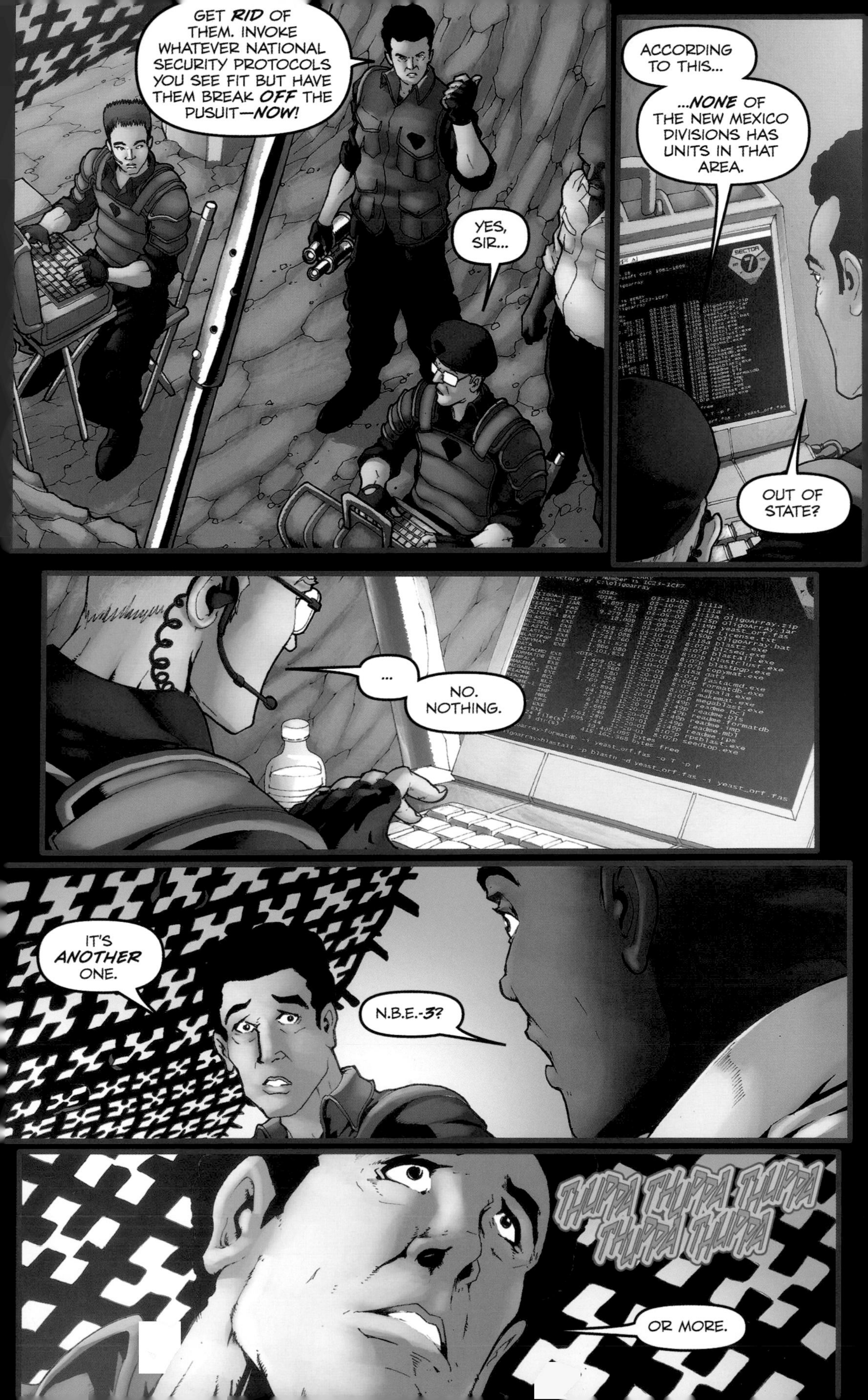
GET RID OF THEM. INVOKE WHATEVER NATIONAL SECURITY PROTOCOLS YOU SEE FIT BUT HAVE THEM BREAK OFF THE PUSUIT—NOW!
YES, SIR...
ACCORDING TO THIS...
...NONE OF THE NEW MEXICO DIVISIONS HAS UNITS IN THAT AREA.
OUT OF STATE?
SECTOR 7
...
NO. NOTHING.
IT'S ANOTHER ONE.
N.B.E.-3?
THUPPA THUPPA THUPPA THUPPA THUPPA
OR MORE.

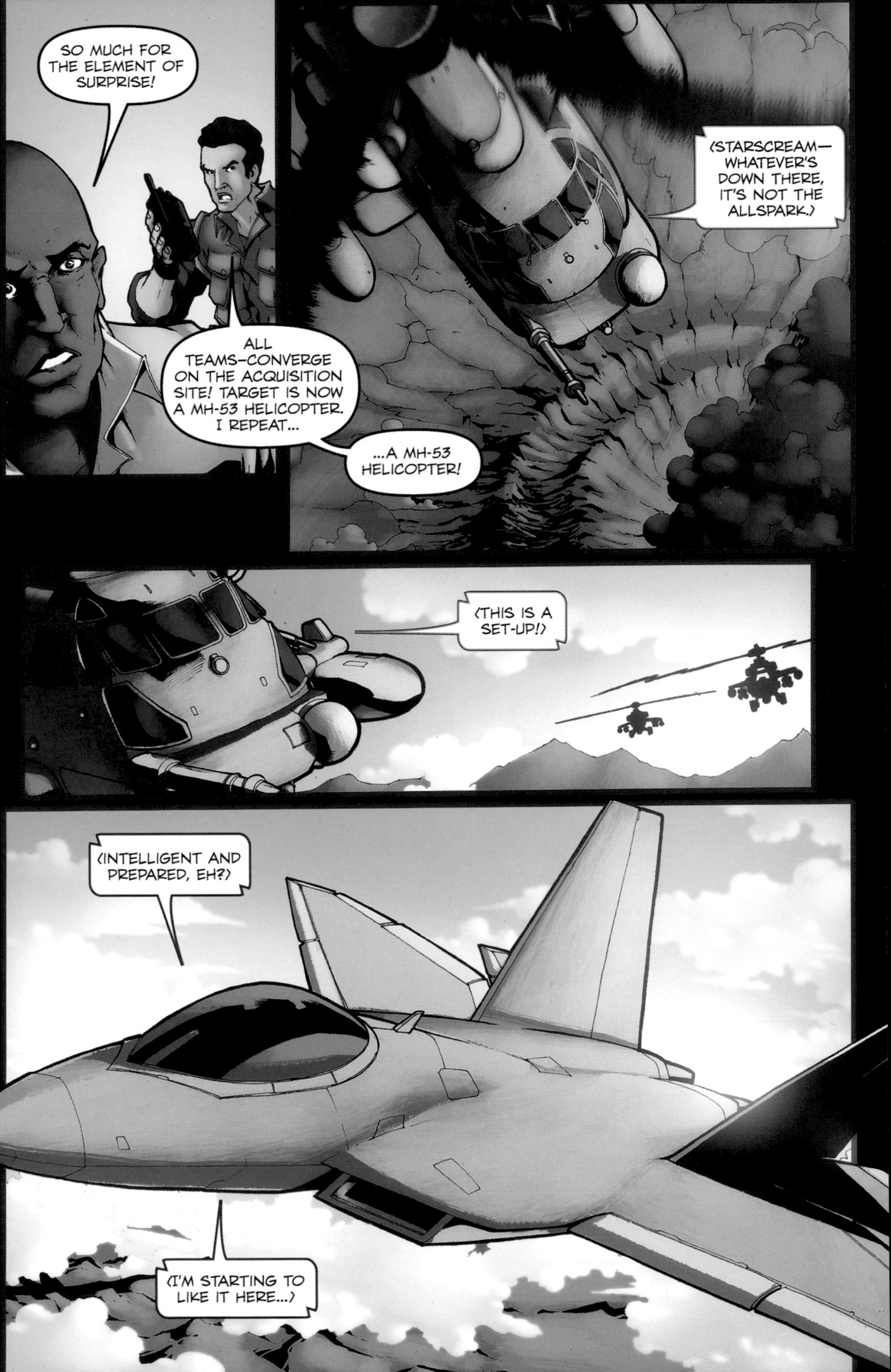
SO MUCH FOR THE ELEMENT OF SURPRISE!
(STARSCREAM— WHATEVER'S DOWN THERE, IT'S NOT THE ALLSPARK.)
ALL TEAMS—CONVERGE ON THE ACQUISITION SITE! TARGET IS NOW A MH-53 HELICOPTER. I REPEAT...
...A MH-53 HELICOPTER!
(THIS IS A SET-UP!)
(INTELLIGENT AND PREPARED, EH?)
(I'M STARTING TO LIKE IT HERE...)

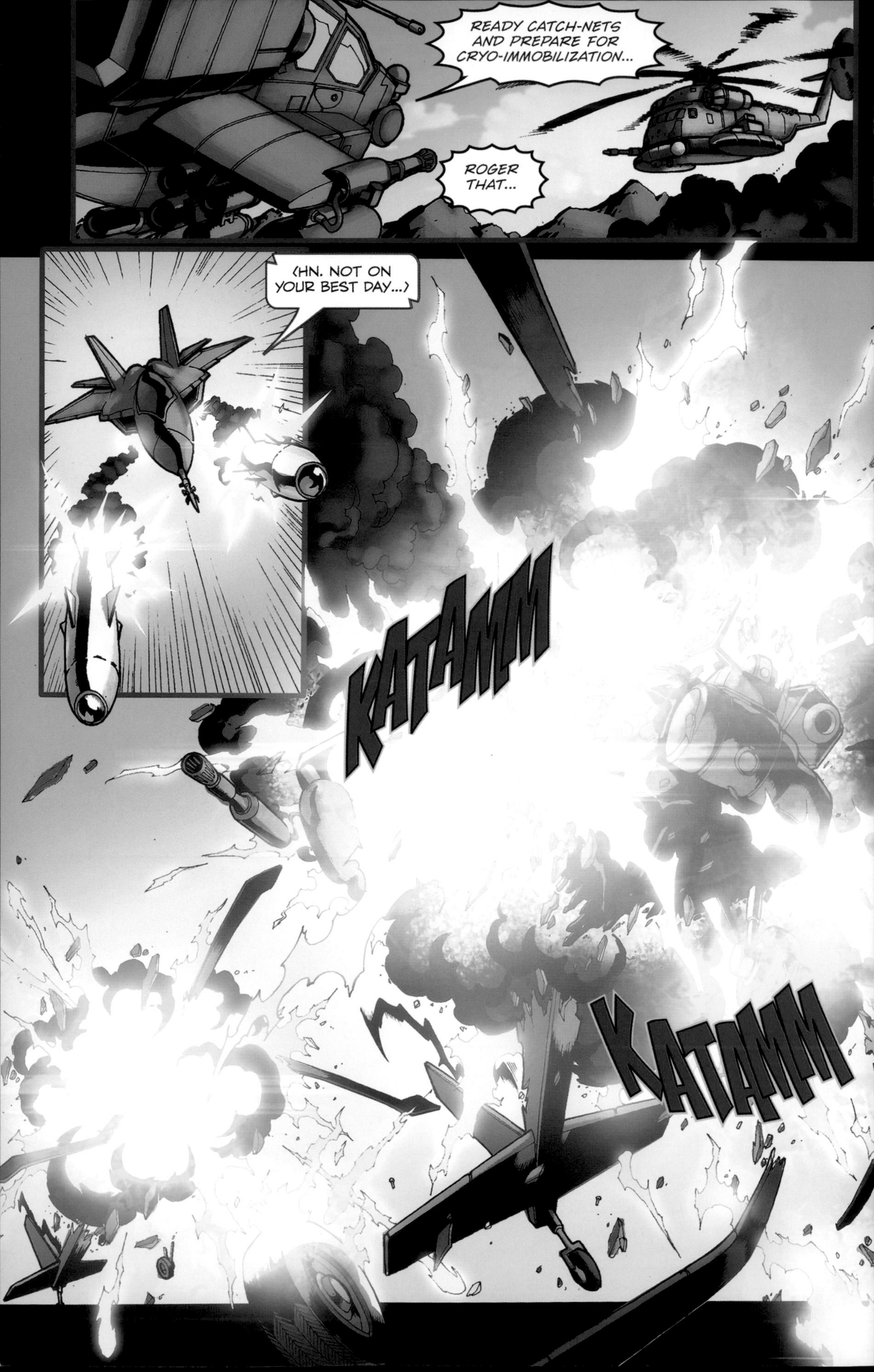
READY CATCH-NETS AND PREPARE FOR CRYO-IMMOBILIZATION...
ROGER THAT...
(HN. NOT ON YOUR BEST DAY...)
KATAMM
KATAMM

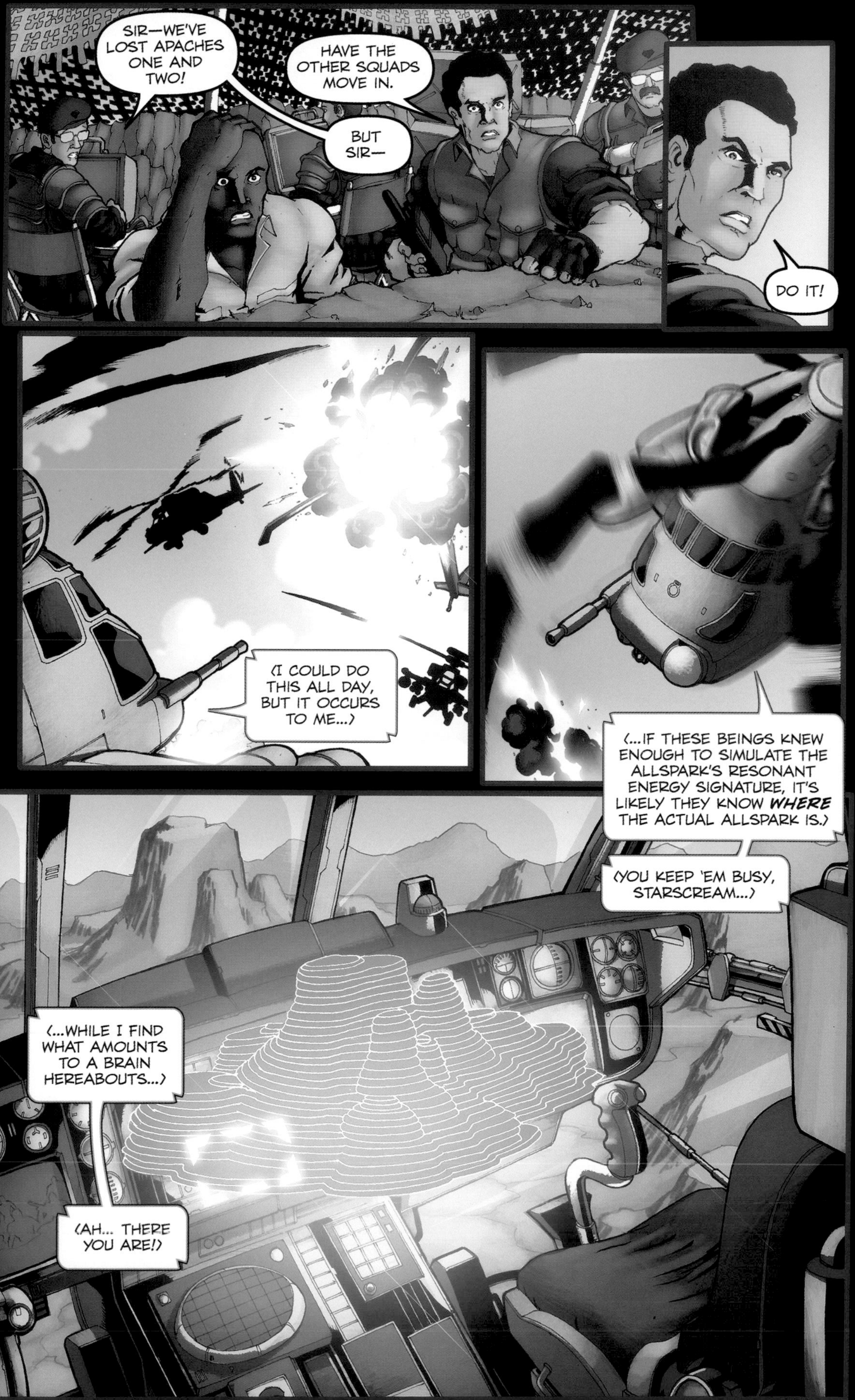

SIR—WE'VE LOST APACHES ONE AND TWO!
HAVE THE OTHER SQUADS MOVE IN.
BUT SIR—
DO IT!
(I COULD DO THIS ALL DAY, BUT IT OCCURS TO ME...)
(...IF THESE BEINGS KNEW ENOUGH TO SIMULATE THE ALLSPARK'S RESONANT ENERGY SIGNATURE, IT'S LIKELY THEY KNOW *WHERE* THE ACTUAL ALLSPARK IS.)
(YOU KEEP 'EM BUSY, STARSCREAM...)
(...WHILE I FIND WHAT AMOUNTS TO A BRAIN HEREABOUTS...)
(AH... THERE YOU ARE!)

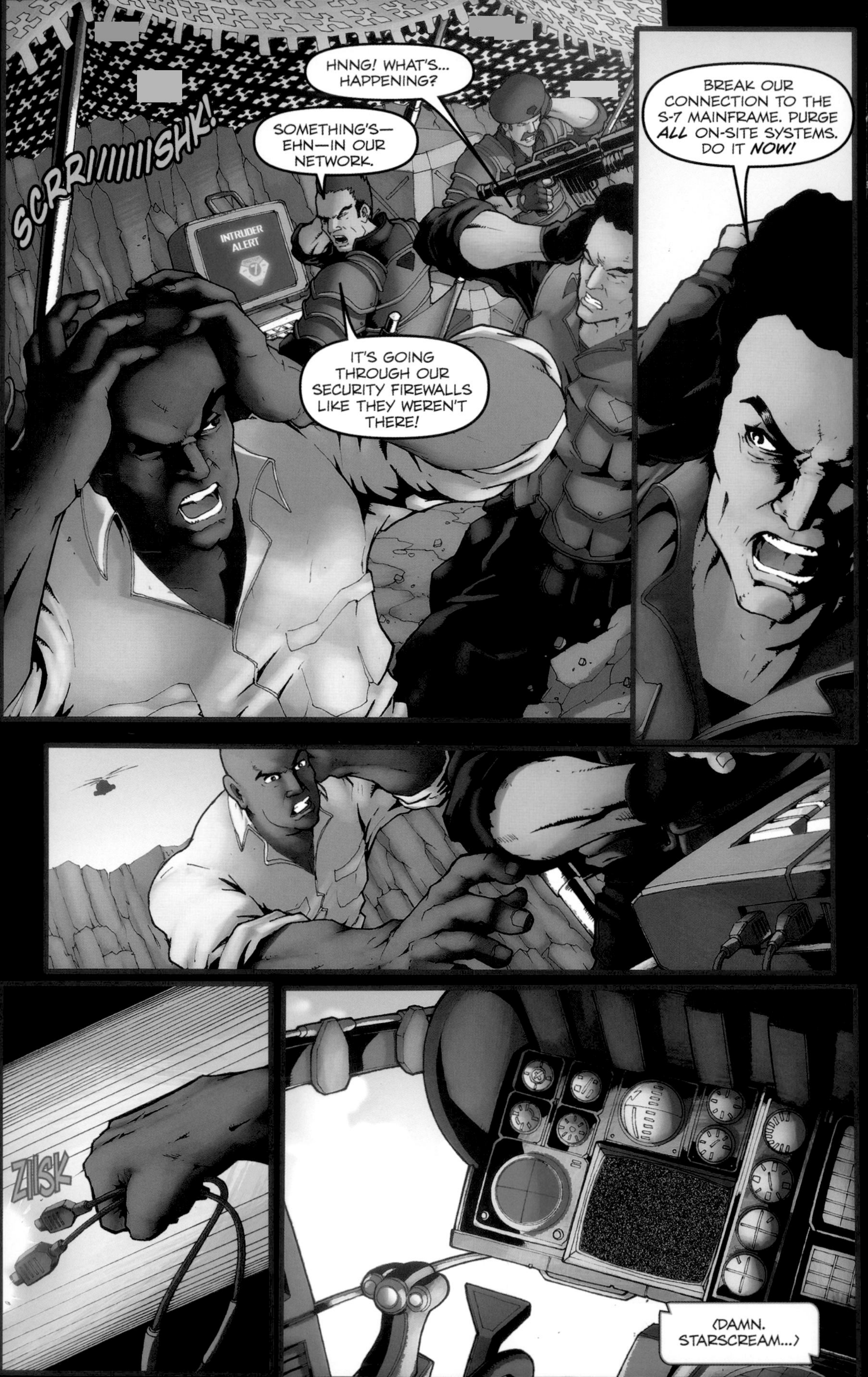
SCRRIIIIIIISHK!
HNNG! WHAT'S... HAPPENING?
SOMETHING'S—EHN—IN OUR NETWORK.
INTRUDER ALERT
IT'S GOING THROUGH OUR SECURITY FIREWALLS LIKE THEY WEREN'T THERE!
BREAK OUR CONNECTION TO THE S-7 MAINFRAME. PURGE *ALL* ON-SITE SYSTEMS. DO IT *NOW!*
ZIISK
(DAMN. STARSCREAM...)

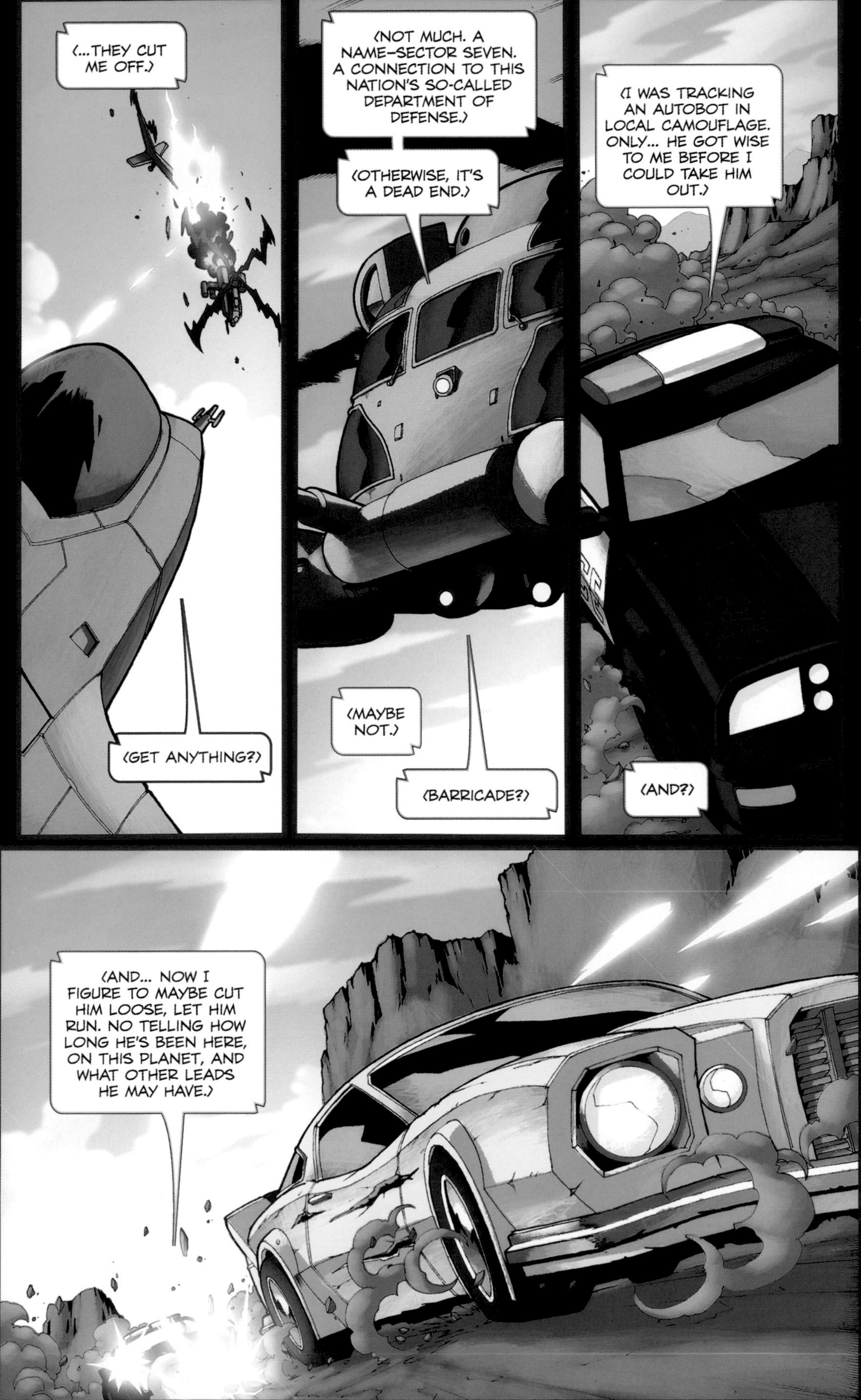
‹...THEY CUT ME OFF.›
‹GET ANYTHING?›
‹NOT MUCH. A NAME–SECTOR SEVEN. A CONNECTION TO THIS NATION'S SO-CALLED DEPARTMENT OF DEFENSE.›
‹OTHERWISE, IT'S A DEAD END.›
‹MAYBE NOT.›
‹BARRICADE?›
‹I WAS TRACKING AN AUTOBOT IN LOCAL CAMOUFLAGE. ONLY... HE GOT WISE TO ME BEFORE I COULD TAKE HIM OUT.›
‹AND?›
‹AND... NOW I FIGURE TO MAYBE CUT HIM LOOSE, LET HIM RUN. NO TELLING HOW LONG HE'S BEEN HERE, ON THIS PLANET, AND WHAT OTHER LEADS HE MAY HAVE.›

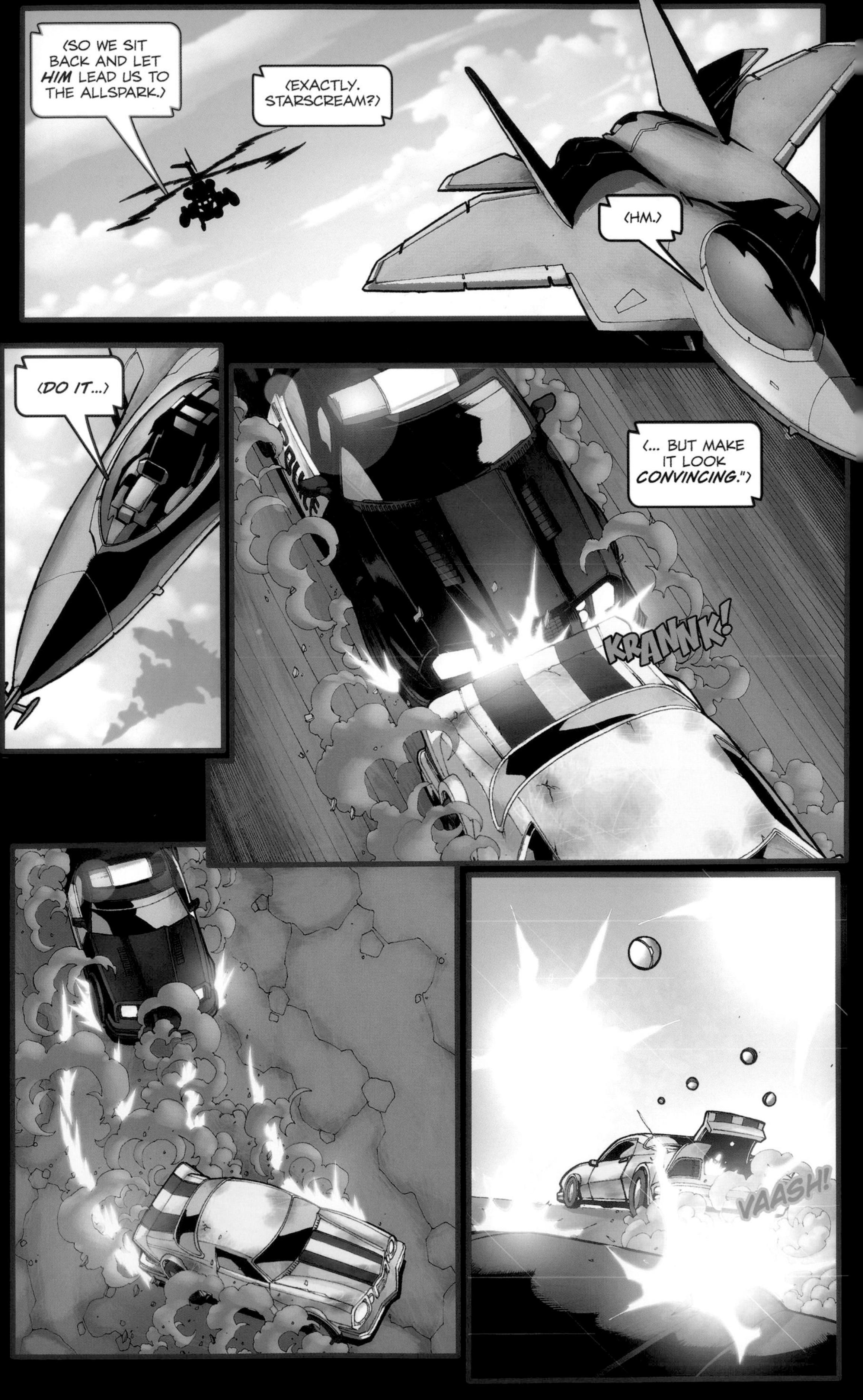
‹SO WE SIT BACK AND LET *HIM* LEAD US TO THE ALLSPARK.›
‹EXACTLY. STARSCREAM?›
‹HM.›
‹*DO IT...*›
‹... BUT MAKE IT LOOK *CONVINCING*."›
KRANNK!
VAASH!

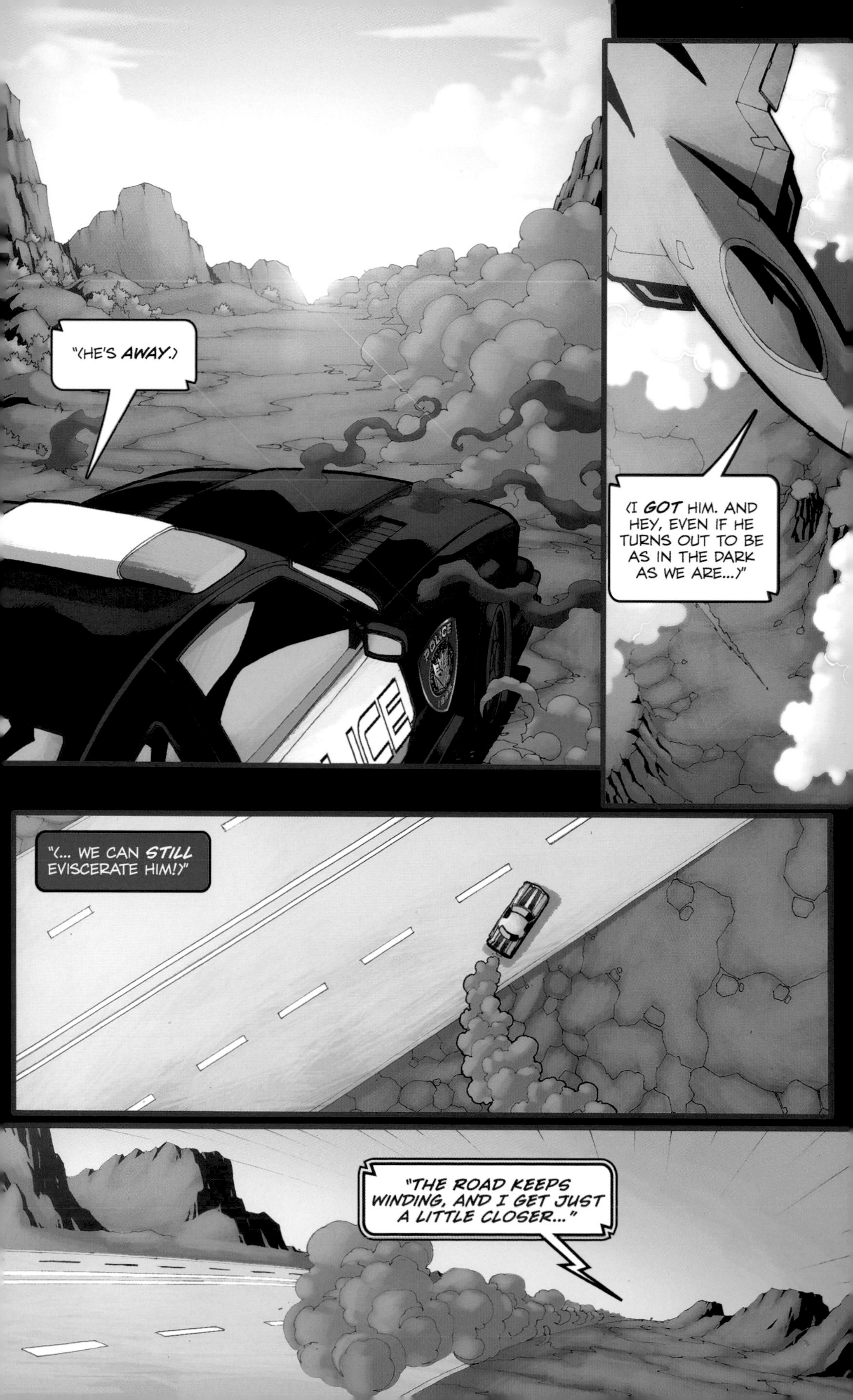
"(HE'S AWAY.)
(I GOT HIM. AND HEY, EVEN IF HE TURNS OUT TO BE AS IN THE DARK AS WE ARE...)"
"(... WE CAN STILL EVISCERATE HIM!)"
"THE ROAD KEEPS WINDING, AND I GET JUST A LITTLE CLOSER..."

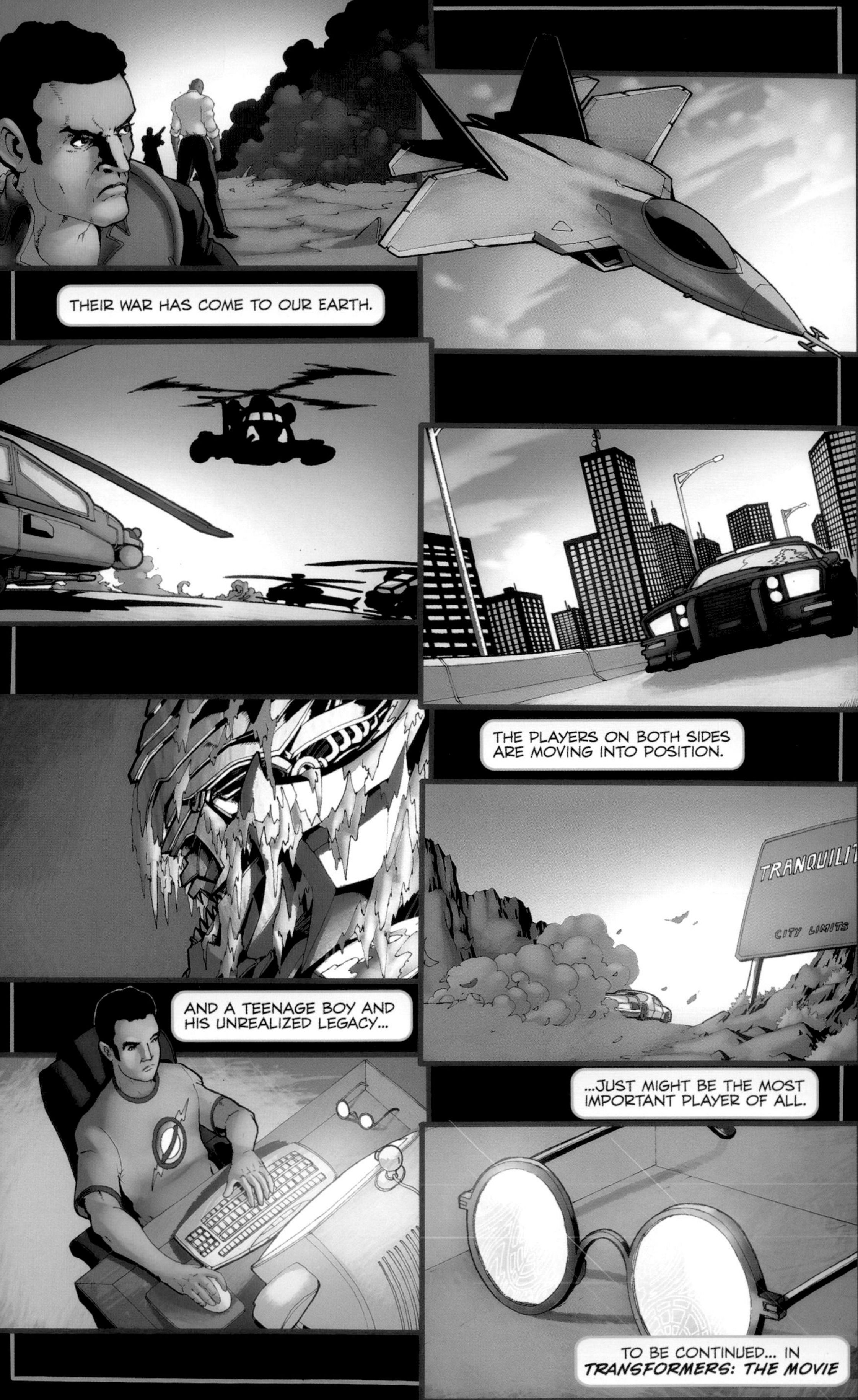
THEIR WAR HAS COME TO OUR EARTH.
THE PLAYERS ON BOTH SIDES ARE MOVING INTO POSITION.
TRANQUILITY
CITY LIMITS
AND A TEENAGE BOY AND HIS UNREALIZED LEGACY...
...JUST MIGHT BE THE MOST IMPORTANT PLAYER OF ALL.
TO BE CONTINUED... IN *TRANSFORMERS: THE MOVIE*

ART GALLERY

ART BY DON FIGUEROA • COLORS BY JOSH BURCHAM

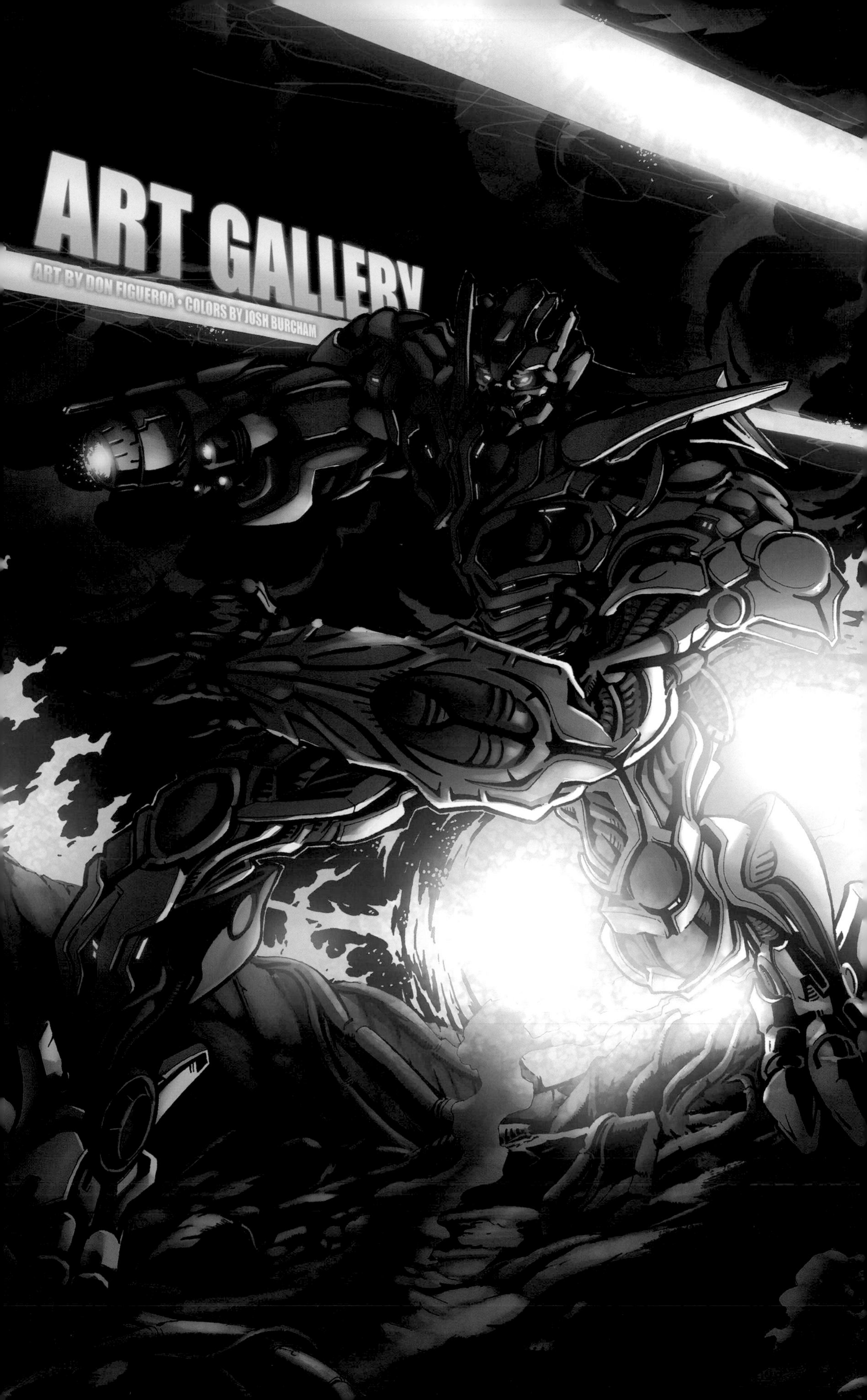

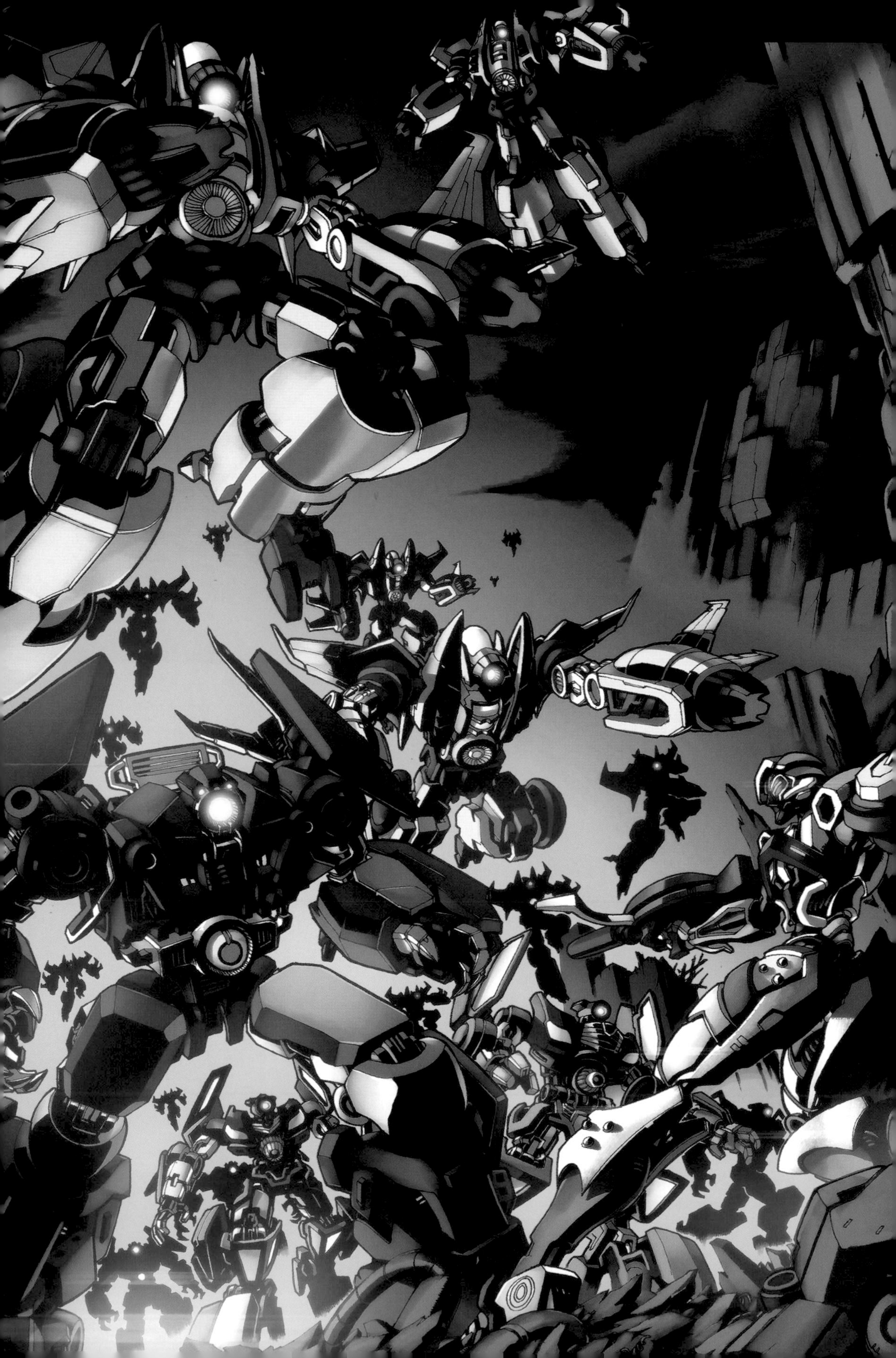

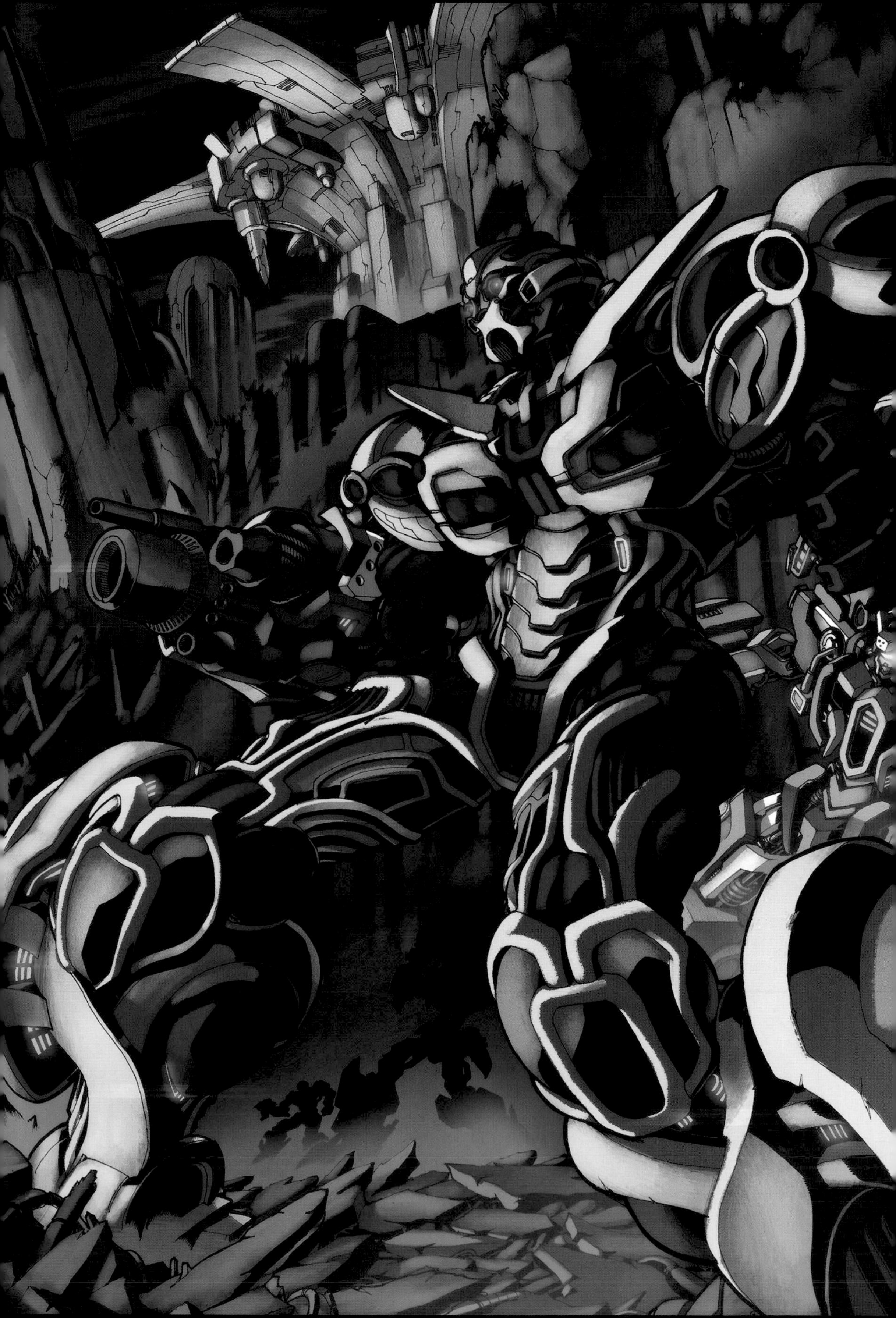

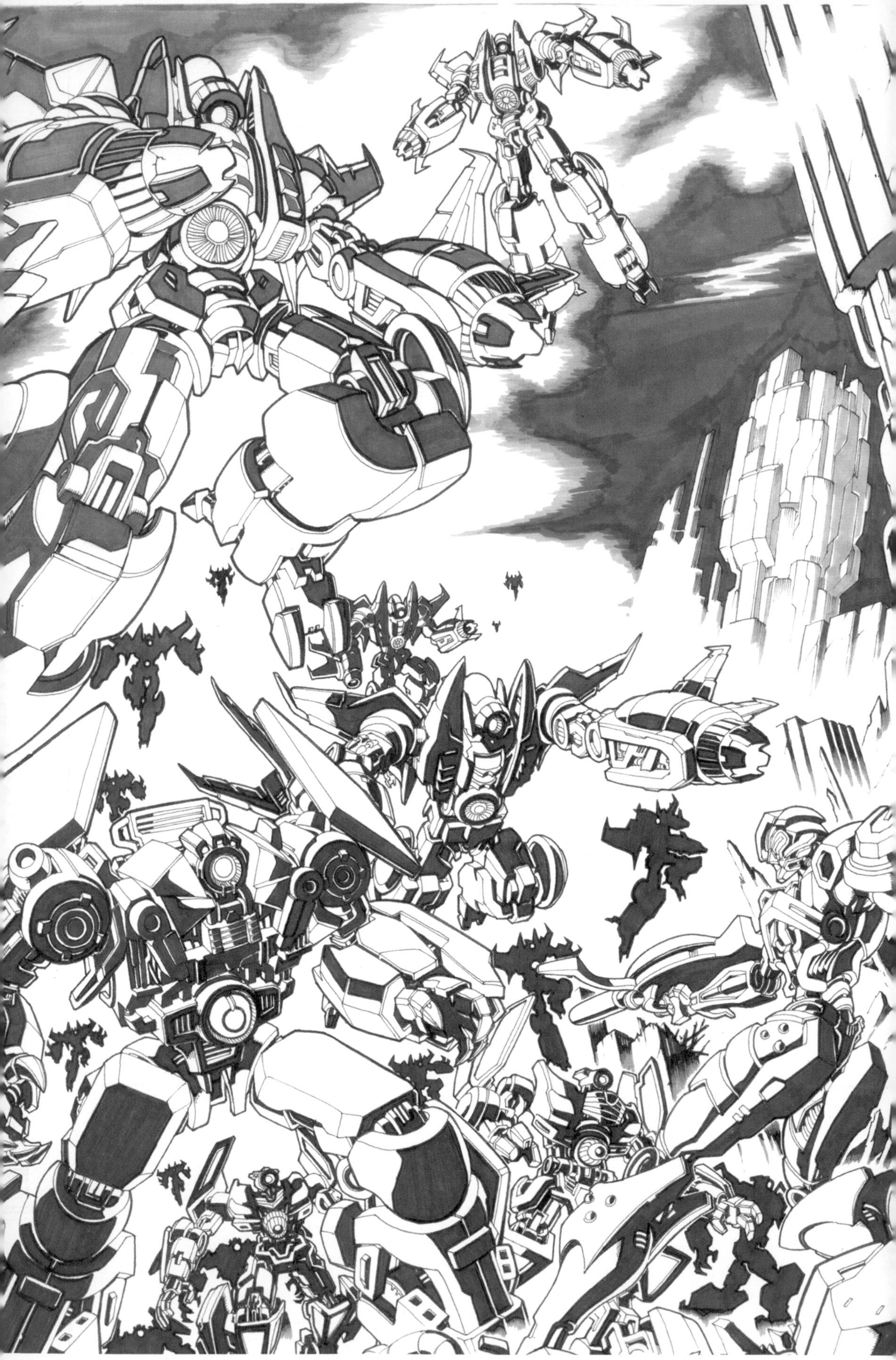

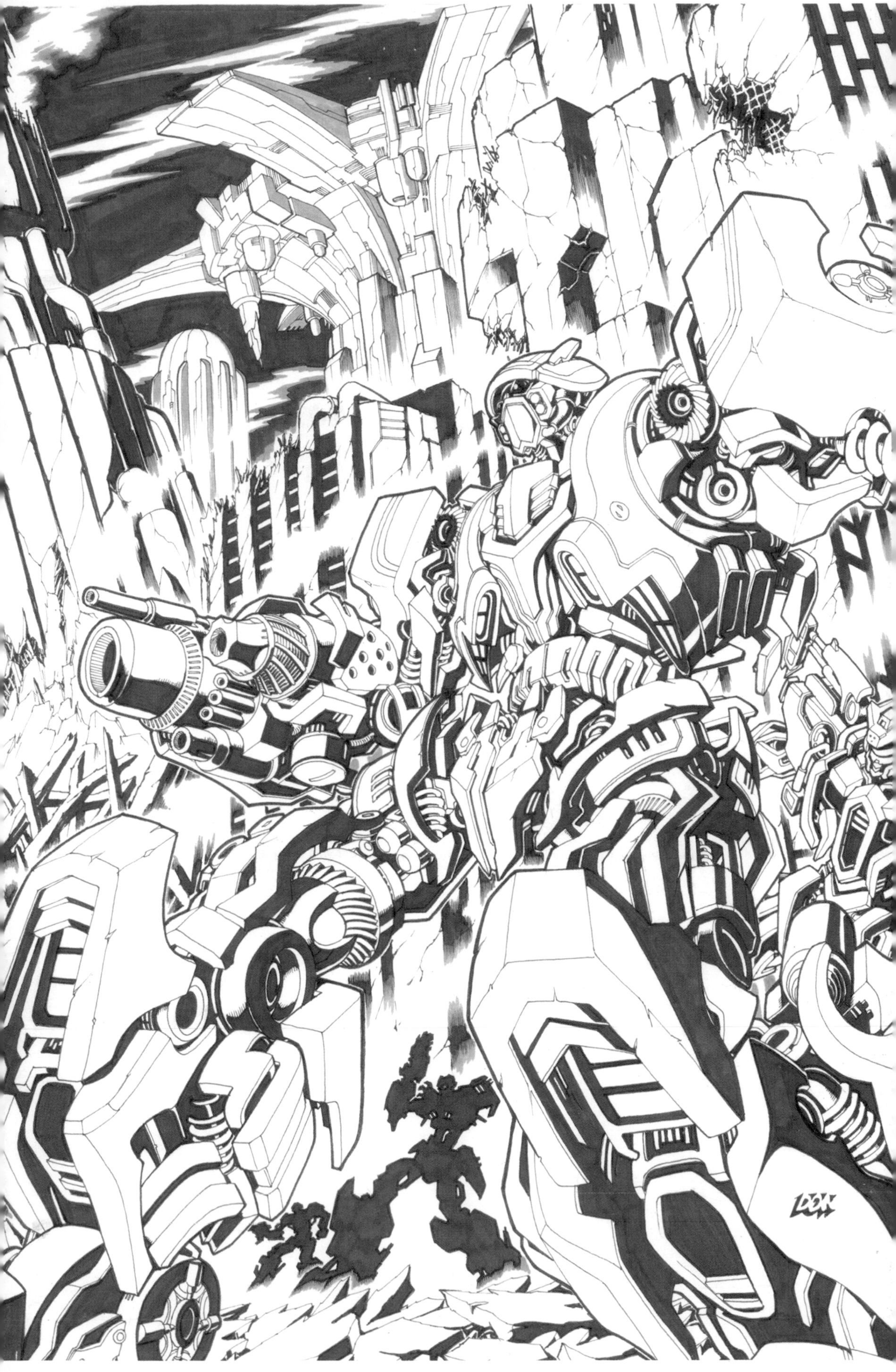
DON

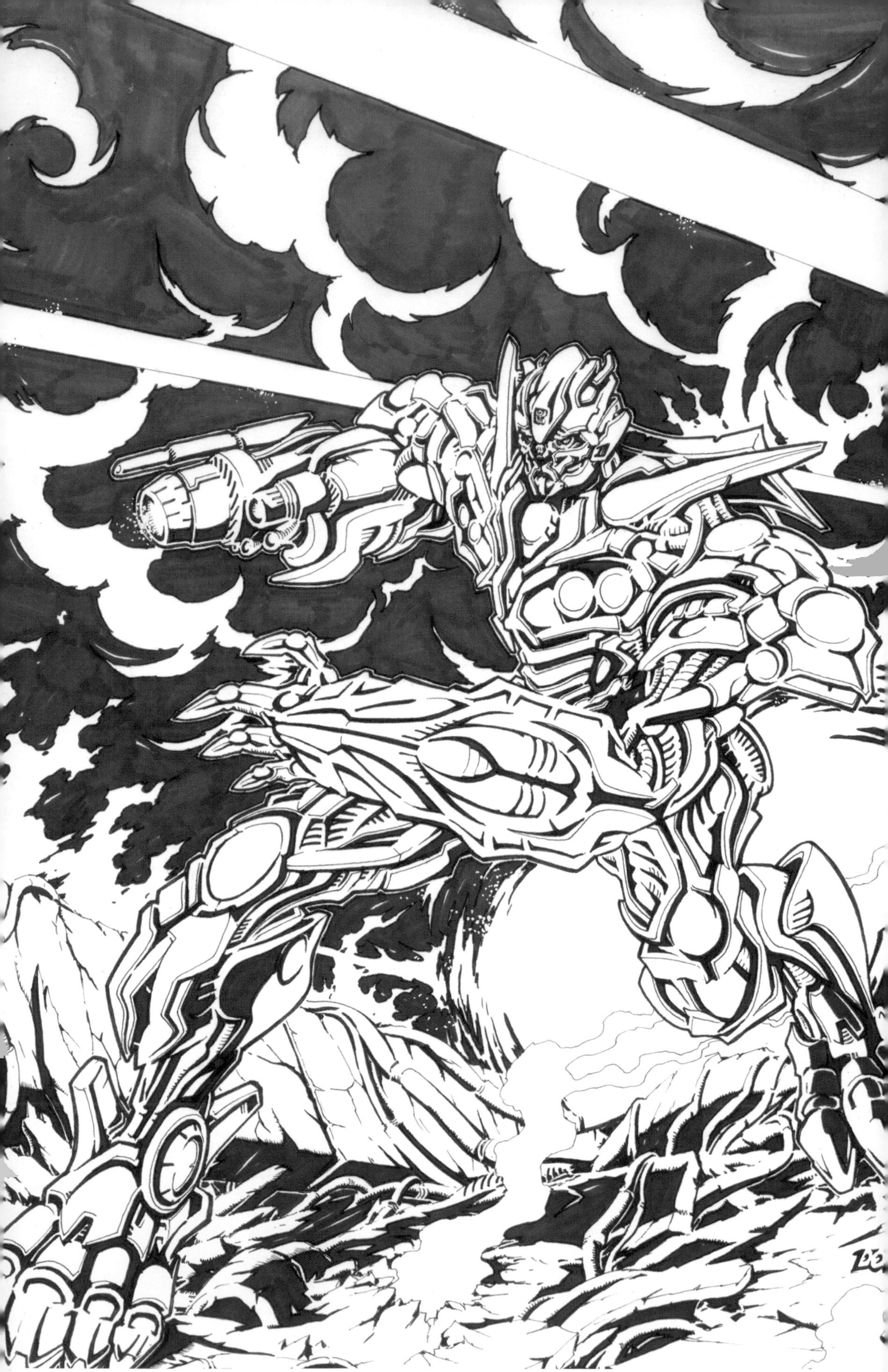

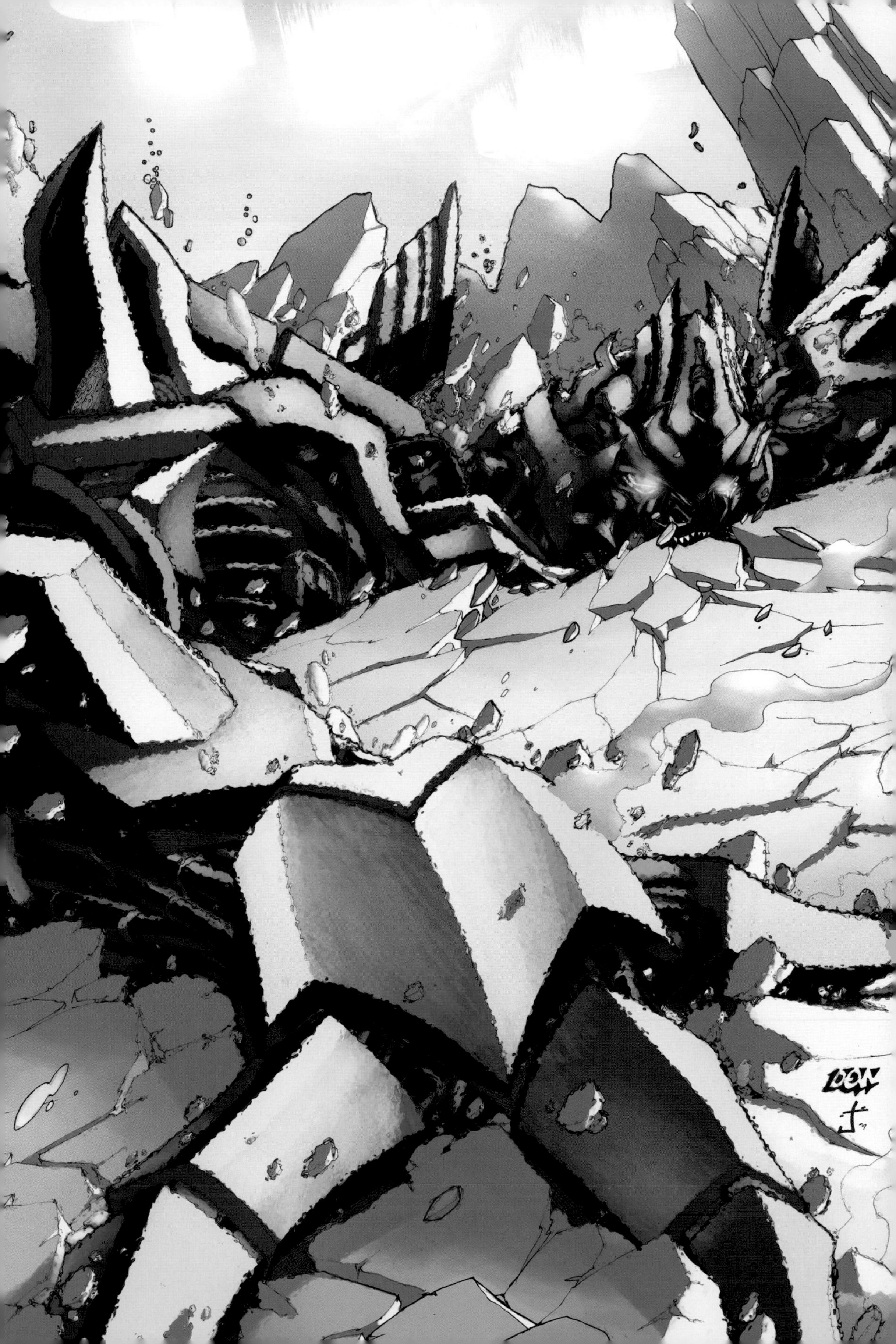

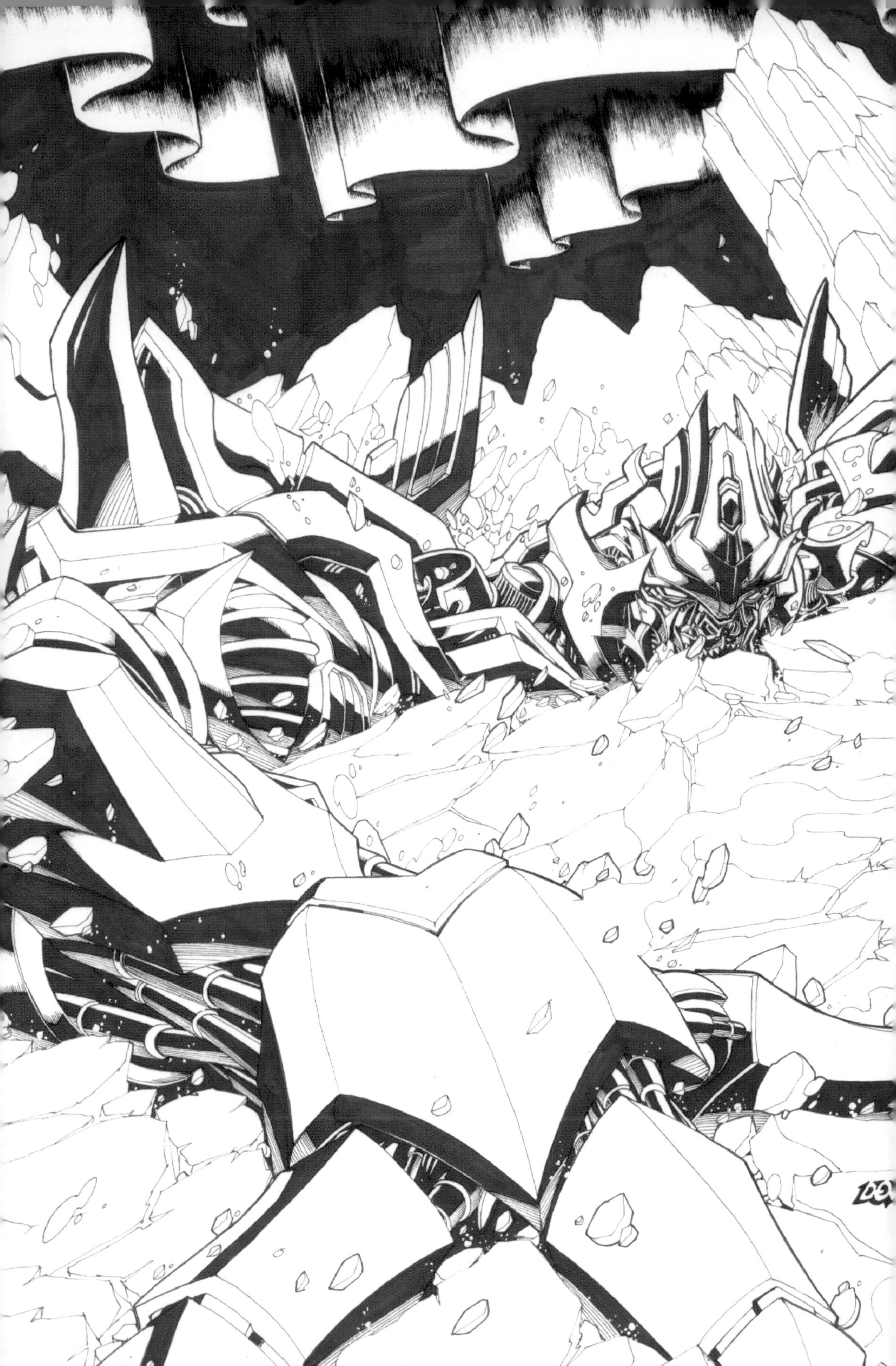

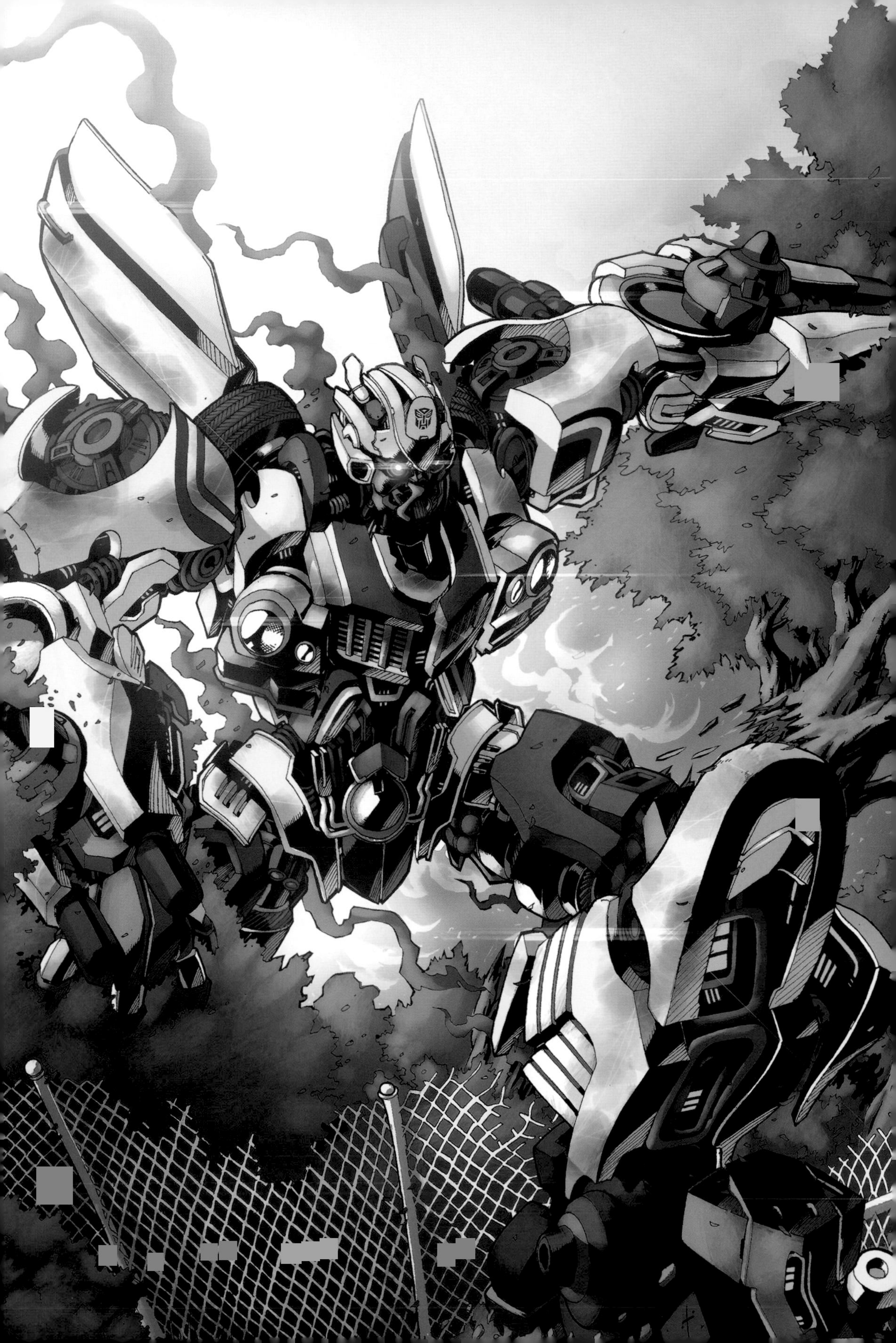

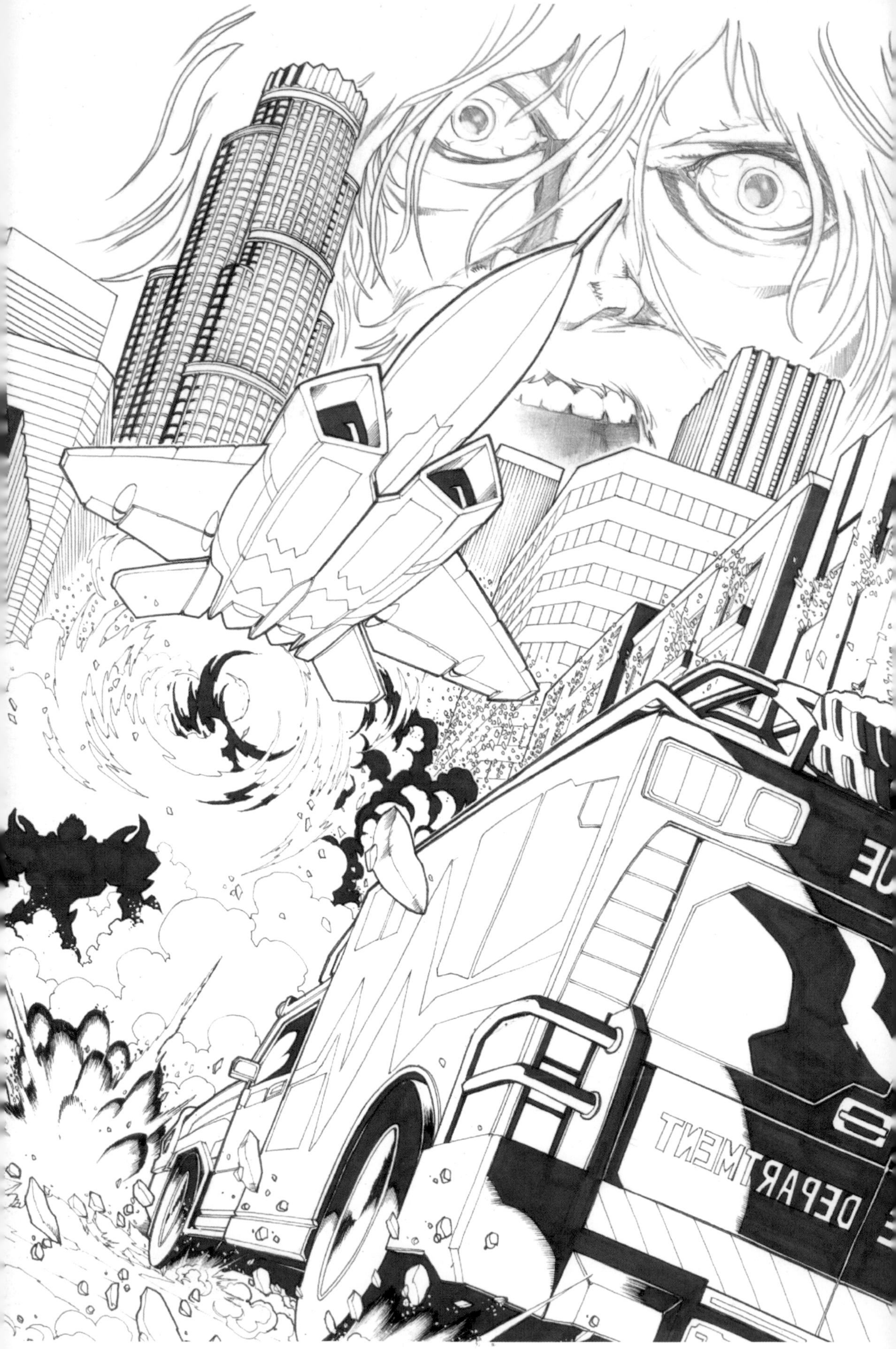
DEPARTMENT

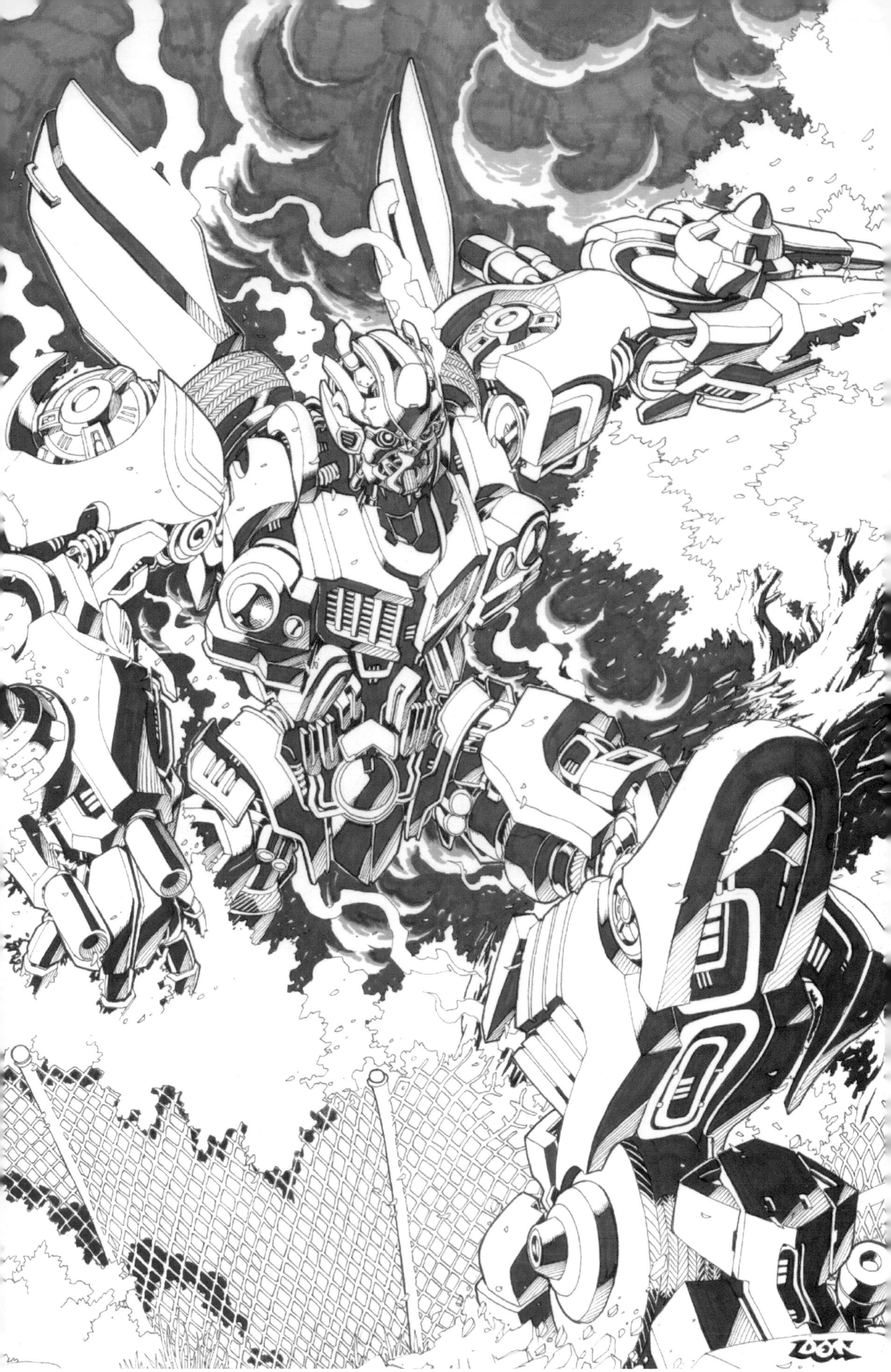

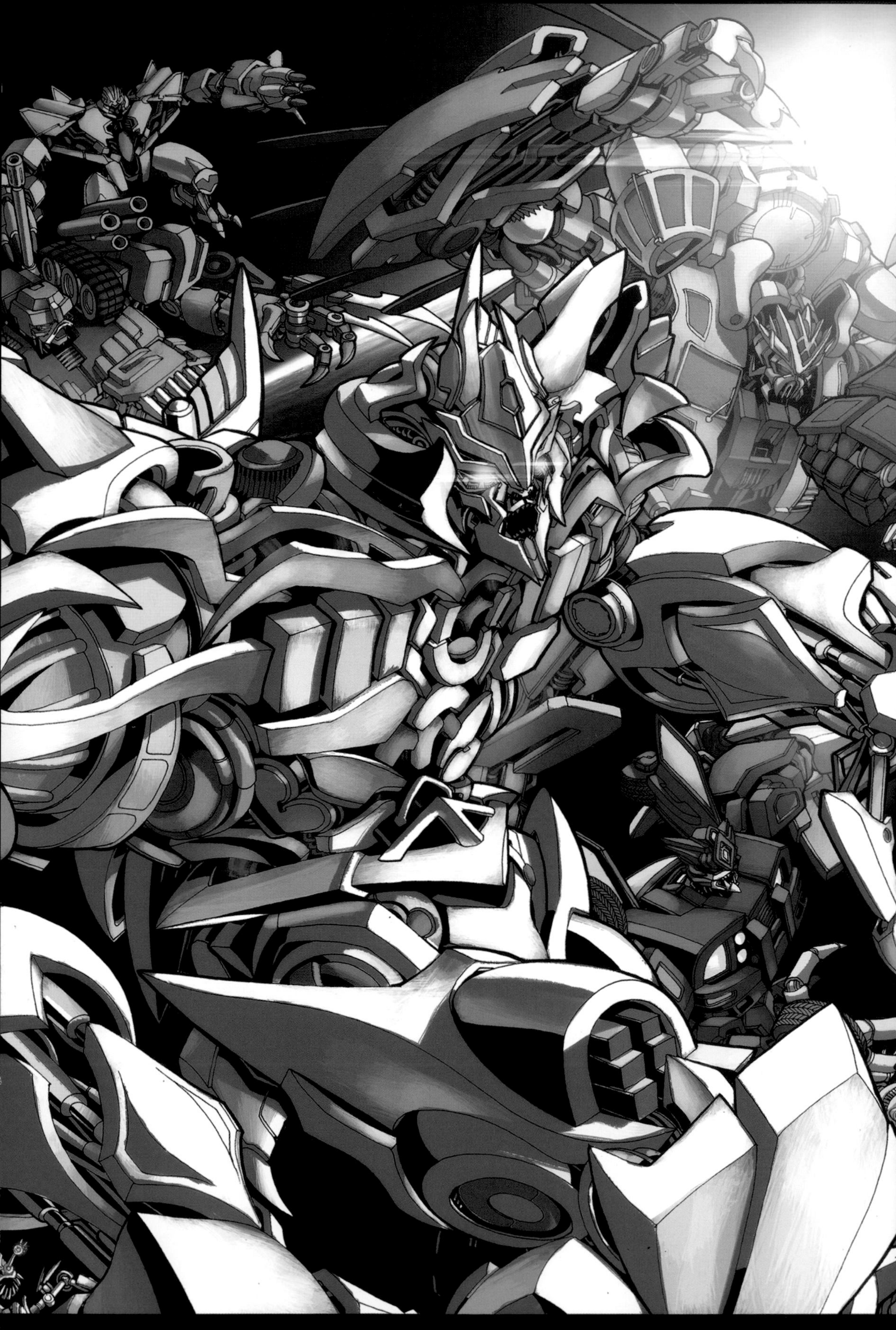

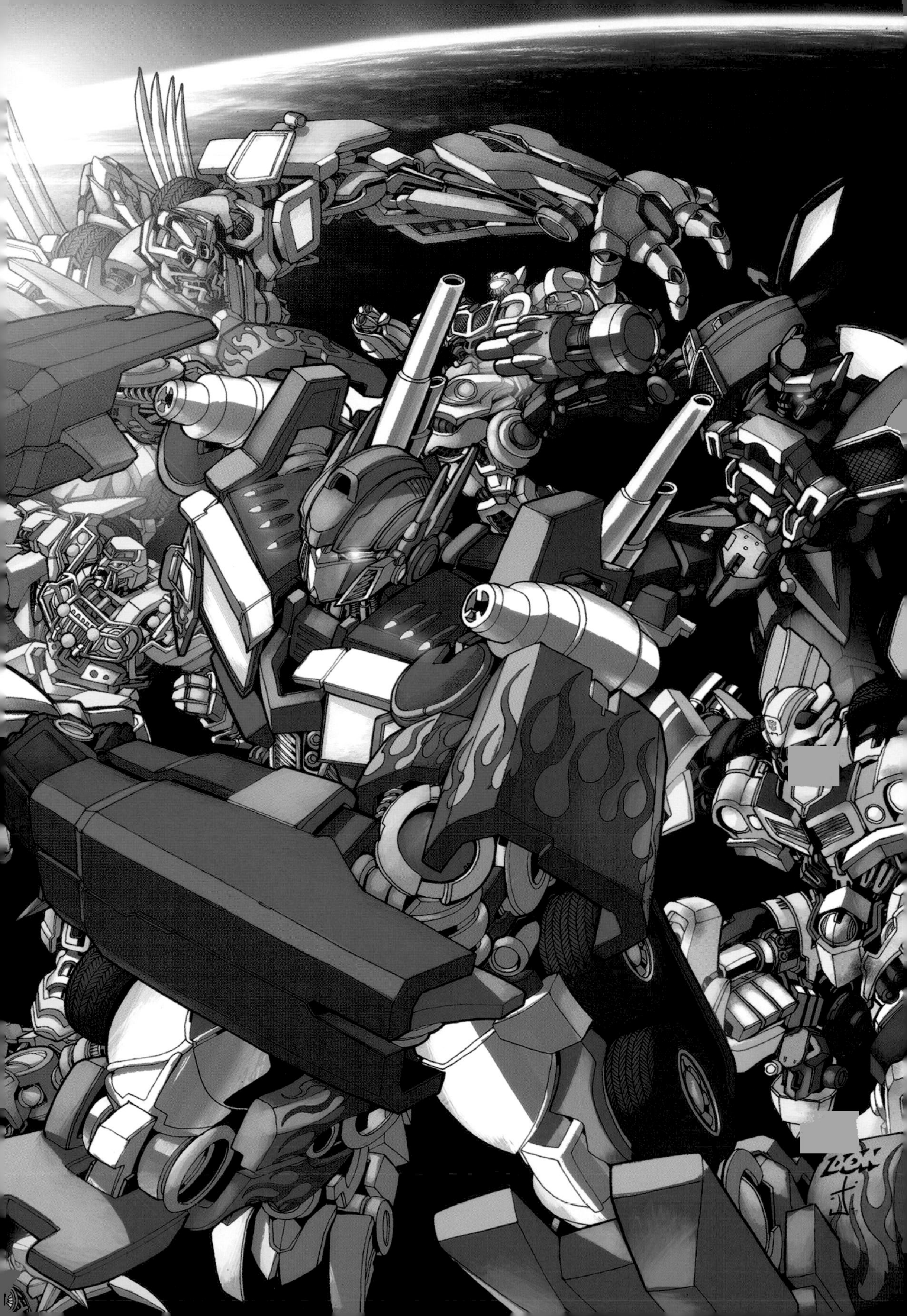

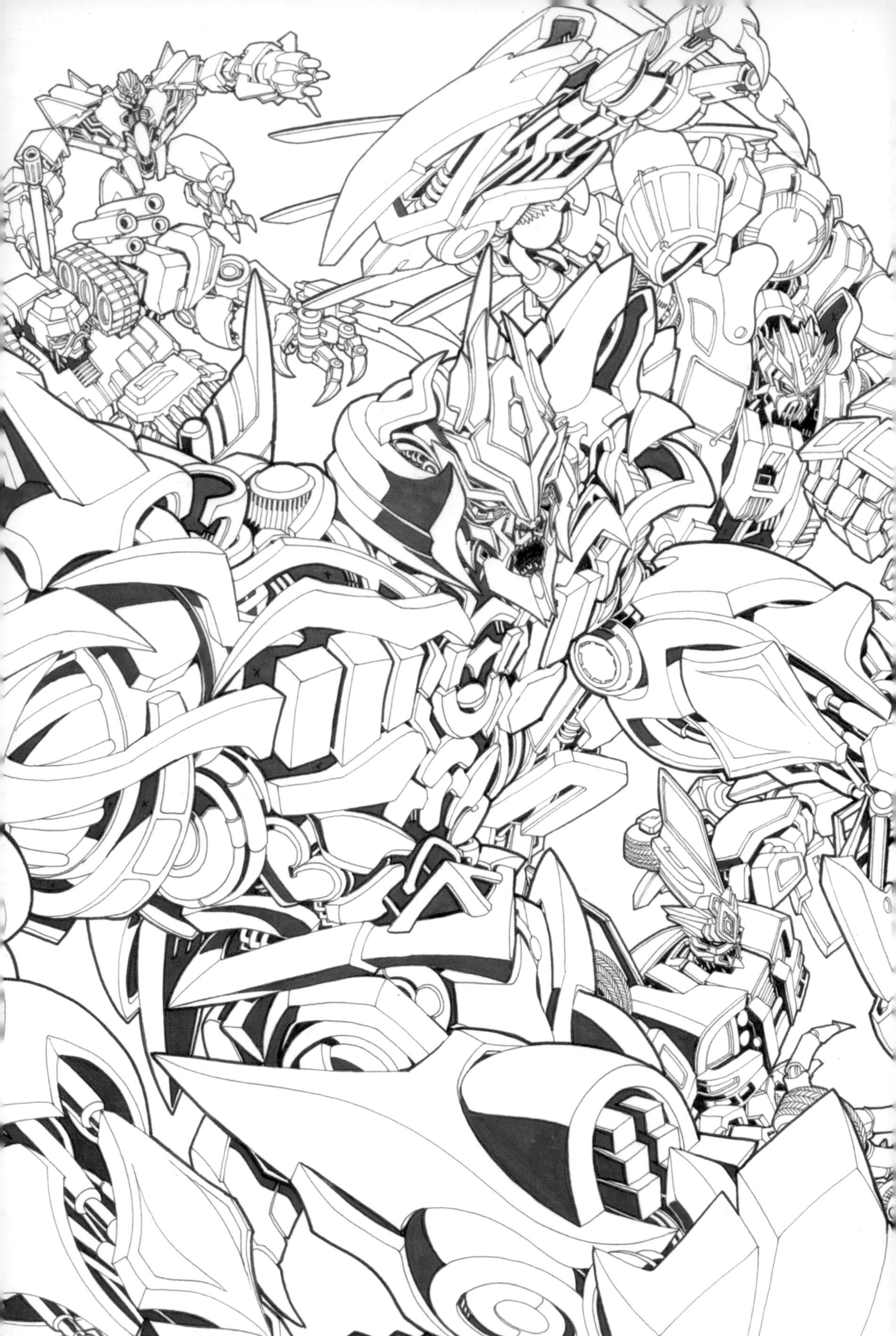

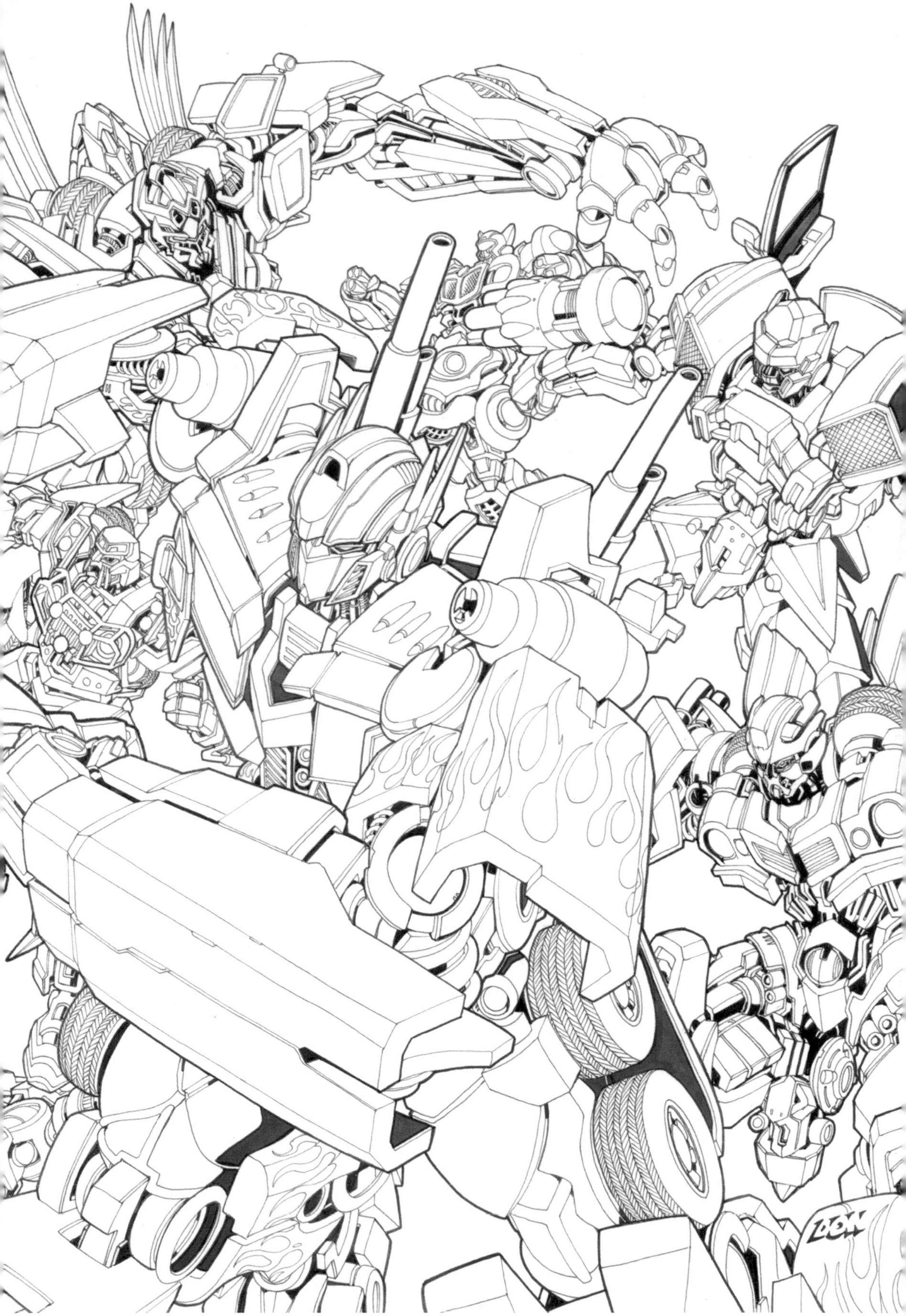

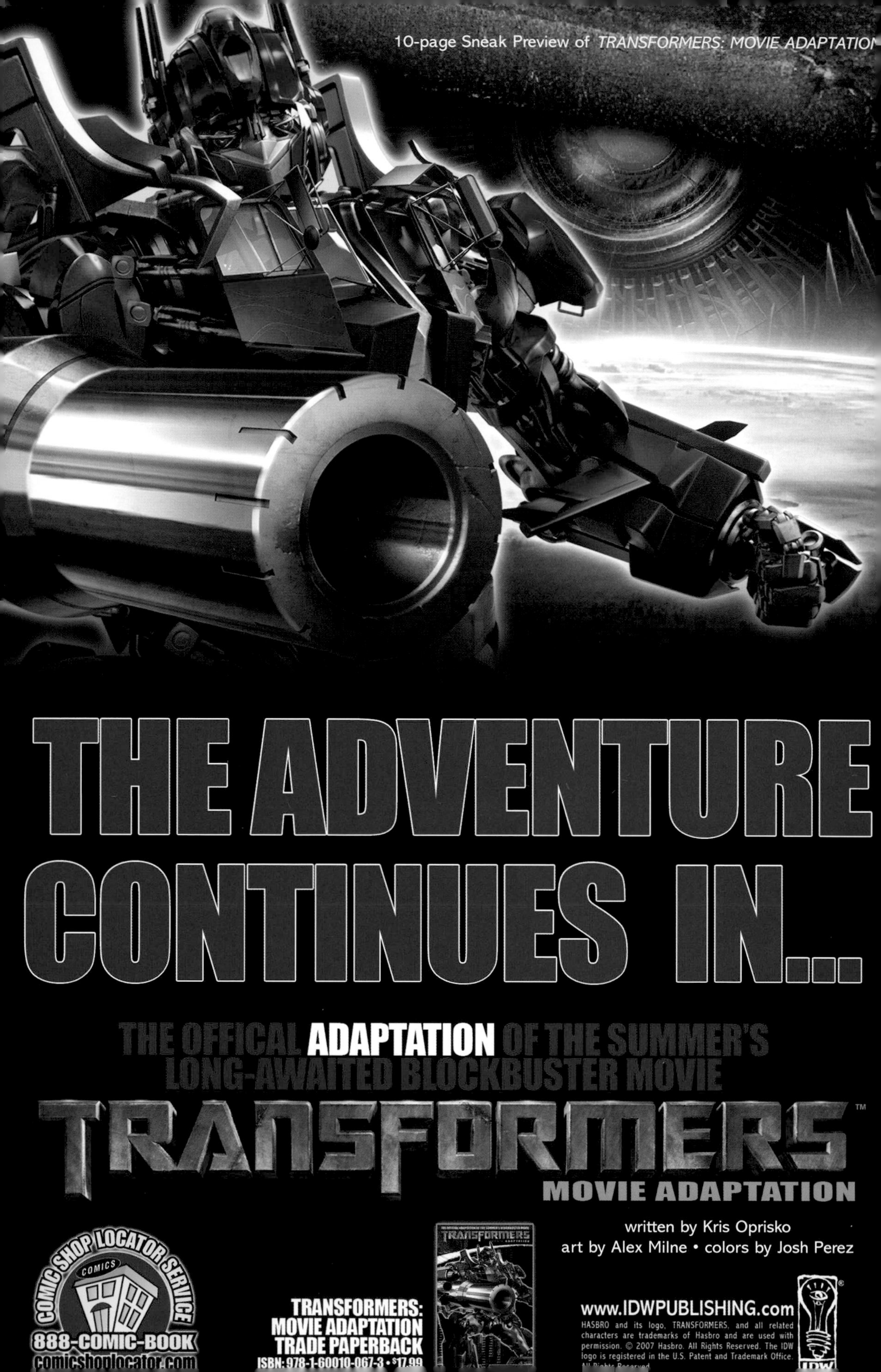
10-page Sneak Preview of *TRANSFORMERS: MOVIE ADAPTATION*
THE ADVENTURE
CONTINUES IN...
THE OFFICAL ADAPTATION OF THE SUMMER'S
LONG-AWAITED BLOCKBUSTER MOVIE
TRANSFORMERS™
MOVIE ADAPTATION
written by Kris Oprisko
art by Alex Milne • colors by Josh Perez
COMIC SHOP LOCATOR SERVICE
COMICS
888-COMIC-BOOK
comicshoplocator.com
TRANSFORMERS:
MOVIE ADAPTATION
TRADE PAPERBACK
ISBN: 978-1-60010-067-3 • $17.99
TRANSFORMERS
www.IDWPUBLISHING.com
HASBRO and its logo, TRANSFORMERS, and all related characters are trademarks of Hasbro and are used with permission. © 2007 Hasbro. All Rights Reserved. The IDW logo is registered in the U.S. Patent and Trademark Office. All Rights Reserved.
IDW

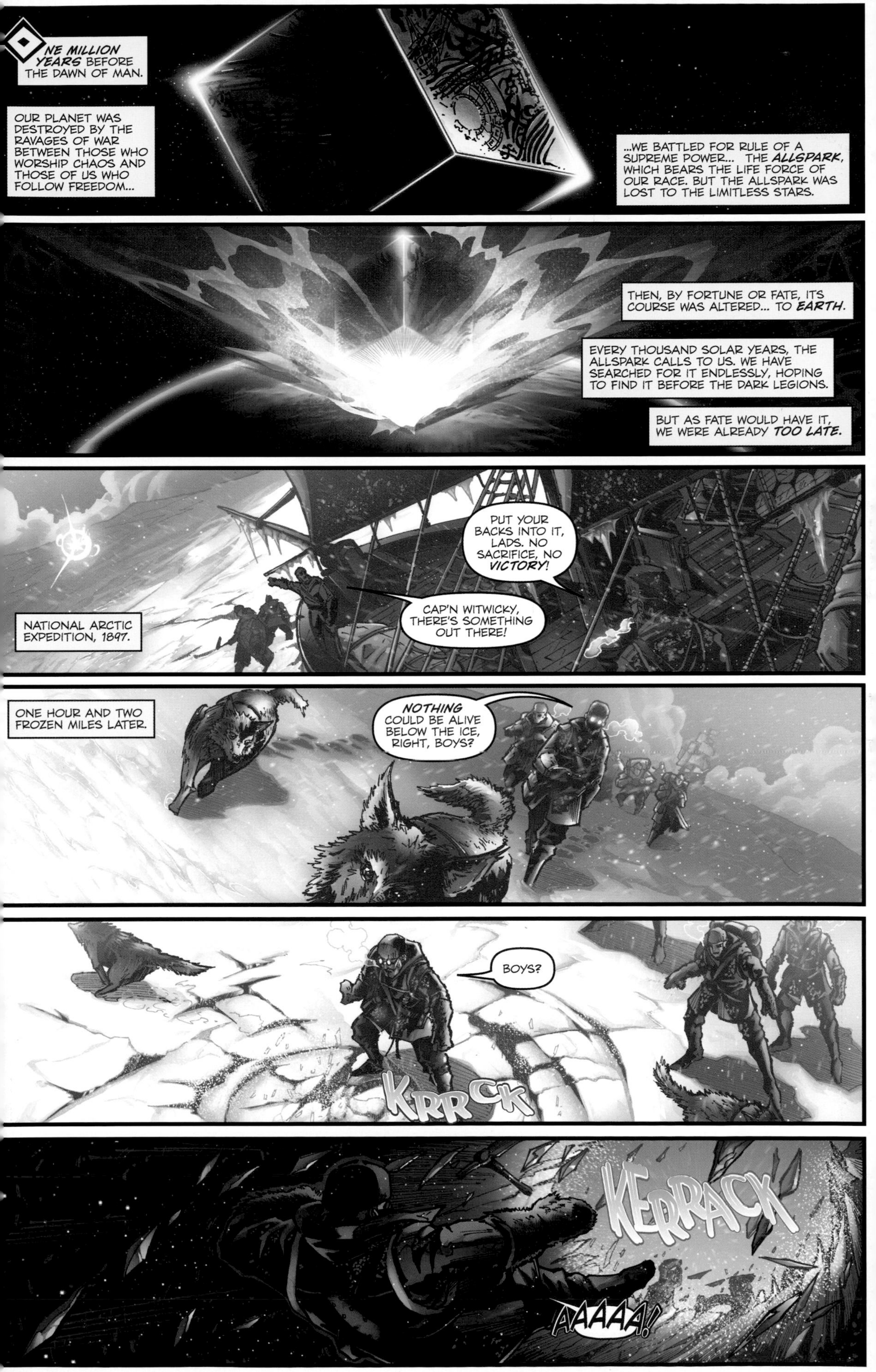
ONE MILLION YEARS BEFORE THE DAWN OF MAN.
OUR PLANET WAS DESTROYED BY THE RAVAGES OF WAR BETWEEN THOSE WHO WORSHIP CHAOS AND THOSE OF US WHO FOLLOW FREEDOM...
...WE BATTLED FOR RULE OF A SUPREME POWER... THE ALLSPARK, WHICH BEARS THE LIFE FORCE OF OUR RACE. BUT THE ALLSPARK WAS LOST TO THE LIMITLESS STARS.
THEN, BY FORTUNE OR FATE, ITS COURSE WAS ALTERED... TO EARTH.
EVERY THOUSAND SOLAR YEARS, THE ALLSPARK CALLS TO US. WE HAVE SEARCHED FOR IT ENDLESSLY, HOPING TO FIND IT BEFORE THE DARK LEGIONS.
BUT AS FATE WOULD HAVE IT, WE WERE ALREADY TOO LATE.
NATIONAL ARCTIC EXPEDITION, 1897.
PUT YOUR BACKS INTO IT, LADS. NO SACRIFICE, NO VICTORY!
CAP'N WITWICKY, THERE'S SOMETHING OUT THERE!
ONE HOUR AND TWO FROZEN MILES LATER.
NOTHING COULD BE ALIVE BELOW THE ICE, RIGHT, BOYS?
BOYS?
KRRCK
KERRACK
AAAAA!

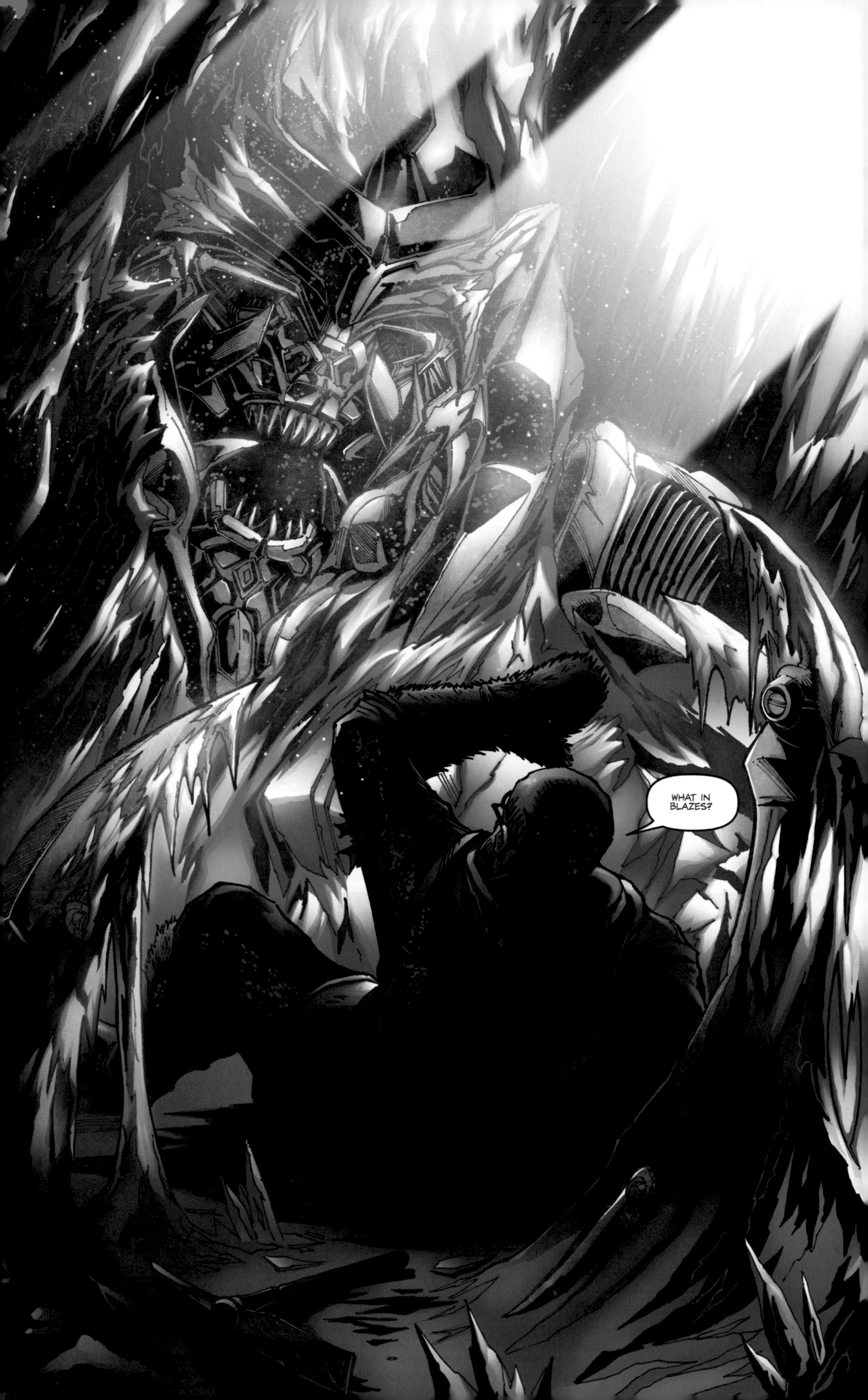
WHAT IN BLAZES?

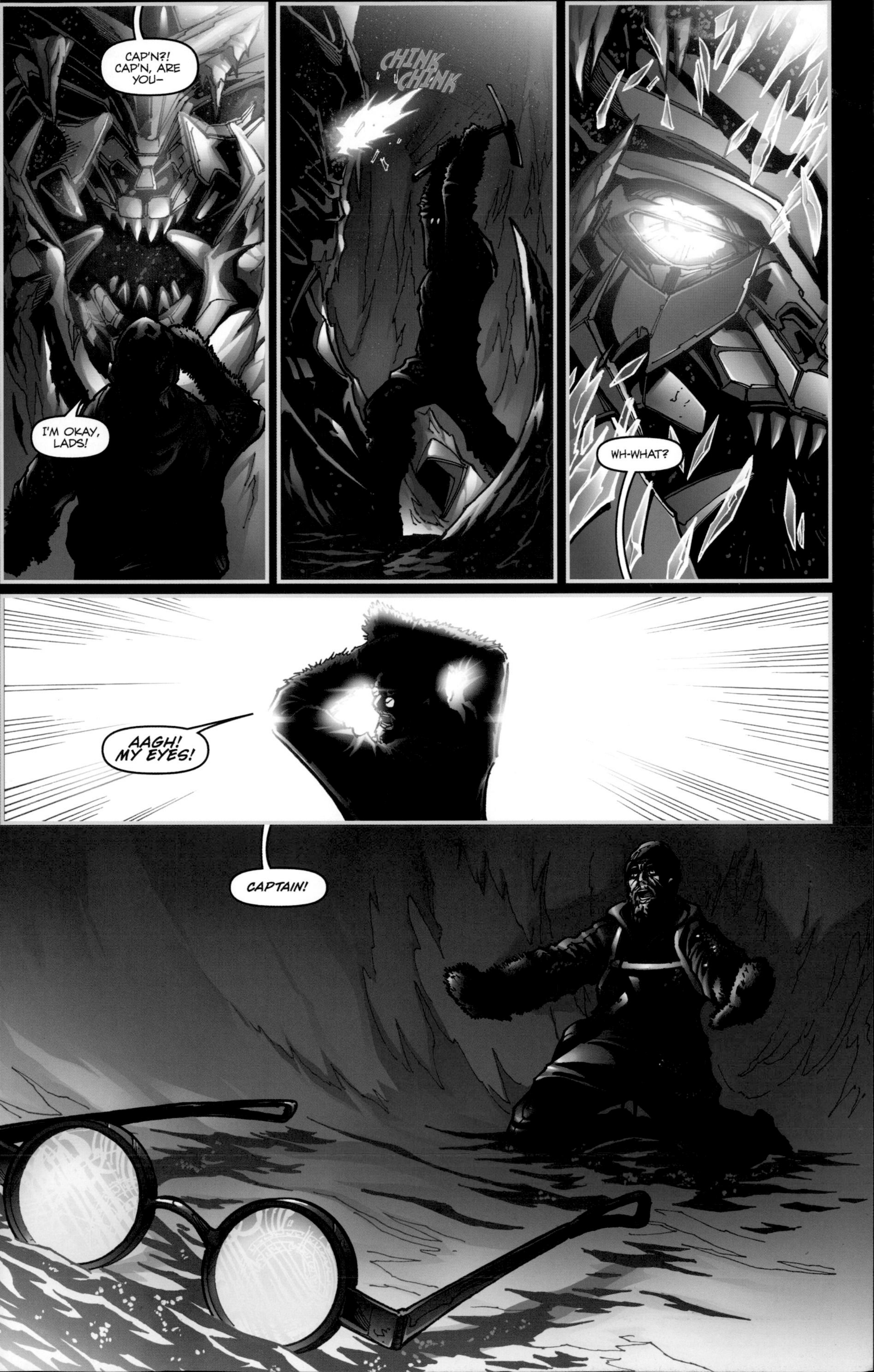
CAP'N?! CAP'N, ARE YOU–
I'M OKAY, LADS!
CHINK CHINK
WH-WHAT?
AAGH! MY EYES!
CAPTAIN!

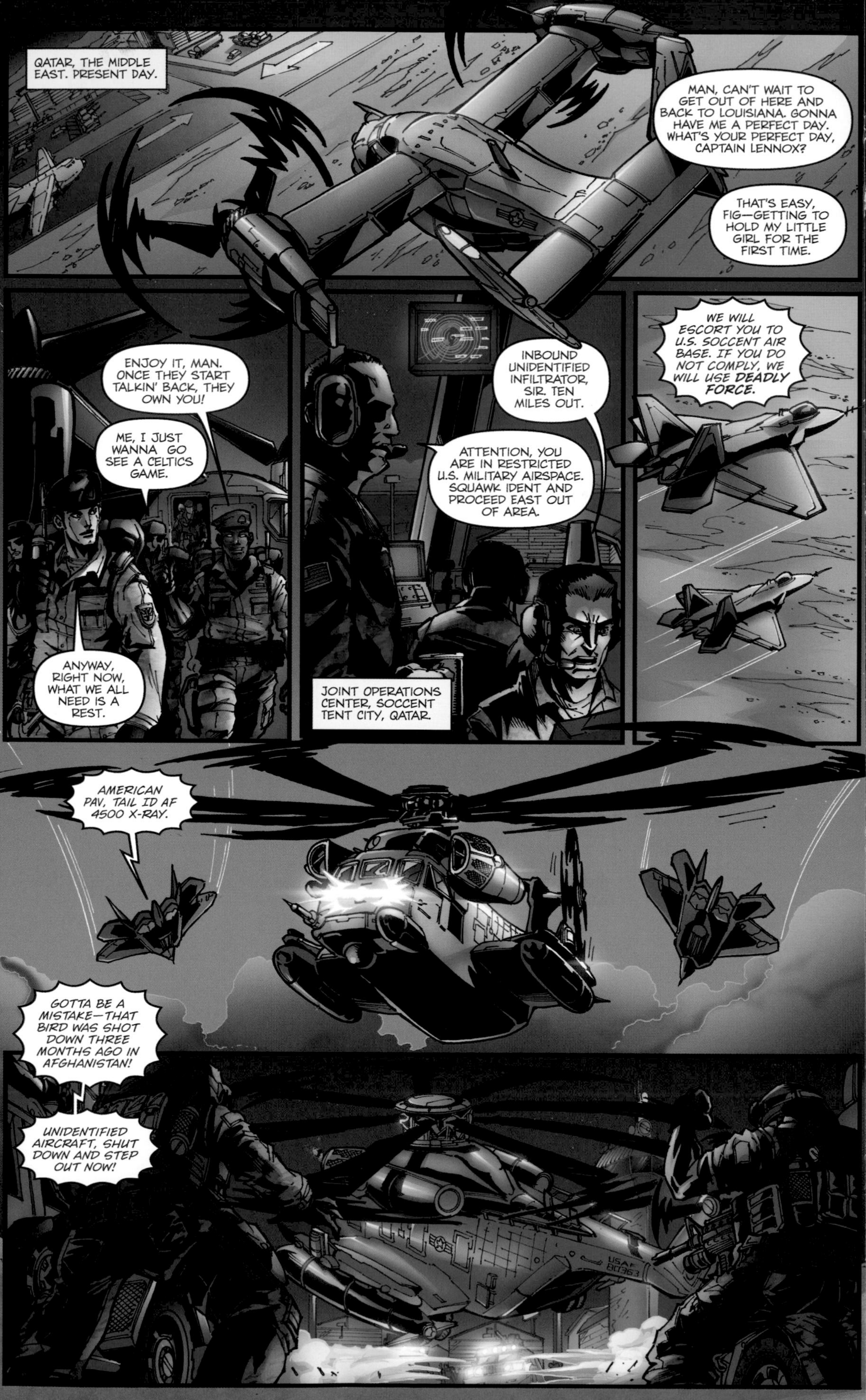
QATAR, THE MIDDLE EAST. PRESENT DAY.
MAN, CAN'T WAIT TO GET OUT OF HERE AND BACK TO LOUISIANA. GONNA HAVE ME A PERFECT DAY. WHAT'S YOUR PERFECT DAY, CAPTAIN LENNOX?
THAT'S EASY, FIG—GETTING TO HOLD MY LITTLE GIRL FOR THE FIRST TIME.
ENJOY IT, MAN. ONCE THEY START TALKIN' BACK, THEY OWN YOU!
ME, I JUST WANNA GO SEE A CELTICS GAME.
ANYWAY, RIGHT NOW, WHAT WE ALL NEED IS A REST.
INBOUND UNIDENTIFIED INFILTRATOR, SIR. TEN MILES OUT.
ATTENTION, YOU ARE IN RESTRICTED U.S. MILITARY AIRSPACE. SQUAWK IDENT AND PROCEED EAST OUT OF AREA.
JOINT OPERATIONS CENTER, SOCCENT TENT CITY, QATAR.
WE WILL ESCORT YOU TO U.S. SOCCENT AIR BASE. IF YOU DO NOT COMPLY, WE WILL USE DEADLY FORCE.
AMERICAN PAV, TAIL ID AF 4500 X-RAY.
GOTTA BE A MISTAKE—THAT BIRD WAS SHOT DOWN THREE MONTHS AGO IN AFGHANISTAN!
UNIDENTIFIED AIRCRAFT, SHUT DOWN AND STEP OUT NOW!
USAF 80363

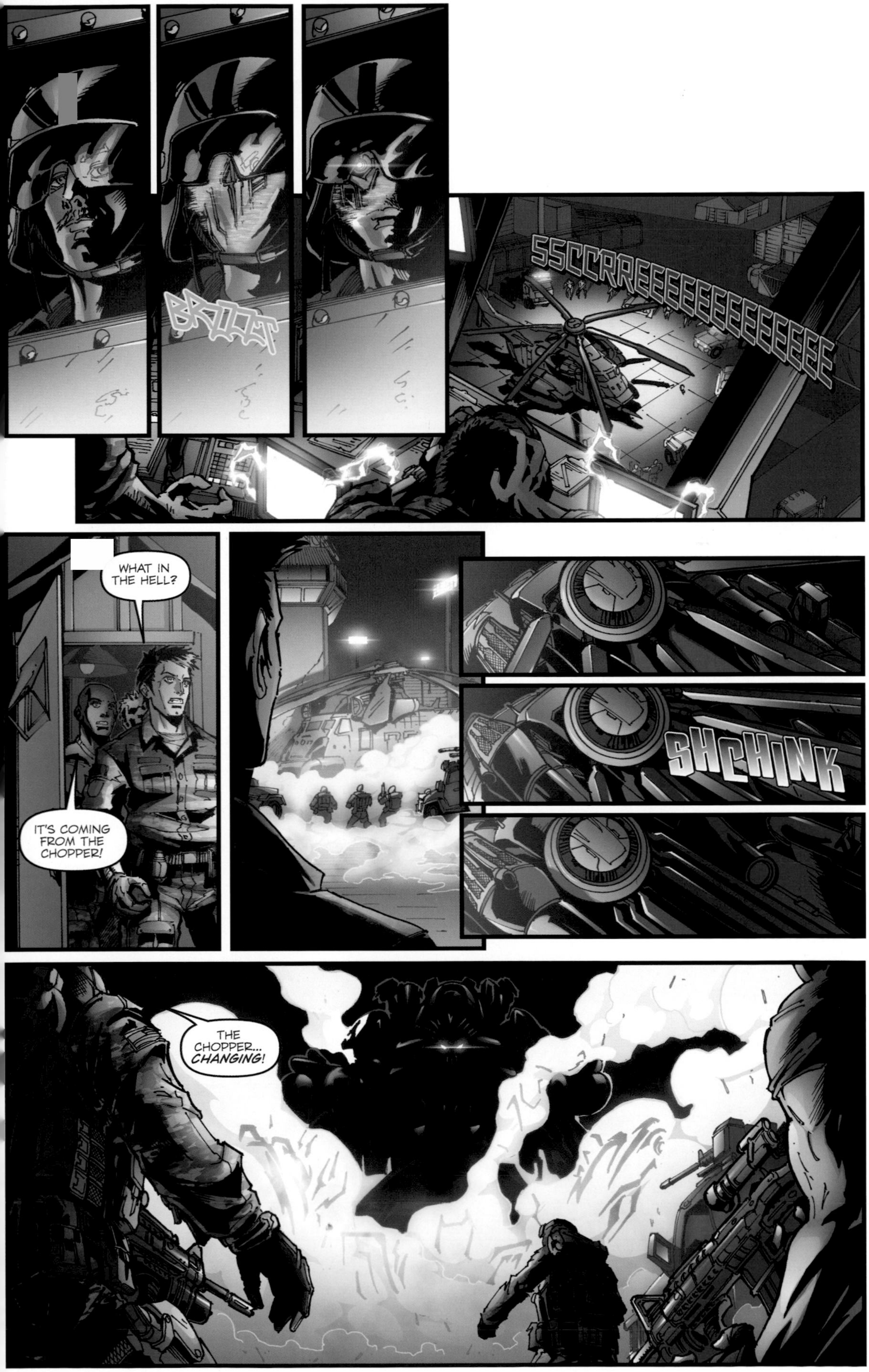
BRZZT
SSCCRREEEEEEEEEEEEEE
WHAT IN THE HELL?
IT'S COMING FROM THE CHOPPER!
SHCHINK
THE CHOPPER... CHANGING!

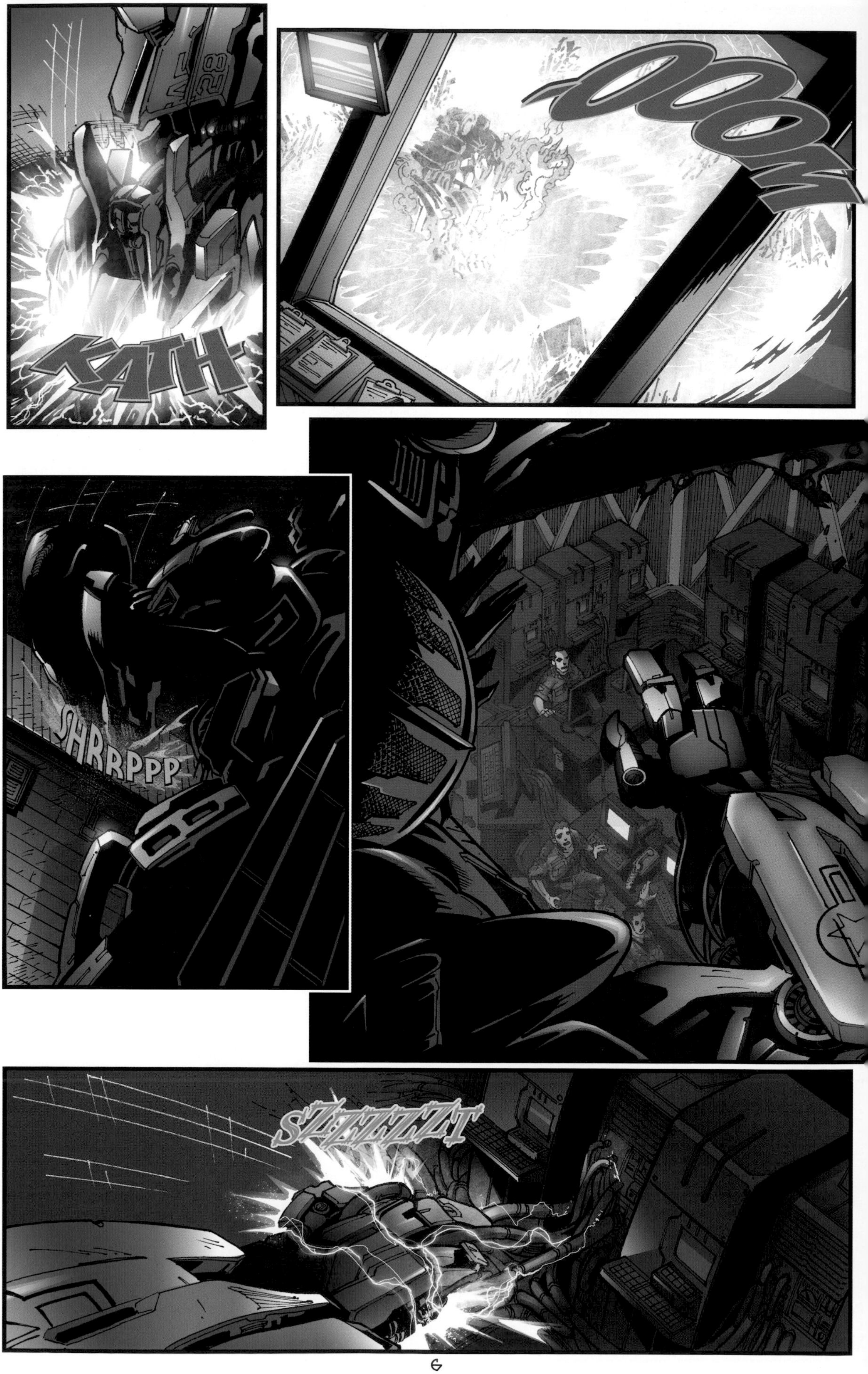
KATH-
-OOOOM
SHRRPPP
SZZZZZT

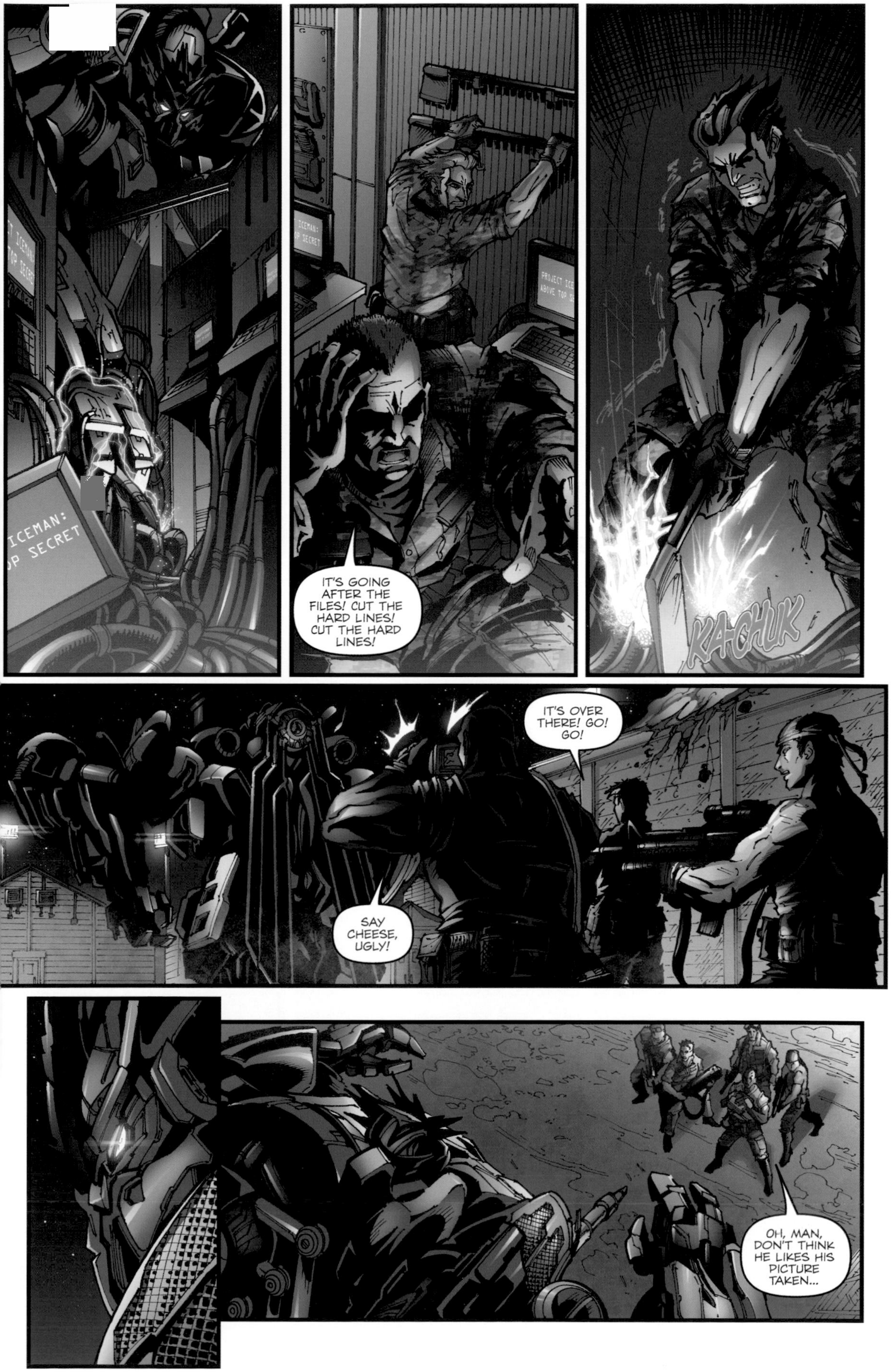
IT'S GOING AFTER THE FILES! CUT THE HARD LINES! CUT THE HARD LINES!
KA-CHUK
IT'S OVER THERE! GO! GO!
SAY CHEESE, UGLY!
OH, MAN, DON'T THINK HE LIKES HIS PICTURE TAKEN...

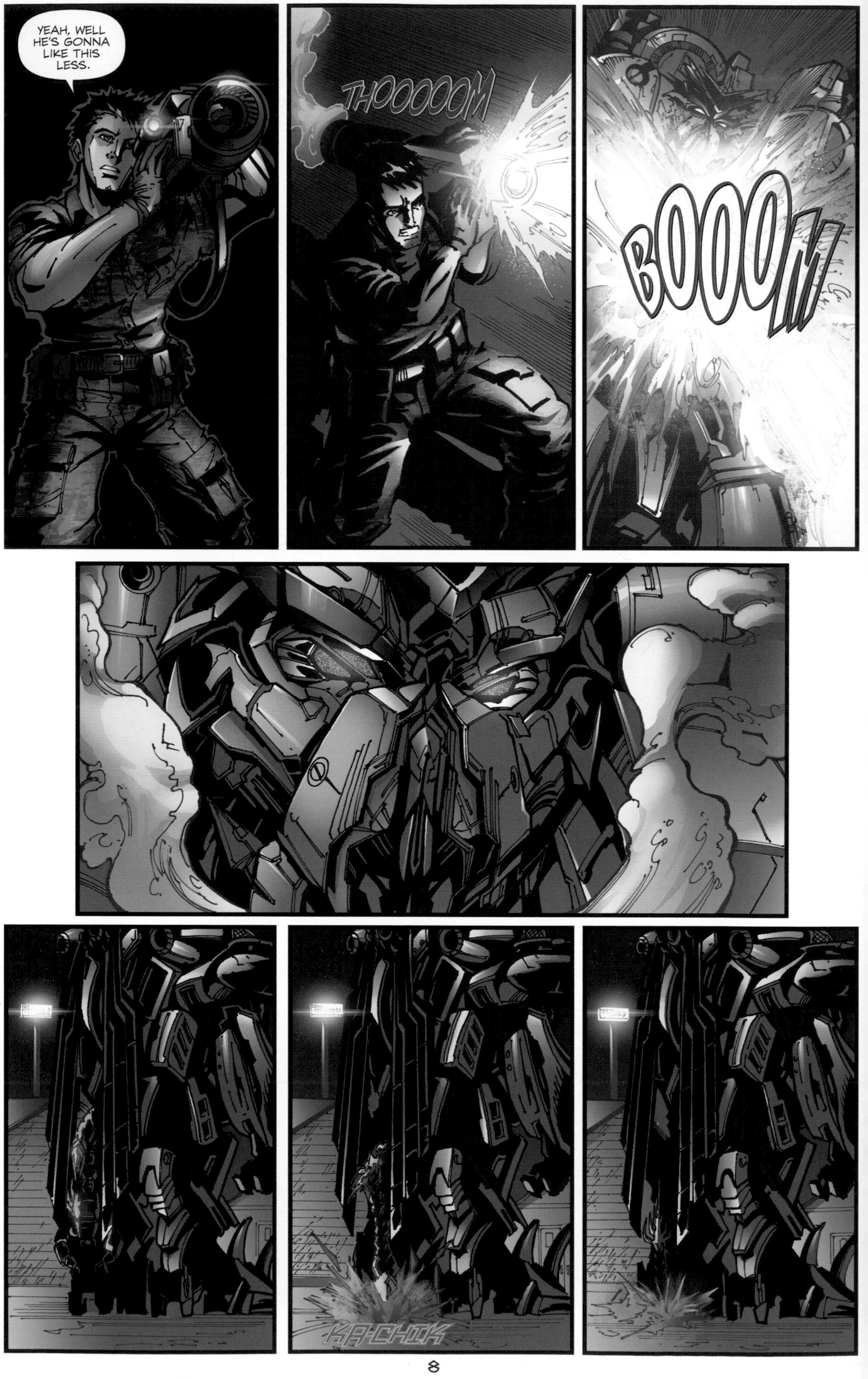
YEAH, WELL HE'S GONNA LIKE THIS LESS.
THOOOOOM
BOOOM
KA-CHIK

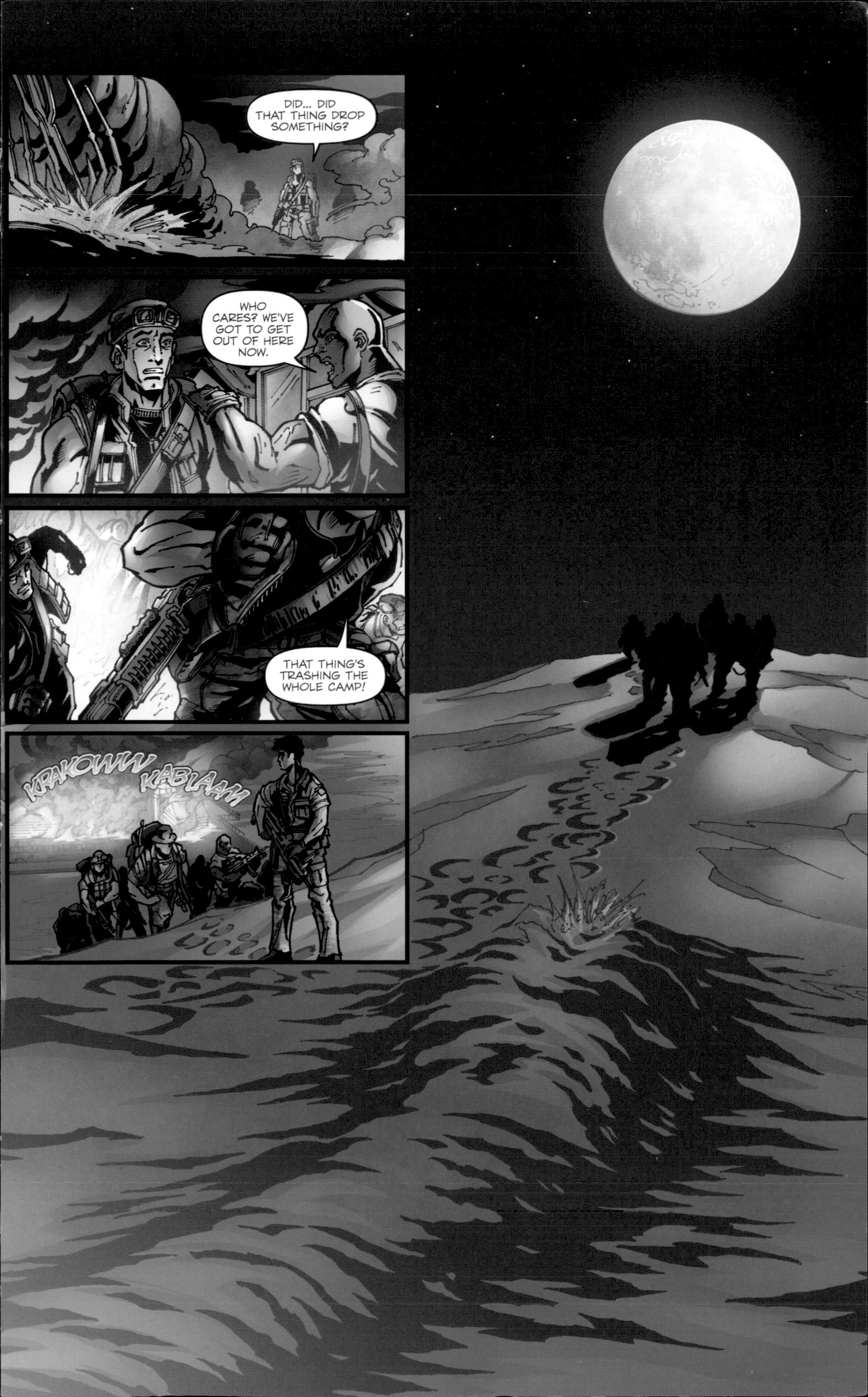
DID... DID THAT THING DROP SOMETHING?
WHO CARES? WE'VE GOT TO GET OUT OF HERE NOW.
THAT THING'S TRASHING THE WHOLE CAMP!
KRAKOWW
KABLAAM

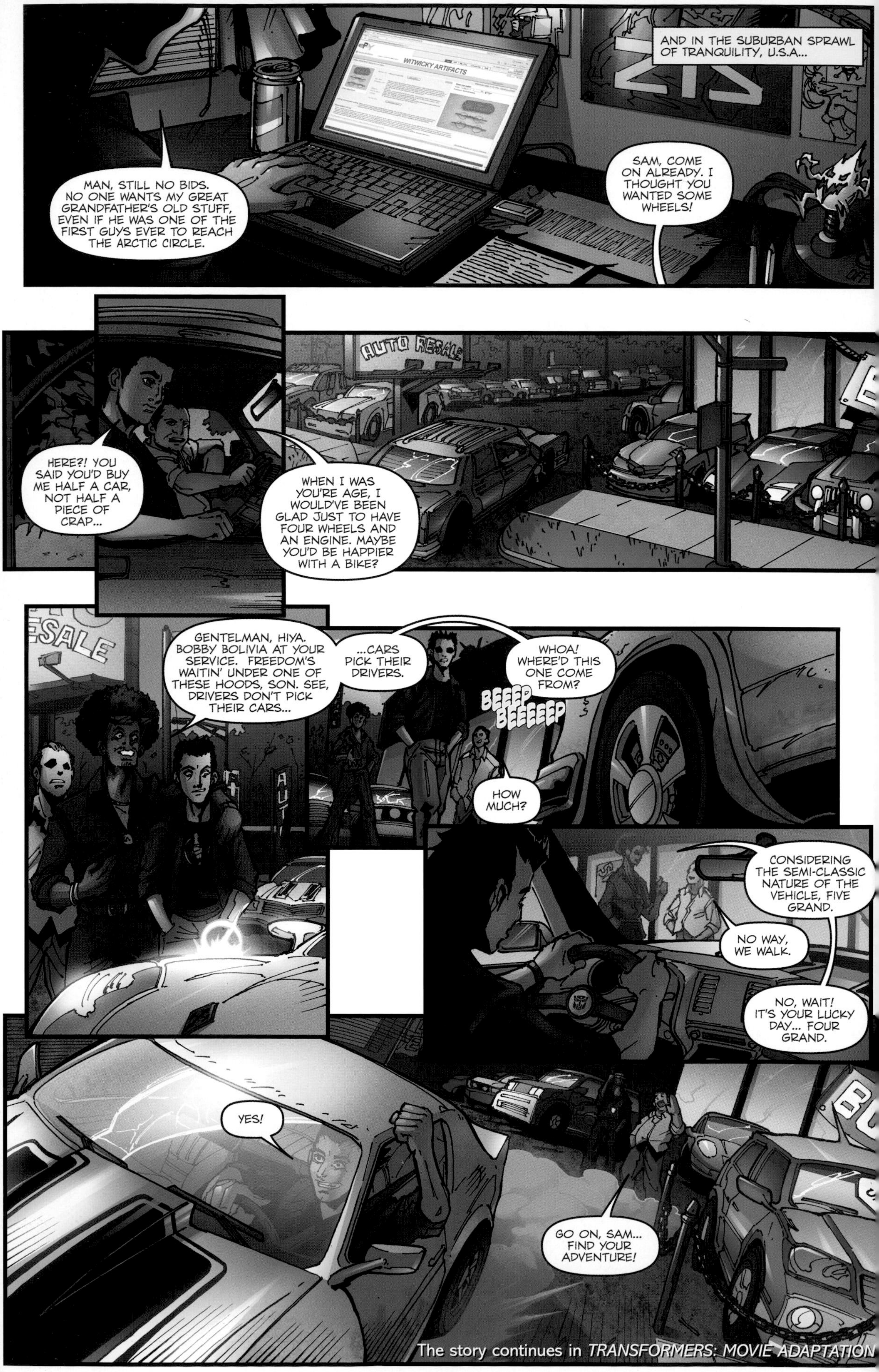
AND IN THE SUBURBAN SPRAWL OF TRANQUILITY, U.S.A...
WITWICKY ARTIFACTS
MAN, STILL NO BIDS. NO ONE WANTS MY GREAT GRANDFATHER'S OLD STUFF, EVEN IF HE WAS ONE OF THE FIRST GUYS EVER TO REACH THE ARCTIC CIRCLE.
SAM, COME ON ALREADY. I THOUGHT YOU WANTED SOME WHEELS!
AUTO RESALE
HERE?! YOU SAID YOU'D BUY ME HALF A CAR, NOT HALF A PIECE OF CRAP...
WHEN I WAS YOU'RE AGE, I WOULD'VE BEEN GLAD JUST TO HAVE FOUR WHEELS AND AN ENGINE. MAYBE YOU'D BE HAPPIER WITH A BIKE?
GENTELMAN, HIYA. BOBBY BOLIVIA AT YOUR SERVICE. FREEDOM'S WAITIN' UNDER ONE OF THESE HOODS, SON. SEE, DRIVERS DON'T PICK THEIR CARS...
...CARS PICK THEIR DRIVERS.
WHOA! WHERE'D THIS ONE COME FROM?
BEEEP BEEEEEP
HOW MUCH?
CONSIDERING THE SEMI-CLASSIC NATURE OF THE VEHICLE, FIVE GRAND.
NO WAY, WE WALK.
NO, WAIT! IT'S YOUR LUCKY DAY... FOUR GRAND.
YES!
GO ON, SAM... FIND YOUR ADVENTURE!
The story continues in *TRANSFORMERS: MOVIE ADAPTATION*